"Who knew that a book about marriage would be part my~~ ~~, ~~ ~~~~~~~~~~~~~~
tale, part how-to manual, part pep talk, and part memoir of a wise and deeply
satisfied wife? And yet, how fitting! In an era when science and technology have
given us so many advancements and solutions, a happy marriage still seems to
remain out of reach for too many. We need guidance from the wisest among us.

Ramona Zabriskie keeps no marriage mystery shrouded. In Wife for Life she
reveals the cheat codes, shares the treasure map, and broadcasts every detail of
the recipe for the secret sauce. She's your tour guide through your own marriage,
but you've never seen it like this before. Truths about your own heart that you
couldn't quite articulate keep tumbling out in her prose. And her deep empathy
for your spouse will melt your heart and send you running to change your ways.

Most refreshing and encouraging of all, perhaps, are Ramona's frank and
funny admissions of her own marital mishaps. Upon hearing about her struggles,
her friend once exclaimed, "I never knew how much failure went into a
successful marriage!" Seeing where she's been and what she's built--nothing less
than a grand marriage--helps banish our doubts that we can, too!

In the short time I've known about Ramona and her work, I've recommended
Wife for Life to more people than any other book in my 20-year career as a
psychologist.

Whether you're a wife or husband, if you... sometimes wonder why you ever
got married... limp along in a serviceable, lackluster relationship... are madly in
love and wonder if things could get even better... spend a few hours under
Ramona's kind tutelage and you'll come back and breathe new life into your
marriage.

Decades from now as you look back and consider your own happiness, your
spouse's, and even your children's and grandchildren's, you'll count Wife for Life
as one of the most important books you've ever read."

—**Mark Chamberlain PhD**, psychologist and
co-author *Love You, Hate the Porn*

"I absolutely loved this book. As a marriage and family therapist, I can say that
this is the best and most helpful book on marriage that I have ever read. It gives
a solid explanation of typical dynamics in marriage and gives specific
suggestions on how to improve a marriage relationship. The author gives
personal examples of the principles she teaches in the book, which makes the
book enjoyable and easy to read. Very few, if any, marriage books lift and
inspire like this book does."

—**Sherry Allen**, marriage and family therapist

"Zabriskie gives us the joyful message that a great marriage is within our own
making and shows us that the power we have as women over this sacred
relationship is awesome and awe-inspiring. That's a message that I couldn't
agree with more. By looking within and loving without, we bring joy to our own
lives and to that of our 'intimate'. This book is an empowering handbook for
women who yearn for a fulfilling and intimate partnership."

—**Emma J. Bell**, author *The True You*

Praise for Wife for Life

"With stories and examples, an extensive amount of marriage research, and her own enthusiasm for empowering women, Ramona focuses on the positive opportunities of being a modern day woman. She raises the bar for marriage higher than any other marriage expert on the market, and gives you the education and the hope to achieve this kind of marriage yourself. I'm a Marriage, Family, Human Development graduate and professional. I've read several marriage books. And Ramona's book is BY FAR the best. I feel her love and hope shine through to me personally. It's beautiful, just beautifully done."

—**Alyssa Evans**, marriage and family professional

"*Wife for Life* is, hands down, the best self-help book I have ever read. It doesn't preach; it doesn't get prosy or bogged down in information that is difficult to relate to. In fact, I would say this author has a future in writing fiction. Not that *Wife for Life* is fiction--it is anything BUT. It is filled with personal experiences of both the author's and all sorts of people with whom she has come in contact and mentored. She has seen marriage from many different angles and really has an accurate handle on what works and what doesn't. Mostly, she is passionate about helping everyone to succeed in marriage--you can feel it in every word she writes."

—**Heidi Ashworth**, Regency author

"What makes *Wife for Life* so successful and so memorable is that Zabriskie does not sugarcoat anything and speaks to women about EVERYTHING. Along with speaking directly to her readers, Zabriskie has a wonderful way of telling stories. Her voice is pleasant and witty and passionate, making *Wife for Life* a very fun and easy book to read… The many stories and pieces of advice Zabriskie share are not, in the slightest, overwhelming, but quite enriching. *Wife for Life* is a book that must be marked in and one that must be read from cover to cover; no skipping and no skimming should be allowed in order for a reader to take away the best possible experience…With an overabundance of information, stories, and pieces of advice that will stick in the minds of any reader, *Wife for Life* is truly a transforming book."

—**Alisha Smock**, Chicago Books Examiner

"If you only read one marriage book, read *Wife for Life!* It is brimming with authentic and deeply personal stories, biographical sketches of "grand marriages" and practical advice any wife can immediately put into practice. Ramona's descriptions of the "crazy ladies" and her list of men's worst fears help women avoid hurtful, "marriage-limiting" behavior. At the same time, she encourages women to take good care of themselves so they have more to give to their marriage. I finally bought a Kindle version because I kept giving my print copies away! Brilliant!"

—**Kristen A. Jenson**, best-selling author *Good Pictures Bad Pictures* and founder Protecting Young Minds

Winner Kirkus Indie Reader Discovery Awards, Reader's Favorite International Book Awards, Indie Excellence Book Awards, and USA Best Book Awards

RAMONA ZABRISKIE

THE POWER TO SUCCEED IN MARRIAGE

A WOMAN'S INSPIRATIONAL GUIDE
TO A GRAND LIFELONG MARRIAGE

WIFE FOR LIFE: THE POWER TO SUCCEED IN MARRIAGE
© 2013 by Ramona Zabriskie. All rights reserved.

http://www.ramonazabriskie.com

ISBN-10: 0-692-27388-3   ISBN-13: 978-0-692-27388-3
Paperback 3rd Edition 2016

Cover design by Grant Zabriskie
Cover photography © Nikolai Sorokin | Dreamstime.com

Dedicated to the *boy* who became the **man** of my dreams.

Contents

Preface

Strong love is not soon forgotten.
—*English proverb*

A younger friend and I chatted in the sun one spring as we planted primroses, bleeding hearts, and forget-me-nots in a little patch of my Washington woodland. Since the flowerbed needed tending as much as our friendship, Sue helped me spring clean while we talked. With so much to catch up on (my husband and I had just returned from an extended overseas assignment), our conversation roamed from topic to topic until somehow we landed on a group of Sue's contemporaries: women in the decade just past adolescence who were already on their second marriages.

I sat back amazed.

"Would you say these women are intelligent, spiritual, grounded, well-intentioned?" I asked.

She said they were.

"Then how do you account for their failed relationships?"

"Too young," she said frankly. "They didn't see, or just ignored, the red flags."

"You really think so?"

"Of course—what else could it be?"

That's when the universe wrinkled. If a bolt of lightning could have zigzagged its way out of the blue and through our piney forest, it would have grounded itself at my feet. Kneeling in the sun, fingernails caked with dirt, I knew suddenly and irreversibly that I had a new mission: I would dig as long and as hard and as deep as necessary to unearth *real* answers. And then I would share the answers with those intelligent, spiritual, grounded, well-intentioned women who long to succeed in marriage, who want to beat the odds and break the post-modern patterns of disillusionment and divorce.

"Sue," I asked, bent over my favorite rosebush, "have I ever told you about the early part of my marriage?"

Her eyes widened with a *you-mean-there's-something-to-tell?* look. I have supported Sue through her pregnancies and acted as a surrogate grandmother to her children. We have shared every holiday, every special event and six years of Sunday dinners. She is the younger sister I never had: as devoted as a disciple, and as indispensable to my happiness and well-being as I am to hers. And yet, for all that, I realized she knew nothing about 1978.

Stalling for a moment, I silently examined the rosebush, noting it would need fertilizer, trimming, and attention to overcome all the cobwebs and aphids in order to blossom again in the summer.

"Dale and I were young, of course, and it felt right to be a wife, but"—I lifted a bare, thorny branch—"I just didn't know how."

Snip. The first bit of dead wood fell to the ground. Memories, long neglected like the flowerbed in my forest, began to breathe again. My friend sat in the shade and the birds listened in while I pruned the sad rosebush and told Sue my story...

After fifteen months of marriage, I found myself residing about as far north as you can go in the continental United States, while my husband lived just as far south. I had taken all the legal steps necessary to keep him in his place (or rather, his parents' place), and life promised fair sailing now that I'd jettisoned the dead weight of a failed marriage. Every single person I knew saluted my decision with a smile: friends, family, even spiritual leaders. To them, the wedding announcement two years ago had been more shocking than the one I made twelve months later: *Dale and I are separating.*

"We all make mistakes," said the silver-haired man at church.

"He was bad news," said my aunt.

"You're meant to be more than a wife," grinned the old boyfriend. (Okay, I should've seen through that one.) Of all the pats on the back, my parents' support reassured me the most; they literally sighed with relief.

"He couldn't have made you happy, honey. He's so spoiled and troubled. You can do much better."

I believed them. And I believed myself. Until out of nowhere sweet thoughts of our honeymoon began to keep me awake at night. Daydreaming about laughter and noisy kisses distracted me at work. (Believe me, an out-of-control imagination makes for a bad bank teller. I never balanced—not once.) Melancholy swamped me, one monster wave after another while doubts floated to the surface faster than I could resubmerge them. Like a sailor on an unwieldy ship, left alone to steer while bailing buckets of remorse, my resolve to divorce sank lower and lower and lower until exactly at the moment when I thought for sure I would drown —Dale called.

That low voice, a gorgeous familiar rumble, momentarily quelled the chaos and muffled the mayhem.

"I've been thinking," he said. "You wanna get back together?"

Freeeeeze.

Did I want to get back together? I mean, honestly, *did I?* Did I want to resume all the uncertainty, all the disappointment, the resentment, the frustration, the anger, the loneliness, and the sadness?

I said I would sleep on it.

So, that's how I ended up sleepless in Seattle (well, about sixty miles south of Seattle, but close enough).

Dreams bobbed to the surface like pesky flotsam and kept me awake night after night until the support of a single girlfriend plus a very romantic movie (which I'll tell you more about in Chapter 3) combined to help me make a momentous decision.

"Come home," I told him.

A few days later, at Sea-Tac International Airport, a new Dale met a new me and we started over.

When I finished the story of my near disaster, Sue dropped her spade and rocked back on her heels, eyes bugging with disbelief.

"I had no idea you and Dale had separated!"

"Hardly anyone does."

"But you'd filed for divorce and everything!"

"We were only days from court."

"What happened?" She was terribly earnest.

"You mean what happened between then and now?"

"*Yes!* What happened!"

I quit picking yellow leaves off the rosebush. What a good question. What *did* happen? How did we turn out so happy? Why did we triumph through thirty-plus years with beloved children and grandchildren to show for it, while many of our friends and associates ended up in divorce?

Even before my talk with Sue, I was a serious student of marriage, learning from and helping other wives along the way. I had read and studied tens of thousands of words and churned out tens of thousands of my own on blogs and in personal writings. I had tested dozens of theories, held hundreds of hands, and listened to decades of emotional spill from my sisters all over the world as a mentor, speaker, leader, and friend of women. Even so, it took me two more years of intense work beyond my lightning-bolt conversation with Sue to piece together a proper response to her question. I am sorry it took so long, Sue, my friend, but I have done my best to give you a comprehensive, truly helpful answer. I call it *Wife for Life: The Power to Succeed in Marriage*.

Now since I assume (hope!) that others beside Sue will want to read *Wife for Life*, it's important I make a disclaimer or two. Readers have to understand that every word coming from me presumes that you are married, or will be married, to a *Nice Guy*. This Nice Guy may vacillate between protagonist and antagonist in your love story, he may one day be your hero and the next day your fool, but for all his faults (which may be many), he does not purposely control, intimidate, or seriously hurt you, physically or mentally.

If you grapple with complicated and critical issues such as unmanageable anger, physical, emotional, or verbal abuse (past or present), substance dependency, pornography addiction, or extramarital affairs in your marriage, I hope you will benefit from *Wife for Life*, but there are additional resources for you (which I strongly recommend seeking out). This book is also not intended to heal childhood trauma or mental illness. Such wounds are the province of therapists, scientists, and the clergy—none of which describes me.

In summary, nothing in this book should be taken in lieu of professional academic, legal, therapeutic, or medical advice. I offer only a voice of encouragement and gentle direction—like a trusted relative or mentor. The values and strategies I advocate are those I have learned for myself as a student, and which I know have proven effective for others. The principles I teach are validated by marriage professionals. Nevertheless, because every relationship is unique, results will unquestionably vary. In other words, only you and your spouse can be responsible for the relationship you create. That gives you the power, not me or anyone else, to make your dreams of a grand, lifelong marriage a reality.

Let's get to work.

Introduction

Love views life from the point of view of eternity.
—*Greek proverb*

I have always thought it was curious how two people—two such different creatures as a man and a woman, who are sometimes wildly different in personality—can behave like magnets, actually feeling drawn together *because* they are opposites. Philosophers, scientists, playwrights, and poets have tried to crack the code of attraction for a long time, and I think we wives should join them. The optimum time to beef up your wifely know-how is before you get married and during the first few years of marriage, but there is also much to be learned even after you have considerable experience. Whenever you choose to start your study, if you will focus on defining why you want to be a wife and then learn as much as you can about *how* to be a wife, and *what* being *his* wife is all about—and not just suppose that...*poof!*...love and happiness will appear at the snap of your fingers or a wave of your wand—then you will have a much better chance of cracking the code; of creating real magic: a grand marriage that is solid and stunning *forever*.

Forever? I hope that word doesn't bother you. I know some people think it's about as real as magic. It's too fantastic, they say, you're overly ambitious, hardly anyone believes in it anymore. But I believe you have to believe if you are going to invest your whole soul into a lifelong partnership. Enduring lovers have faith in *forever*—in the constant, endless nature of their love, if not their bodies. Whether figurative (as in your legacy lasting generations), or literal (as in living together in an afterlife), believing in *forever* is essential if you want to take your marriage from good, to great, to grand. So, although it may take a little mind-bending, the first thing you have to come to terms with when incorporating *forever* into your relationship is how way-way-way far away it is.

Or is it?

Brace yourself for the here-and-now truth: *forever* is happening even as we speak.

Each one of your days is a piece in your *forever*. Imagine how your marriage would be affected years from now if you and your husband acted as though your forever unfolded with every act, with every choice. A slight move in one direction today and you will be heading towards *forever*. Turn a tad the other way, and you will eventually run smack dab into *temporary*. The first road brings you closer and closer to the kind of intimacy you long for: holding your loved one's hand with your hearts in sync, looking out over the world and feeling safe. Follow the other path, however, and instead of creating a shared view of life, you will eventually hit a dead-end: just you, all alone, with nothing but a messy pile of what-could-have-beens.

Let me share an email I received not long ago to illustrate what I mean. It is a cry for help from the lonely end of the road after twenty years of marriage:

> "I am losing the other half of myself—I cannot understand. He is the love of my life and I am having hard time breathing. The despair of this is killing me. No words can convey the depth of my misery. I have tried talking to him and he just doesn't want anything to do with me. He said, "You just aren't getting it...I don't love you." I will never understand this and I will never get beyond it. He is the love of my life and he doesn't love me back...how do you move on from there? The pain is too horrible."

Compare that to a comment from a follower of my blog:

> "What love he has for me! No wonder it becomes more and more baffling to me that he remains constant. There is more history behind us of hurt and disappointment washed away by his charity and forgiveness than ever before. Here we are and he continues yet to invest, support, serve, and love me repeatedly in spite of our numerous backslides. I can think of no greater acceptance than to say: "Yes, I take you, your flaws and all, and I will let go of the mistakes and cleave to the strengths. Here together we shall stand!" Bless that man! Bless him!"

Before you jump to crediting the guy in these examples, let me assure you that I know both of these men and they are just guys: ordinary individuals, with no more faults than your husband or mine. I also know both of these women very well: they are good, productive, well-intentioned people. How then do you explain their completely opposite outcomes?

The answer lies in how these wives and their husbands oriented themselves: the little choices each of them made along the way and how their partner reacted to those choices. In the latter case, the wife, for instance, is embracing the fact that her husband is her *opposite* or her *other*—as in a completely different person and gender who has the right to his individuality and to his dreams and to her respect—which is drawing him steadily to her like a magnet. That is the road to intimacy.

In the first case, however, the wife, by choice or by ignorance, pointed herself in the opposite direction, towards the conviction that a husband must think and act exactly like his wife—including fixating on her and fulfilling all her needs precisely as she prescribes. In the end, her actions repelled instead of attracted him. That is the road to *alienation*.

Introduction

I thought I understood this principle (in a very rudimentary way) as a young wife, and I tried to orient myself toward intimacy, but I did not have a clear idea of how to go about it. I goofed up lots. There was no one nearby to cheer me on, to boost my confidence, to suggest ways of handling our relationship as it developed. They all thought I should toss him! Many of my family and friends shook their heads in disbelief when they heard we had reconciled after a six-month separation. Some disapproved so severely that they threatened to disown me if I got back together with Dale. For years and years I had no mentor to tell me what to expect, how to remove the obstacles, how to reconcile my femininity with his masculinity, how to fix my mistakes or deal with his. My commitment to *forever* carried me through the rough times, but too often I felt like a child spinning blindfolded who, when her eyes are uncovered, feels dazed and disoriented.

You don't have to go through all that. Patiently work your way through this book, chapter by chapter, and you will learn what I have learned about loving a man for a lifetime. If you follow my blog posts, podcasts, webinars, and videos at *ramonazabriskie.com* or participate in Wife for Life University, the principles will become even more meaningful and lasting for you.

Wife for Life know-how is carefully crafted into a framework that is meant to inspire as well as inform. Concepts are woven into stories and analogies that will help them stick in your mind and heart. The book is divided into three parts, with chapters progressing in order to build your understanding and your skills, piece by piece:

- Part I: "*Why* You Both Want a Grand, Lifelong Marriage" lays out the foundational understanding you will need.
- In Part II: "*How* to Avoid Becoming a Dream Breaker", I will continue to teach by precept and example, but will also give you concrete *how-tos.*

- And by Part III: "*What* to Do to Make Dreams Come True", you will be ready to work the *whats* of dream making into your life.

Warning: skipping ahead to look for a quick fix or instant inspiration won't work. Though I'm more and more tactical as the book progresses, if there is one core value you must internalize, it's that becoming a Wife for Life *takes time...*

"We have been married 42 years—wish I had known all of this long ago!"

"Your ideas connected the dots for me. I wish I had heard you years ago!!"

"Forty-three years of marriage and it just clicked tonight!"

"I wish I had heard you years ago—I'll have to start now after 39 years!"

"If I had heard you 20 years ago, I would not have divorced my husband."

"You may have just saved my marriage. I've been married 47 years."

"I wish I had heard this 40 years ago. I agree with everything you said but I didn't put it together for myself!"

"I've been married 52 years, and I can't wait to put into practice the things you taught us tonight."

These are all comments from women who heard in my live presentation only a small portion of what you hold in your hands. Commit yourself right here, right now, to the time and effort it will take to assimilate everything in this book and you will never have to moan, "I wish I had known." You can do it. I know you can. You've just taken your first step on the Road to *Forever.*

Part 1

WHY YOU BOTH WANT A GRAND, LIFELONG MARRIAGE

1

The Pioneer and the Creator

There is no life as complete as the life that is lived by choice.
—*Shad Helmstetter, Ph. D., author and behavioral researcher*

Lela Avis Pollan wanted her own homestead, so she settled into an abandoned cabin seventy feet above the Salmon River. Surrounded by nothing but nature, Lela woke up every day at four a.m. and watched the sun splay its spectacular rose and lavender hues over the hills, canyon, and lava beds. Then she went to work. After she milked her cows (they walked off the job if she didn't see to them first), she took care of her horses, geese, chickens, and lambs. The ramshackle shack needed a new roof and windows, so she started that project in-between her other chores. Of course, swinging a saw and hammer will stoke a girl's appetite, so Lela loaded her rifle and bagged pheasant, rabbit, and pigeon for dinner. But that's not all. What would a day in the country be without a close encounter with a rattler? She skinned all seven feet of it and hung its eighteen rattles on the fence to dry.

Although Lela missed her parents, she relished solitude. Rich soil and plenty of space made for good gardening and peaceful afternoons. Evening rides over the moonlit mountain filled her with serenity. It was well over a year before Lela had any wish to see civilization again. In all that time, no one came to visit except her father.

When she finally came off the mountain, Lela met and fell in love with a young man named Chandler Schroeder, who ran a business in town. With a little house in the middle of the hubbub, the new Mrs. Schroeder soon found herself doing more cooking and cleaning for drop-in guests than she felt comfortable with—but it was a live-in mother-in-law who finally drove her back to the hills. Resuming life at the homestead all on her lonesome, she planted, harvested, and canned a large garden, living and working without a husband right up until her eighth month of pregnancy, when she got on her horse and rode into town.

She was twenty years old.

Obviously, my great-grandmother Lela (who I grew up calling Gammy) acted as independently as her cows. She may have shocked the city-dwelling women of 1914, but she would fit right into Manhattan's financial district today. She displayed the kind of self-determination our suffragette sisters fought for. Because of the sacrifices and efforts of pioneer progenitors like Lela, twenty-first century women with her brand of tenacity and gumption now have choices bunching like apple blossoms in spring. Consequently, many of us try to pick every piece of fruit we see, unwilling to let precious rights rot on the ground. But the orchard can ripen all at once—education, career, romance, marriage, children—and time is at a premium. It becomes very difficult, if not impossible, to eat the apples all at once. Inevitably, whether we like it or not, basketfuls of choices will go unclaimed or half-eaten, while others spoil.

Lela made her choice. She eventually left the autonomy of the homestead. And while it is true that the birth of her baby (my grandmother) brought Lela physically off the mountain, it is also true that she came down to earth at that moment, fully embracing a new reality. In making that paradigm shift, my Gammy actually began to live life on a higher plane as she focused on living with, and for, others. She and Chandler left town together and headed West to begin a whole new life big enough to grow both his dreams and hers.

Building an enduring reciprocal relationship like that requires nothing less than what I call a *Pioneer Woman:* courageous, stubborn, pliant, resilient, centered, and most of all, self-reliant. In order to preserve herself and her stake, a Pioneer Woman takes responsibility for acquiring the skills she needs.

- She learns how to take care of herself, emotionally and physically, so that she can give with abundance (from a full heart and a strong body) and receive with confidence (from a deep-seated belief that she deserves nurturing and attention).
- She makes, and sticks with, difficult choices and lives from the heart.
- She believes in her own objectives, but finds a way to meld them with the hopes of others, particularly those of her husband, so that in the end, her little homestead has turned into a thriving estate, humming with activity, life, and love—a fully orchestrated piece of music instead of a lonely solo.

As an elderly matriarch, round in the hips and shoulders, Gammy's spirit still stood strong and independent. A widow for many years, she traveled alone all over the country to see, and do, and be with her progeny. One thing her whole family could count on: whenever there was a new baby, Gammy would arrive like the cavalry, just in time. Since I was the oldest of her great-grandchildren, she and I waited for Mama to come home from the hospital every two years or so, watching game shows on daytime television while she ironed. Occasionally, during the commercials, Gammy would reminisce about the old days. Whether her story included herding cattle, quicksand, or friendly Native Americans, what impressed me most was how she ended forays into the past with the same line, acted out in the same way. I can see her lifting a wrinkled shirt with one hand, holding the hot iron in the other, her voice quivering like old fingers.

"And you know," she would conclude her stories each time —"*all* my best dreams and wishes have come true."

Lela clearly did not forfeit or bury her aspirations when she chose marriage and a family; that would have been counterproductive. No, when she forged ahead with forever as her compass, she was bound for the Promised Land: a land of abundant opportunities for making her dreams come true, as well as the dreams of her loved ones.

Just before she died in her nineties, Gammy composed a poem entitled "Happy People Live Longer":

Happy people live longer.
Happy people tend to be ill less often.
Happy people age more slowly and recover more quickly.
Happy people have bones and tissues that heal better.
Happy people have better color and glossier skin.
Happiness and health go together.
The art of living is never, ever impossible.

What an irony that a girl born in the nineteenth century, one who matured during a period that we associate with female oppression, actually created and sustained a truly happy, fulfilling life—an achievement that escapes many women in this century. Rough-and-ready Lela Schroeder, Pioneer Woman, became what you can become if you choose: a strong, smart, sure woman, refined by love, a virtuoso of the heart, a Wife for Life cultured in the art of living.

The Art in the Art of Living

While Gammy embodied the art of living, another lady I admire is the absolute picture of it.

With a veil that never flutters, though it traces an animated face, and with a satin dress that never shifts, even when she crosses her hands, this grand woman has the ageless expression, the composed bearing, and the gentle smile we all wish we could maintain for as long as she has. Forever poised, forever restful, forever serene, our lady is nothing less than omniscient. She is majesty, mischief, and mystery. She is eternal. She is Mona Lisa.

The tour guide's Parisian-accented English came through the wireless headset loud and clear. I didn't entirely understand what she was talking about, but at least I could hear her: "This portrait is painted to a realistic scale in the highly structured space where it has the fullness of volume of a sculpture in the round." I only wished my view of Mona was as clear as the docent's voice. Millions of tourists pour into the Louvre each year (the world's most visited museum), and it seemed to me that at least half of them had chosen to come on the same day I had. The crowd in the *Salle des Etats* (like the crowd every day) was as thick as the red carpet on Oscar night and as manic as a mob circling a rock star. Hundreds of digital cameras and cell phones hovered in the air overhead on the arms of tourists who were perched precariously on tiptoe, simultaneously snapping photos. Poor Mona. She is the most famous, most critiqued, most replicated piece of art in the history of mankind.

And I love her.

Furthermore, I know she loves me.

Best.

My birth certificate says *Ramona*, but I've been called every conceivable variation of that name. Of course, my mother used the whole thing—*Ramona Jeanette*—like an epitaph, whenever she thought I deserved it, while my four little brothers barely dignified me with a monosyllabic Mo. But of all the nicknames all the people in all my life bequeathed me, the one that became the most common (and the most precious to me when Dale began to use it) was Mona. Add to that little moniker the fact that my ASL name sign is the same as that for *smile*, and you will see why I naturally borrowed da Vinci's *señora* to define and decorate my internet presence for years.

Mona is more than a name and a smile, however. When she and I were photographed (as close together as possible—darn those velvet ropes) I was sure we looked an awful lot alike. At least I hoped so. Mona Lisa, also known as *Portrait of Lisa Gherardini, Wife of Francesco del Giocondo,* represents to me the glory of femininity: the wisdom and elegance and joy I aspire to. She is a woman. She is a wife. She is the art in the art of living.

Think about that for a minute. Think about *you* for a minute. What if I handed over a set of fine brushes and a palette of oils and asked you to paint an ideal version of yourself, what would it look like? How would you capture yourself in a painting? And how would you illustrate your mate? What would he look like on canvas? Don't pretend you haven't thought about it; we both know that you've spent a big chunk of your feminine life envisioning exactly the man you would hang on the wall and spend your life looking at. That's totally okay, completely natural, part of the process. Unfortunately, it is also natural for us to jump on the first model that superficially resembles our visual ideal and start eagerly painting, only to be let down when the relationship ends up a crumpled reject. Of course, the higher our reject pile, the more cynical, and the less trustful, we become.

Since I want to help you feel confident about marriage, I think it's important to understand why those earlier sketches did not mature into masterpieces. Obviously, there are lots of reasons men don't turn out to be The One, but the primary culprit is the mother lode of disappointment: false expectations.

When we dewy-eyed damsels try painting our romantic interest as a dreamy imitation—superimposing our vision of a heroic lover upon the poor guy, rather than seeing what he really is—we are in trouble. On the other side of the easel, the guy may be fantasizing about an irresistible, adoring woman, portraying his sweetheart more as a still life than a three-dimensional woman. The immature lovers end up with a relationship that imitates instead of authenticates. Surreal images act like a wall between them, rather than a window to the heart and soul. Frustration is inevitable.

As noted author and Jungian analyst Robert A. Johnson wrote in *We: Understanding the Psychology of Romantic Love:*

> "Romantic love, true to its paradoxical nature, fools us: It looks as though it aims at making a human relationship to a person. After all, one is not meditating in a temple; one is 'in love' with a human person. Or is one? It is difficult for us to see the difference—the vast difference—between relating to a human person and using that person as a vehicle for one's projection" (p. 138).

In addition to playing house instead of dealing with real life, inexperienced artists can also ruin romance by acting impatiently. Hasty lovers are in danger when they attempt to paint in oils before they've even learned to draw. Wide brushes and bold colors might feel exhilarating to begin with, but relationships that move too fast gloss over the details or forfeit personal preparation, and they predictably can end up with all the perspective of a finger painting.

On my tour of the Louvre, I learned that the Mona Lisa took forty-plus years to create—at least it took that long for consummate Renaissance man, Leonardo da Vinci, to become expert enough to craft what is considered by many art historians the world's greatest painting. He began his journey toward Mona as a teenager, apprenticing in the workshop of an accomplished master, Andrea del Verrocchio, of Florence. Young da Vinci worked with a team of other apprentices, gaining exposure to a myriad of tools and techniques. Because he started with very little knowledge, his first twelve-hour days were spent sweeping, cleaning, and running errands. It didn't take long, however, before he began to fashion brushes, apply plaster, make charcoal, mix tempera, and prepare wax for sculpture.

During this period of tutoring, a fortunate tipping point

occurred for Leonardo: fine art began to change dramatically. Rather than paint the flat, unrealistic religious scenes dictated by ecclesiastical authority, artists began to depict humans and nature precisely as they saw them. Leonardo was on the cusp of this new wave, and his powers of observation and keen desire to learn (his prolific notes are legendary) played to his great advantage. Having digested rigorous lessons in geometry, he took easily to a whole new technique called *perspective*: a way to create the illusion of three-dimensionality on a one-dimensional surface.

His responsibilities at the studio increased in importance and complexity as his abilities steadily progressed. New privileges included transferring the master's drawings onto walls or wooden panels, applying the first layer of a fresco, creating backgrounds, or adding small objects to a painting. He kept at it for a long time, all the while experimenting with perspective on his own, letting his playful, imaginative, slightly rebellious spirit have its way.

A lot of his experimentation involved painting with oils. This newly popular medium appealed to the young artist as an alternative to the more commonly used tempera paint, which dried too quickly, forcing the methodical Leonardo to make corrections by painting over the original. In contrast, oils remained moist long enough to allow him to blend and alter on the surface, composing slowly and making changes as he went along. With this more flexible approach, he began to perfect the three-dimensional look, using contour and shadows to profound effect. His oil work became so smooth that hardly a brush stroke could be detected. The final glow was lifelike.

After six years of studying everything around him, Leonardo da Vinci completed his training and earned the title of master craftsman. He joined the painter's guild, for he was now a respected professional in his own right. Even so, he continued to collaborate with Verrocchio for some time before setting up his own shop.

Many, many years later, after he had spent decades studying all kinds of enriching fields (among them, science, mathematics, geology, aeronautics, anatomy, architecture, and philosophy), da Vinci, now an old man, finally sat down to create Mona. She was so special (or so I like to think) that immortalizing her image called for a whole new approach to portraiture: a groundbreaking perspective that focused closely on the sitter in half-length, painted precisely and to a realistic scale. This revolutionary formula took weeks of planning, preparing, and organizing, as well as hundreds of mathematical calculations and sketches. With the composition complete, a drawing was transferred to a wooden panel, which was then covered with the first coat of light underpainting, followed by darker shadows, and then—and only then—when all of that was done and dry, when all the years had added up to this moment: Mona was finally ready to be painted.

How detailed and tedious the process seems! I can just picture Leonardo concentrating, bending toward the easel, holding a palette in his right hand and using his left to sort through a haystack of brushes to find the best one for this first stroke. He raises it, surveying the pricked-and-penciled outline one last time. Satisfied, he dabs the tip into the oil, then sweeps his brush gently across the canvas with supreme sensitivity...a pinpoint finesse that could only come into being after a lifetime of preparation.

Does imagining that scene leave you as breathless as it does me? Was all that time, effort, study, and practice worth it? Of course it was! Who can argue with perfection? Mona Lisa, wife of Francesco del Giocondo, will live forever. And so can your marriage.

Like anything truly worthy, a marriage that is destined to become grand (the *forever* relationship in which you will feel cherished) requires not only inspiration (falling in love), but education, even an apprenticeship (which you may be just beginning). It is a given that you have, or will have, a maturely chosen subject (your husband), and good lighting (your *why*), as well as the proper environment (the *how-tos*). You will also need to learn to use the right brushes and techniques (the *whats*). Most importantly, fashioning that great piece of fine art will require mixing palettes of patience, persistence, and practice, each one absolutely required to succeed in marriage. The three Ps act more like oil than tempera: if you use them to full advantage, you will be able to correct and blend as you go along.

Beautiful living then takes all of that perspective and perseverance *plus* a whole lot of imagination. Crafting relationships is definitely an art form, and artistry connotes mastery, a unique flair, a stroke of genius. Stay open and flexible, playful and imaginative, even slightly rebellious. Be as curious and as observant as a Renaissance woman, and you will, in the end, have your masterpiece. It will happen! You can do it!

A modern Renaissance man named Steve Jobs once said that some things have to be believed to be seen. If you want to see what *forever* might look like, if you want to know what it is to be cherished, then you have to believe. Believe you are as splendid as Mona Lisa and as brilliant as da Vinci.

You are a woman. You were *born* to create.

2
The Talent and the Dream Maker

Creation means bringing into existence something that did not exist before—
colorful gardens, harmonious homes, family memories, flowing laughter.
—Dieter F. Uchtdorf, ecclesiastical leader

One of the great myths about creative people is that they are
somehow naturally talented. Granted, thinking outside the
proverbial box may come easier to some, but while I believe we
are all born with gifts, I also believe we can develop almost any
talent we really set our mind to. For instance, Gammy Lela may
have been more comfortable confronting a rattler in the desert than
she was facing her mother-in-law in the kitchen, but when she
made her choice to master family life, she eventually grew
relationships as beautifully as she grew vegetables. And think of
Leonardo! The world considers him the most talented man in
history, yet you and I now know it took years of concerted study
and practice for him to earn that position.

It is just too easy to adopt the *que sera sera* attitude that fate is
responsible for our advantages or disadvantages. Observing a
woman who is remarkably adept at choosing just the right words,
in just the right tone of voice, and with just the right expression to
interest the man of her choice and hold his attraction indefinitely—
we may be tempted to attribute her success to some kind of good
luck or instinctive aptitude that we just don't have. Or in
considering the wife who appears adored by her husband, we may
almost hope her happiness away, because if it is real and lasting,

31

we would have to acknowledge our own imperfect situation, pretensions, or shortcomings. It is just too great a disturbance to our performance-based paradigm (I am good at___ and bad at __) to attribute a beloved wife's expertise to genuine effort instead of luck of the draw.

No, talent always begins in a raw place and is purposefully formulated over time so that it looks to the outsider, the admirer from a distance, as though it were a natural, effortless gift. You can be absolutely certain though, that not only did every grand marriage begin awkwardly, surviving repeated fiascos, but that you personally have as much of the right stuff as the next girl. I don't know which may be the greater revelation to you—that near-perfection is acquired or that it's possible for you—but I do know that you cannot absorb and hone the Wife for Life skill set I'm going to teach you until you believe that becoming your husband's Intimate is a talent, a worthy talent, perhaps the ultimate talent, and one that any woman can boast of achieving, with application and time.

I recently asked my lovely, accomplished friend, Debbie, a woman whose marriage I have admired for twenty-plus years, how she became her husband's Intimate. Her answer revealed not only her Wife for Life philosophy, but also how her marriage facilitated the development of her many other remarkable talents:

> "My husband used to say, 'If you and I can make it, anybody can.' I have to agree with him. We have certainly had our trials in learning how to live with one another. Raising a very concentrated family of eight children, balancing work schedules and other major responsibilities, dealing with financial setbacks, health problems, both being imperfect people...all these marital challenges could stretch our very best selves to exhaustion. But what kept us going and made him want me to be his wife for a lifetime? I learned that I needed to show I believed in his worth, and

through those efforts, he learned to trust my desire to live up to the promises I made to him when we chose to spend our entire lives together. Trust is the one value that can never be compromised. Through trust, all my other pursuits, ambitions, and desires are being realized. I was free to run in the direction I felt I had to go because he supported me and trusted the intention of my heart."

As Debbie articulates, prioritizing your relationship with your husband actually has the effect of freeing you for a vast array of other creative endeavors. Think how much time and energy women spend in angst over their relationships with men, how much brain function is wasted on distrust, negativity, and self-pity. Of course, even more resources go down the drain with divorce. Another, less obvious method of squandering creativity lies in tracking the mythical Mr. Right—looking for the Lost City of Gold in the Land of Opportunity. Other energy zappers include lifestyles or behaviors that are based in fear: fear that you won't succeed, or that he's not the one, or that you will lose him otherwise. Living conditionally, with a love based on trepidation, is like ascending a rickety staircase in the dark. Every step requires so much concentration—clinging to an unsteady rail, tensing at every creak and loose board—that productivity is incredibly compromised. In a committed marriage, love is given and received, not like some high-stakes gamble, but more like pennies in a piggy bank, steadily accumulating over time. In a marriage like Debbie's, a woman becomes rich day by day, ascending the stairway of her life with confidence, free to create to her heart's content, to plan ahead, to pace herself through each stage of womanhood, to enjoy and make the most of her peculiar talents and ambitions.

In order to experience personal development and freedom as a married woman then, becoming your husband's Intimate must be your most prized goal, your primary pastime, your preferred creative endeavor. It must be what I am going to call *The One*

Talent Left Standing—the one buoy kept afloat, the one plate unbroken—no matter what other pursuits you necessarily and voluntarily take on.

Do you feel the potential in the idea? It may sound paradoxical at first, but full-hearted partnership with your Nice Guy is, I believe, the most brilliant, dynamic way to realize your dreams while feeling loved and emotionally supported for the rest of your life. If you still have a hard time accepting that, maybe what you really doubt is yourself: *is it possible for me? how can I be sure of success?*

While no writer, counselor, researcher, or mother-in-law can guarantee the outcome of your relationship, there is one person you can turn to with confidence, one person who holds the power to make your castle in the sky a real one on earth, one individual who can translate your intent into talent, one partner in this whole affair whom we can rightfully call your Dream Maker.

That person is you.

You Have the Power

A recent article on the state of marriage begins with this statistic: "From 1970 to 2010, the number of American women heading to the altar tumbled from 76.5 million to 34.9 million...." Interesting. This e-zine report about the factors contributing to a long-term marriage (based on a national nonpartisan, nonsectarian, and interdisciplinary analysis of the social and cultural forces shaping contemporary marriage) leads out with a statistic about women. Not men, not couples, but women. Whatever the researcher's rationale for focusing on our gender, it is clear that how we women feel about marriage, and our actions in relation to it, is setting the marital bar.

Over the last few years, I have devoured book after book after book on marriage, amassing a personal library that represents a cultural wealth of research, experience, and viewpoints. Bent on acquiring a deep and well-rounded understanding, I have studied (and continue to study) material written by Jewish, Christian, New Age, and agnostic or atheistic scientists, psychologists, anthropologists, and sociologists, as well as journalists, philosophers, and novelists. I have also considered the works and opinions of governmental, educational, and faith-based leadership.

After analyzing marriage from a multiplicity of angles, what has struck me overall is how each of these sources (regardless of the author's personal background, purpose, or professional credentials) assert, or at least assume, these general trends in the Western world:

- There has been a titanic cultural shift in the roles of men and women.
- This social transformation has left many men in a quandary over their identity. The lack of definitive social expectations leaves men at a disadvantage compared to their male progenitors, who knew for thousands of years exactly what was expected of a man.
- This adjustment is affecting men's personal and professional relationships with women.
- On the positive side, men are increasingly looking to strong women to help them direct their energy, inspire their ambitions, and channel their nature in constructive ways.
- This progressive view is allowing more and more men and women to act as true partners in achieving family and professional goals.
- Of all the strengths women bring to partnership, one of the most vital is their natural orientation toward relationships. Women, by virtue of biochemistry, social tradition, contemporary cultural developments, or all of the above, are generally more adept at

relationship dynamics than men are.

Thus, in a nutshell, women today, either by design, development, or accident, depending on your belief system, are in a very powerful position when it comes to creating and maintaining truly rewarding relationships with men. As anthropologist Helen Fisher asserts in *First Sex: The Natural Talents of Women and How They Are Changing the World:*

> "Most important, women are better educated than at any other time in human history. They also have more business opportunities, more personal and professional networks, fewer children, and more freedom to develop themselves socially and intellectually. Women are becoming capable, worldly, and interesting—as wives, as lovers, as friends, and as companions. If ever there was a time in human evolution when men and women have had the opportunity to make fulfilling marital attachments, that time is now" (p. 283).

One of the most striking illustrations of women's power in relationships comes from *What Could He Be Thinking?* by Michael Gurian, cofounder of the Gurian Institute, which conducts research on the difference between men's and women's brains. The entire book is to our point, but I was particularly struck by what a professional associate of Gurian's told him:

> "In the words of therapist Pam Brown," he writes, "'If the man telephones me to set up marital counseling, I know the marriage is finished. The woman has decided to leave her commitment behind. I know that when I meet with this couple, I'll learn that he thinks he's been a good husband,

but she doesn't. The marriage only has a chance if she's the one who calls. Her call means she hasn't walked out the door yet'" (p. 161).

I hope you felt the same *wow* reaction I did on reading that passage. That *wow* should be accompanied by a clearer vision of your womanly strength, even a sense of your opportunity and responsibility in marriage.

Musing over the idea that a woman wields significant control or influence in a relationship, I am reminded of a conversation I once had with a girlfriend. She reacted excitedly to the announcement that I would be speaking on romance in marriage at an upcoming event. Realizing that her husband would be attending the lecture with her, my friend grabbed me by the shoulders. "I hope Jim will really listen!" she said. I looked into her desperate eyes and thought, *Oh, boy—is she going to be surprised.* My talk on romance in marriage would be zinging straight toward her, not Jim. My friend was sure to be caught off guard by the revelation of her *own* responsibility for romance. For twenty-plus years she had blamed her man and their circumstances instead of looking at the obvious answers inside her.

Each of the four types of women described in this and the previous chapter are *you*: the Pioneer Woman, the Creator, the Talent, and the Dream Maker. Each of these titles became part of your womanly identity when your man slipped that ring on your finger. Like Dorothy in Oz, you have the power to make your dreams come true. You have had it all along.

Of course, any relationship is a two-way street, linking two people who share responsibility for its outcome. But the truth of the matter is, women have a disproportionate amount of influence on both the day-to-day and the long-term tenor of their marriage. The feminine energy we bring to the partnership is intuitive, relational, receptive, connective, intimate, and inclusive. We are therefore, the keepers of the relationship.

Most women sense this innately–deep down—and we try to stoke the fire on a Friday night. But what bewilders and frustrates us is that the flame too often dies out by Saturday morning (and frequently stays out until the following Friday). Supposing the fault to be with our man, we bemoan his lack of romantic inclination, his inattention to our needs, and his insensitivity to the pressures of our lives, to the rarity of give and take, to the infrequency of care and closeness, to sporadic intimacy and affection. Yet the truth of the matter is that most Nice Guys would be devastated if they knew just how far short they were falling. Your man would love nothing more than for *every* night to be Friday night—which brings me to a certain Friday night many years ago, the one where I learned this lesson.

After seven days of caring for four children and taking half the day to start the day, I was crazy for a date night with my husband. And at that stage of my life, date night to me meant all-about-me night. I expected to be wined and dined, ooohed and ahhhed over, and listened to with rapt attention. To his great credit, my honey managed to pull this off nearly every Friday night (his cue was the entrance of the babysitter). However, if my prince, on rare occasion, slipped off his steed in the slightest—if he was anything less than perfectly charming (due to worries which I could not and did not try to comprehend), his Cinderella, who had miraculously gone from apron and headscarf to ball gown and crown, would turn into one cold pumpkin come midnight.

This particular Friday night had started out all right. We had a nice dinner out and a movie. When we got home, the kids were already tucked in and fast asleep. Things were going so well for Prince that he let his guard down. While I disappeared into the bathroom to get ready for bed, he paused at the computer for a quick checkup on some business matters. Baaaaaaaaad idea. For some reason that I can't really explain all these years later, I had gotten it into my head that getting on the computer was violating the Date Night Prime Directive: *You shall not take your eyes or ears off your woman—even after returning to your native environment.*

As soon as I realized that I was talking to myself in the bathroom (because of course I was jabbering incessantly), Cinderella morphed into the Wicked Queen.

We went to sleep fairly miserable that night. If I remember right, it was one of those nights they tell you *never* to have: hurt husband, sulky wife, back to back, on opposite sides of the bed.

Early the next morning, the phone woke us up. The leader of our congregation was inviting Dale and me to be at his office within the hour. Ooooookaaaaay. We bypassed our usual morning kisses and cuddles and got ready in silence. The moody cloud dampened our spirits all the way to the church and followed us right into the building.

I was called in first.

"Sister Ramona," he said, "we would like you to speak at the upcoming conference for husbands and wives in our congregation."

I nodded numbly. Speaking was all right with me; even though I didn't feel too brilliant at the moment, I had no doubt I could come up with an impressive topic.

"What we would like you to speak on is—" *Oh, no!* I thought. *An assigned topic!* He cleared his throat, adding a second to my suspense, then pronounced—"strengthening marriage through patience and understanding."

I went ashen.

I exited. Dale entered. I could not even look him in the eye as we passed.

Four minutes later, he emerged. The door closed behind him. His head was hanging—so much so that I became concerned. I rose from the couch where I had been waiting.

"What is it, honey?"

He lifted his chin to look at me, a tear about to wriggle down his cheek.

"I'm speaking at the conference."

"I am, too. Did he say what he wants you to talk about?"

"Yes."

We just stood there. I wanted to hold him and be held by him, but humiliation held us both.

With more than a little awe in his voice, he finally said: "The importance of romance in marriage."

On that never-to-be-forgotten morning after, we had *both* learned a lesson. Yet, somehow, deep in my womanly heart, I felt especially convicted. No one but Dale knew what had happened the night before. No one but my husband had endured my stonewalling, heard my accusations, seen me brood, and felt the door slam in his face. And only I knew how it had disturbed my sleep. There was no way anyone could be aware of any of that: no one, that is, except God.

I had received a direct revelation that romance was about the two of us, not one of us, and from now on I had to do my part to inspire it.

That important realization led to the grand marriage we have today, and it can lead to a grand marriage for you. It is the comprehension that you have the power:

- the power of choice
- the power of happiness
- the power to affect your marriage

Just imagine! To a far greater extent than you ever knew possible, your relationship with your husband can be as cool or as fuzzy, dark or bright, flat or colorful, quiet or intense, chilling or thrilling, limiting or liberating, dull or mesmerizing, long or short —as you make it. Part of that power lies in your spirit, your imagination, your intelligence. Another part lies in the social changes that are empowering women in general. Yet another part—an aspect of your gender which you are perhaps only subconsciously aware of—lies in your biological makeup. As the Nigerian proverb says about women: "It is a beautiful necessity of our nature to love." Nothing can be more basic than that.

Do not postpone believing in or practicing this most basic of basics, the power you have over your relationship, until it is too late. For many women, this first principle, the one that provides a foundation for marital success, somehow never sinks in, until it suddenly becomes their only hope—a last-ditch effort to save the relationship. By then, of course, a woman's power is depleted; she has never developed The Talent, and her husband is beyond reaching. End of story. The wife's victimization is set, and tragically, she may pass down her distrust of men and her cynicism about marriage to the next generation of females in the family.

Take a hard look at where you are standing. You are teetering on a very critical precipice. The next step you take will send you flying into *forever* or tumbling into *temporary*. Your powerful position as a woman can carry you just as certainly toward alienation as it can toward intimacy. Alienation is not where you want to be.

Where you want to be (way down the pike) is with your great-granddaughter, telling her about your adventures as a Wife for Life. At the end of those rabble-rousing, heart-pumping, bodice-ripping tales, you want to be able to say, and mean it, "All my best dreams and wishes have come true. But before I tell you *how* they came true, dear granddaughter, let me tell you *why*..."

3
Your Power Begins With Your Why

The supreme happiness of life is the conviction that we are loved.
—*Danish proverb*

Marriages without a why are easy to spot: the relationships are more like a contract (if you do this, then I'll do that) than a covenant (I pledge to do this no matter what). The contractual marriage without a *why* behind it is like a couple of inexperienced skydivers who neglect their training. A man and woman may stand at the open door of a plane, suited up for the dive, but when it's time to take that leap of faith called marriage; it's more like a free fall than a team jump. They speed toward the ground in a panic, unable to resist the gravity of self-interest, when they should be experiencing the exhilaration of flying in tandem. I don't mean to sound dismal or pessimistic; I am all about celebrating marriages that never leave the sky. I just want to be sure you understand that in order to live in the clouds, you've got to be grounded in *why*. You've got to go beyond skills and knowledge. You have to start with a foundational rationale, a deep-down motivation, a philosophical backdrop to give your efforts sincerity and staying power. This is what I call your *why*. It is a reason for marriage that will inspire your marriage.

Most relationship advice falls far short of explaining the importance of *why*. I have dog-eared, sticky-noted, marked up, and torn apart dozens of books looking for *why*. The Marriage and Relationships section of the bookstore is full of the whats and the hows, but amazingly bereft of *why*. When I discovered that a highly respected professional who now heads a national movement in support of marriage admitted to a gap between his training as a therapist and his understanding of *why* (in a keynote address at a national marriage conference, no less), I was not surprised. The fields of family education and therapy, he said, "had forgotten what marriage was really about." Another therapist writes that he cringes when he thinks of some of the therapies he's prescribed in the past, and yet another admits that he and his associates never understood what made marriages work; they were so preoccupied at the time with what made them fail.

Now, I don't mean to discourage couples who are having serious marital issues from seeking professional counseling—on the contrary. There are obviously plenty of honest, effective professionals and programs. It's just that some experts focus their writing, or speaking, or counseling on merely avoiding or resolving conflict— which is important, especially for those who are sinking or who are already in deep water—but those same guides struggle to articulate a truly inspiring message. One very experienced professional admits as much when he relates that after helping hundreds of couples save their marriages through intense workshops, a surprising number of wives returned asking for something more. A stable home life, a marriage without obvious struggle, is not necessarily satisfying to today's woman. I believe it comes down to the stunning fact that very few, if any, marriage advocates and professionals are zeroing in on a *why* that sticks, that really resonates, especially with women.

Part of that failure is buried in the confusion of twenty-first century relationships. Since *she* does not necessarily need *he* to bring home fresh meat or fight off the barbarians any more, and *he* doesn't have to have *she*, or rather, a wife, to have sex, a lot of men and women are wondering if marriage is even necessary. Some argue that wedlock is hardly the road to either productivity or happiness, while others would produce equal evidence that it is.

Social scientists and researchers assert all kinds of societal factors for us to consider, such as the needs of children, or economic growth and stability, or even the general health of the population; but even those extremely significant considerations rarely override a woman's rationale for bailing out of a marriage if she's really unhappy. No. We still don't have a *why* that will convince more women, no matter their beliefs or traditions, to hang tough over and around and through the ups and downs, the thick and thin, the black and white, that is life with a young man, a middle-aged man, and a very old man. Even love itself can be such an unrelenting taskmaster that some women would rather give up on it than give in to it.

So, we have got to answer this one big question before any others if we are to enthrone the role of wife in the minds of sophisticated women. And the sixty-four million dollar question (as the old game show used to call it, and adjusted for inflation) is this:

Why do I want to be a Wife for Life?

When I undertook the mission of tracking down this elusive creature, the *why* of a lifelong marriage, I searched every nook and cranny, asking every villager and castle dweller for their insights, peering down every wishing well and looking through every dark cave, dank forest, and hollow log I could find. In the process, I became convinced of one thing for certain: the real *why* lay far beyond fantasy and fairy tales.

And that's where I was wrong.

Cherish Is the Word

Do you ever think about what life will be like when you and your spouse have spent decades together? Will your loved one be there for you? How well will you know him? How well will he love you? Of course, as a twenty-something I rarely gave it much thought: at least, not until the day I watched *Heaven Can Wait*

(Paramount Pictures, 1978). In this popular film fantasy about the eternal nature of love and identity, a man and a woman become involuntarily separated. Fearing they will not recognize one another should they meet again, the lovers swear to remember; to give each other a chance; and to not be afraid. Those promises turn out to be the magic that makes their reunion and, we assume, their happily-ever-after possible.

I was as vulnerable as I have ever been when I watched that movie in 1978, but I will never regret the decision I made while the credits scrolled by. Though Dale and I had voluntarily separated months ago (we were only days away from court), and though everyone in my life thought divorcing him was the right thing to do, I knew suddenly, absolutely, brilliantly, that I was ready to love him for better, for worse, forever. I made an about-face because one thing—and one thing only—had changed.

My *why*.

Like most women, identifying *why* I wanted a man (and the same man) in my life, for the rest of my life, was not something I worried about. To tell the truth, I had never even considered it. But on that particular night, as my imagination was unleashed, I became aware of a spiritual hunger for a real partnership; a grand, reciprocal relationship. What I needed most, deep down, I decided, was a beautiful love, even a holy love, to sustain and lift me. If I had that kind of marriage, I told myself, I could forgive both Dale and myself as we grew and morphed through life—as decade by decade, he became a different man from the one I married, and I a more mature woman—as long as I felt sure…

- that he needed me—to achieve, and that he would help me to achieve.
- that he desired me—to be happy, and that he would try to make me happy.
- that he hoped through me—to reach his destiny, and that I could trust him to help me reach mine.

- that I was the most wonderful creature in the world to him, and he to me; that we could become the truest of friends.

In order to endure to the point of no-fear, no-doubt, I had to be convinced that, just as in the fairy tales, my man would treasure me as I treasured him, that he would never leave me as I intended to never abandon him, and that he would live his life for us, forever, just as I hoped to live my life for our family, no matter what.

I wanted to cherish and to be cherished thus.

As a mature woman, that same desire to cherish and to be cherished is still at the core of my nature, sewn into every fiber of my being. It is a source of life for my spirit, just as sleeping or eating is for my body. Having now cherished, and felt cherished, on a daily basis, I can tell you that the sensation in its fullness comes from more than appreciation, more than admiration, more than understanding. In fact, even the word *love* has such a wide range of valuation that when used tritely, it is a monochromatic shard of glass compared to the kaleidoscope inside "I cherish you." To cherish is beyond words. It is a thrilling, tender regard, a lasting spiritual impression. And such a priceless gift must come from more than a friend, more than a sibling, more than a child, more than a parent. It has to come from, and be given to, a partner, your soul mate. To experience the closeness of *cherish*, a woman must become her husband's Intimate.

If you are familiar with the Eden story, then you know the way God planted this need in women: "Thy desire shall be to thy husband" (Genesis 3:16). If you prefer biology, then you are familiar with the hormones that make up a woman, the chemistry that ignites when you feel loved by a man. However you explain its origins, there is a natural and healthy desire in a woman (healthy, that is, when balanced with a strong sense of self-worth, wisdom, and patience): an irresistible combustion of heart, body, and spirit. That desire, in its most hallowed state, is not about grabbing, clinging, or pushing in desperation for more, more, more from a man, or about wanting a partner to be different from or better than other men. It is not about satisfying a deficit in yourself, or making up for some childhood hurt or fear of abandonment. And it's not about over-nurturing, subservience, dependency, oppression, control, or giving without limits. Oh, no!

The sweet, spiritual longing that is the womanly need to cherish and to be cherished is the luscious cherry center in that proverbial box of chocolates called life, the beautifully designed ticket to bringing two people together and making the union last for a lifetime.

Of course, at that early point in our marriage we did not come close to the *cherish* level of supernal joy, security, and knowing. We were barely out of courtship. The fact is, we hadn't had enough of life to develop the reverence for one another that is necessary for two people to cherish each other—but I was committed to experiencing it someday. I was determined to become wise, generous, and courageous (a Pioneer Woman). I wanted to have an abundance of love to share with everyone, but especially with my husband (the Talent). I hoped to wrap silken strings of worth, faith, and desire around us so tight that there would be no chance of falling apart (the Creator and the Dream Maker).

Over the next several years, that is exactly what I did, by trial and error, and that is exactly what I'm going to teach you systematically. Though preparation to write *Wife for Life* included a great deal of reading and research so that I could present my experience in a sensible way, nothing proved as helpful as my own journals. Digging through nearly thirty-five years of personal letters and records, the pivotal event that stood out first and foremost was the crisis of near-divorce. Youthful diaries reminded me how the imaginary lovers of *Heaven Can Wait* had crystalized my *why* and changed our direction forever. Not only that, I realized the same movie had prompted me to wonder for the first time about *his why*: his reason to need me and to love me for a lifetime.

Even way back then, with so little understanding really, my feminine intuition sensed truth inside that fairy tale.

There was something powerful—and I could feel it—about a heroine believing in her hero.

4

Finding His Why

The ultimate adventure, when all the barriers and ogres have been overcome, is
commonly represented as a mystical marriage of the triumphant hero-soul with
the Queen Goddess of the World. This is the crisis at the nadir, the zenith, or at
the uttermost edge of the earth, at the central point of the cosmos, in the
tabernacle of the temple, or within the darkness of the deepest chamber of the
heart. —*Joseph Campbell, American mythology professor, writer, and lecturer*

In the fall of 2010, Israeli friends led us through the labyrinth of
ancient passages and landmarks that is Jerusalem. We were
working our way toward the city's famous Western Wall, a remnant
of the vast structure that was once Israel's Second Temple: rebuilt
by Herod, frequented by Jesus, and considered a holy site of
pilgrimage to practicing Jews. People from all over the world
worship there: writing hopes and wishes on scraps of paper,
tucking them between the ancient stones. Petitions at the Wall are
said to ascend directly to God.

It was after sunset by the time we arrived, and moonlight
spilled onto the courtyard. From our elevated position, we could
watch the multitudes approaching and lining the Wall: a living
spectacle, underscored by a haunting melody, a single disembodied
voice. We stood in silent reverie for a few moments, then, gratified
by the wonder in my face, our friends gently encouraged me.

"Go to the Wall," they said.

"Oh, no! Me? That's allowed? Really?"

I caught the current, flowing by footsteps into the crowd as it
separated by gender. We walked together, yet apart. The desert air

filled my lungs and fluttered my lashes while every hesitant step brought the Wall closer and closer...higher and higher...brighter and brighter...louder and louder until I heard *it*...the sound of the earth, the song of humanity, the Wailing of the Women.

Mothers, daughters, sisters, and wives rocked back and forth or swayed side to side, comforting themselves like they would a crying baby. Some mumbled, some sang, all prayed. It took only seconds before I too stood weeping at the Wailing Wall, tears streaming into the well of community. My heart wanted to burst— the emotions of so many others competed for space there: women and children from all over the world and from every corner of history, folding their wishes into the tiny crevices between my *own* dreams and disasters.

Jerusalem affected me deeply. For days I mulled it over, finally putting into storage my goal of writing a novel, choosing instead to write an inspirational book for women. That decision demanded a major relocation of imagination, but I embraced it almost instantly. My dreams, after all, have survived three decades of improvisation, postponement, and reinvention. At twenty-one, for instance, I delivered my first-born, a child with severe disabilities. Consequentially, the idea of becoming an actress morphed into becoming a public speaker and advocate. The vision of directing live theater transformed into organizing a complex therapy program involving dozens of volunteers. You see, mine is a life of contingencies: a life that is actually a composite of many other lives. I cannot help it. I am a woman. I am a relational creature by instinct. Like all the mothers, grandmothers, daughters, sisters, and wives at the Wailing Wall, my whole life, my every prayer, is about relationships.

If you think you are different, if you perceive life as something you can control outside the realm of others (as in, "I do my own thing")—I don't buy it. Even if you lived alone in the middle of the Pacific Ocean, the ebb and flow of your life as a woman would be discontinuous, constantly interrupted. Puberty, menstrual cycles, menopause, and aging wreak havoc on the best-laid plans. Introduce a baby to your island and suddenly pregnancy, breastfeeding, and scraped knees waylay you. In the real world, relatives and children arrive and depart this life unexpectedly. Friends and associates and opportunities come and go. So, no. Uh-uh. There is no way around it. In fact, you should be proud of it. You are a woman and you are an expert at adapting to new circumstances, at revising or reworking dreams as you go.

The days you take pride in that expertise should be many. However, you will undoubtedly have other days, maybe even extended periods of life, when you feel like a klutz of a woman, more fallible than malleable. As astute as we may become at keeping our balance in the surf, you and I both know the waves of change can sometimes overwhelm us. To keep your sanity—your sense of continuity when the tide changes and waves pull the sand out from under your feet—pause to consider the thread that keeps you upright. What makes it all make sense? What is the theme of your life? I long ago realized that mine was unifying people. All the crazy, diverse episodes and projects of my life have, at their core, a desire to unify. Your thread will be different, but you can find it if you think hard enough.

And when you think hard enough about the underlying principles you hold fast to, about the focus of your life that is actually linear, you will come closer to understanding the person that is your husband.

The Nature of the Male Quest

Of course, we all have dreams in common with one another, with all man-and womankind. We want to be happy, for instance. And we want to be healthy. We want to be loved and respected. We dream of having the necessities and comforts of life for ourselves and for our loved ones. But that's where it stops; our paths diverge from there—one great big human dream divides into a hundred million parts. Looking around me at all the people at the Western Wall I wondered: how do we dream alike? how do we dream differently? I sensed that the women and I dreamed at least in the same style. But I wasn't so sure about the men. What were they praying about? The mystery ate at me for several weeks. I finally decided to treat it as a riddle...

What do men dream about and how do their dreams affect their feelings towards a woman?

The riddle turned out to be far easier to solve than I'd expected, the answer hardly elusive. I found it repeated again and again, over and over—clearly, obviously. The secret lies in a universally acknowledged aspect of manhood, woven so completely into our concept of masculinity that it is represented in the facts and fables of every culture in every century. For all that ubiquity, however—even with men from historic Hercules to the Hollywood hero enacting it for us—the obvious remains surprisingly obscure to most women. Primed these days to think feminine energy is equal or superior (if not at least preferable) to male energy, a wife tends to overlook or discount what *really* makes her man tick. In doing so, she not only annihilates her husband's dreams, but contributes to the demise of her own. On the other hand, if she can try to comprehend and honor his dreams, weaving them into hers—or hers into his—both of their *whys* are fulfilled and she will draw him steadily to center, to real intimacy. And that is what makes a marriage grand.

So, here it is: the bull's-eye that leads straight to the center of the earth. If you haven't solved the mystery of his *why* by now, I'm going to give it to you:

In order to thrive, a man must have a quest.

The specific nature of the male quest varies from man to man and from stage to stage, but your husband innately casts himself as the protagonist on a Hero's Journey: the classical but highly personal tale of exertion, competition, and conquest. He is performance-driven: a biological imperative that is not going away just because some consider it passé, even ridiculous. After thousands, if not millions of years, the male nature is not likely to be relegated to folklore anytime soon. The Odysseus of Homer's epic poem, *The Odyssey*, is alive and well and tenaciously determined to win. He can overcome. He *must* overcome. He *will* achieve. You can see the male quest playing out in every office and sports arena, every church and court, every stage and studio, every marina and airport, every hospital, firehouse, and commercial kitchen, every city hall and world capital, every lab, library, and classroom, on every construction site, every farm, every mountain, every jungle, every battlefield.

Women are in all those places too, of course, right beside men. So what makes his quest different from her dream? At first glance, not so much; as we've said, he wants to be happy, you want to be happy. But if we compare *dream* to *quest* inside an ocean metaphor, the differences rise to the surface. A woman's dreams, which come from the heart, are like the waves of the sea, undulating with the tug and pull of life's tides, receptive to and inclusive of external forces. A man's quest, on the other hand, is more like the Gulf Stream: a one-directional current, forceful, self-contained, and utterly tied to his identity.

He believes that what he does is who he is.

This defining journey for a man—again, like the Gulf Stream —accelerates as it progresses, propelled by tension and strain, just as ocean currents are driven by wind stress. We can compare the young man to an arrow strung in a taut bow (perhaps searching for a direction), the slightly older man to the arrow just released, and the mature man to the arrow arching through the air. Regardless of the stage, his trajectory rarely changes once he has settled on a quest—only out of the greatest necessity, certainly not as frequently or as gracefully as a woman's might. She thinks on a grid. He thinks on a line. The linear narrowness of the quest has a purpose, however. It helps him compress energy and gather strength, developing the laser-beam focus required to power through his most impossible dream.

Of course, the ultimate outcome of the ultimate adventure is a decisive victory. If his quest is completed in this life, then he will live and die a happy man. But if his quest is involuntarily delayed, interrupted, or aborted prematurely because he has miscalculated, or worse, because he was emasculated, he will live, and eventually die, a tired, sick, angry, corrupted, or broken man. We all know examples. Either outcome is possible for a man because his biological and spiritual essence is not about nurturing relationships as a woman's is (though he will learn much about that from her). Rather, his value and distinction come from nurturing a personal quest. He is impelled by nature to chase, to capture, and to tame his own wild side: to discover, then wrangle, preposterous plans into logical, glorious goals.

Believe it or not (and if not, you soon will), Mother Nature is a perfect genius for designing him that way. She's a sista' and when she bequeathed a mission to your man...she did it for you.

His *Why* for Living

I remember the kiss. I remember the exact kiss, which came fully, passionately, in a tirade of kisses. The difference in this particular kiss was its shocking tenderness. Its red-hot delicacy so astonished me, I pulled back and gasped. He begged for more, as if in holy agony: a state of fear and elation that bordered on frenzy. It amazed me. Then and there, at the fulcrum of our give and take, at the fork between physical and spiritual, a new world opened up to me, and I apprehended my husband.

He needs me!

The revelation sank deep. The plainness of it filled my soul. Its simple beauty turned me inside out. With one full-throttle kiss, my man had let down his defenses and exposed his raw, ravenous *dependence* on me. Just as surely as if he had sliced open his chest and handed me his heart, I knew in that moment that I held his every hope...his every hurt...his every opportunity.

Once, as a preschooler, I visited a petting zoo. Fluffy things fascinated me: bunnies and kittens of course; but the most intriguing creatures of all were tiny baby chicks. Diminutive size communicated vulnerability to me, and I yearned for a touch. Someone finally noticed me hanging over the cage and put a squirming chick into my fingers. Yellow fuzz, warm from the heat lamp, made me want to squeeze it like a hot water bottle. I would have, except hovering hands snatched it away.

Good thing. And too bad male hearts can't be rescued like that before wives (acting more like little girls than women) thoughtlessly crush them. I understand a lot about why they do. There's a whole list of whys, actually, which we'll discuss in Chapter 8, but the most common reason women squash their man's crusade (and thereby his heart) is plain old ignorance. They just don't know. Here's a man, probably bigger and thicker than she is. Who would guess that he's as susceptible to her careless treatment as that little chick to a child's? It's not something he can tell you. He won't verbalize his sacred need. In fact, he will do his best to cover it up, because a man's aim is to impress his woman with strength. To be so blatantly sensitive would let you see how easily he is humiliated, and that would make him dangerously vulnerable —something he cannot tolerate. Failing translates to ultimate mental, and therefore physical, stress.

So, since he cannot explain that you are like air and water to him, your man gives you kisses instead—and prays you understand that his why for living is the same as his why for loving!

There is no quest without his woman. For a married man, all roads lead to his wife.

If a married man begins adulthood as a normal, well-intentioned guy, the support and enthusiasm of a Wife for Life will turn his ordinariness into greatness. Personal strife will turn into a crusade—if she believes in him. The goal is irrelevant: it might be starting a business, curing cancer, remodeling the house, or pitching a no-hitter. The point is that she believes he can do it and that he should do it. He can outrun fear, doubt, and insecurity—the demons nipping at his heels—if she sets the pace. His wife is the springboard as well as the finish line. She makes him reach. She also makes him accountable because she is the only other person in it for the long haul and the only one who cares as much as he does. She is the most intimate, immediate witness to his grinding investment, the only one who can truly appreciate the payoff because she paid too. And that's why he needs a (committed) Wife for Life. A lot of quests can take decades to discover, achieve, and glory in. You earn that ticker-tape parade together.

As you know, I made the decision after our separation, to buckle in and hold on no matter how long or bumpy the ride. Most of the turbulence that followed involved his search for a quest. Of course, I only added to the tumult by refusing to comprehend just how desperate he was to find it. I fought exasperation and impatience, longing for roots while he behaved (from my perspective) like a nomad. *Why look to square off with a giant?* I thought. *We're happy enough in our little cottage—aren't we? In fact, if a quest is so important, how about changing that dirty diaper, or offering to sweep the kitchen?*

Obviously, I didn't get it. And it wasn't until I did get it (years later I'm embarrassed to admit) that he began to fly and real happiness came home to stay—literally. Since my man finally took aim at his pie-in-the-sky nearly fifteen years ago (we've been married thirty-five), he has clocked more than two million air miles in his work as a professional speaker. Which leaves me where? That's right, at home. We had four children, who were, by choice, my life for many years, including our daughter with developmental disabilities. Giving him permission to go full bore with my full support meant I had to become a strong, secure person, responsible for my own development and happiness, a real Pioneer Woman. I could not become the vested partner Dale needed until I let him go. Then, when he came home to us (which was often enough to be an engaged father and a loving husband), I generally felt calm and together, and he, in turn, was vigorous and content. His arrow was flying high. He became a hundred times more effective as a family man because of it. And as our relationship advanced this way, we *both* found joy, because something truly magical had happened: *his quest had become one of my most important dreams, and my dreams had become part of his quest.* He did everything in his power to support and facilitate whatever I visualized for myself and the children as the years went by.

This is more than our story; it is a mythic tale, an epic of a quest replayed a million times, always framed in the context of a struggle between man and God, or between man and nature, or man versus man. On the surface it may appear egocentric, as if the proverbial world revolves around storybook him. However, the down-to-earth truth of it is, the protagonist becomes a hero only when he self-sacrifices: it is how we define the archetype. The story cannot really be about him. Everyone knows it. He knows it.

His impossible dream is only possible, only noble, only beautiful and worthwhile, if it is for someone else.

And that someone must be you.

He wants with all his heart to believe, and wants you to believe, that he does what he does not only because of you, but for you—a magnificent obsession born of love. He offers you a reason, through his quest, to admire him, to desire him, to hold fast to him—sensing innately that you crave the kind of man you can respect. And when you gratify this longing in your man's heart, receiving his quest as a gift, he is enlarged and emboldened. *You have inspired him.*

I remember how Dale once, in pursuit of a professional certification, spent weeks preparing for an intense immersion course that encompassed a vast amount of highly technical knowledge. The fact that those who passed the six-hour test had spent their entire education and career in the field, while he was relatively new to that body of knowledge, stacked the odds hugely against him. But, like biblical David, he took his shot.

The whole process filled me with ache and awe, truly something for a wife to behold: her man determined and magnificent. It was also heartrending to see the after-effects: the weight of the commitment, the pressure of investment, and the uncertainty of success doing their best to derail his hopes and dreams.

I did all I could to distract and build him up as weeks passed without word of the results. It was not the first time he had tried to take a mountain down, and I knew, based on experience and chemistry, that my faith in him would mysteriously contribute to the outcome. When he dropped his slingshot, I picked it up and tucked it back into his belt.

Weeks after taking the test, he burst into the room, breathless, shoving the screen of his smart phone in my face. There it was: the long-awaited email with his score. I wrapped my arms around him and we wept. My man had slain his Goliath the way a hero—when his woman believes in him—always does. We rejoiced in this triumph for hours, and as we celebrated later that night, I got my revelatory kiss, the one that left all the others behind.

So there it is. I've given you the answer. Our hunt for a man's *why* for marriage has led us to an unlimited source of glittering gold: a treasure trove hidden in plain view...

Inspiring wives are cherished by their husbands. If riches make things grand, then this knowledge can make you a very wealthy woman for the rest of your life.

5
Your Husband, Positively

You have lifted my very soul up into the light of your soul, and I am not
ever likely to mistake it for the common daylight.
—*Elizabeth Barrett, English poet*

Talk of wealth and riches is always heady stuff. You knew though
(because you know your fairy tales), that sooner or later, the wise
old woman would enter the fable and extend a word of caution.
That would be me. So here is my advice (which, I admit, would be
more memorable in iambic pentameter): Beware the temptation to
grab the money and run. Please do not approach him tonight with:
"So, honey, what quest are we on today?" It won't work, and it's a
recipe for disaster. Though I hope you found the discussion of how
his why fulfills *your why* provocative, there is much more to
comprehend before you can inspire him through the decades. You
will have to gain access to his innermost self—patiently passing
through the steps (the time and effort) it takes to become his
Intimate. The *hows* and the *whats* involved in that process (which
make up the rest of this book) won't ring true unless you respect
something very basic to both your evolution and his.

The masculine brain.

I wish I had time to research and write up a set of
encyclopedias on the subject—it's *that* interesting—but I don't,
and besides, there are already shelves full of great books by
contemporary researchers. Suffice it to say, the old hardline
position that there is no difference between men and women has

been thoroughly, soundly, scientifically debunked. Perceptions about gender have swung from one extreme to the other over the past century and are now closer to a realistic middle. While real progress has been made in eliminating discrimination against women, at least in Western society, today's men suffer a subtler prejudice. Women sometimes forget that the well-intentioned man in their life craves and deserves validation as much as anyone.

So, with all due respect, let's take a closer look at that man of yours.

First of all, I know what you're thinking: What in the world is he thinking?

To answer that question, I could recommend a number of fascinating books, but the most helpful to me was Michael Gurian's aptly titled work, *What Could He Be Thinking? How A Man's Mind Really Works*. A social philosopher specializing in neurobiology, Gurian takes into account both nature and nurture to determine male biological trends. Though he focuses on the commonalities among men, he carefully points out that, for all their similarities, men do vary by degrees. He explains this in terms of what he calls "the brain spectrum." At one end of the human continuum, structurally and hormonally, is the most intensely male brain imaginable (think "action hero"). At the other extreme is the most female brain (think "the most talk-oriented, nonspatial woman").

Your man falls somewhere within that spectrum, as do you, depending on a combination of biology and psychology, and it will be your work as a Wife for Life to figure out and make allowances for him as a man and as an individual. It is also your commission to emphasize his particular strengths, for both your sakes, and to be grateful for his maleness. Mother Nature intended for masculine drive and feminine energy to harmonize. If balanced, complementary dynamics create grand marriage. If disrespected, the two forces create sparks igniting the dynamite that blows your dreams to smithereens.

Another way to put this warning is that getting fired up over a long list of frustrations will only generate pain. Contempt is hazardous. A long list of negatives about him is like a fuse leading to a suicide bomb: you and the innocent bystanders (i.e., children) are bound to get hurt. Since the motivation behind this project is to spare women and children unnecessary pain, I am going to bundle up a few of the most dangerously common complaints wives have about their husbands and send them to the hinterlands. I want to blow them up by the time you finish this book. I want to help you obliterate, eradicate, and annihilate that way of thinking by sharing my perspective, my experience, and the findings of brain mapping and modern research.

This chapter will be a brief treatment of the subject—an overview. We will explore his psyche and nature more in depth in other parts of the book. Here, however, we will examine some of the most common of the derogatory clichés about men—clichés which some women actually believe—then turn each one upside down to help right your perspective. (Remember, your man may be a lot like these clichés or only a little, depending on that cocktail mixed up for him in the home and gene pool.) You see, the same male foibles that annoy you as a woman can also be seen as masculine traits that enhance the feminine part of yourself. These particular attributes can be necessary to fulfilling the male quest, which you now know can help support and facilitate your own dreams. It all depends on how you look at it, how you orient yourself. You have the power to not only live with his differences, but to learn to love them.

Of course, we are talking about Nice Guys here—that is, generally well-intentioned men. Extremes in any of these cases can be imagined and debated and all kinds of personality differences discussed, but that is for psychologists to deal with. It is not our purpose here. We are addressing *common annoyances* that can be better dealt with just by a change in your attitude. So let's consider the following clichés and some alternate ways of looking at men's idiosyncrasies.

Cliché: Men are pig-headed. They won't seek out help or advice.

In fact, a man's tendency to solve problems analytically and independently is vital to overcoming obstacles on his quest. It's important for men to be able to think for themselves, to be intellectually independent and incisive under pressure. During times of crisis, you'll no doubt be grateful that your husband is an autonomous, self-confident thinker.

How this plays out:

She: Come on honey, you've been trying to unstop that toilet for an hour. Let's forget it.

He: No, I've almost got it.

You can scold him for not buying a better plunger, complain about the age of the apartment, or suggest calling a plumber. But remember that he loves to solve problems and has to do it in his own way and in his own head.

Cliché: Men are insensitive, judgmental, and unsympathetic.

Men are hard-wired, generally, to stay level-headed and focused, to process logically and rationally, not emotionally; they try to reach a solution by the shortest distance possible, using a take-action paradigm. These characteristics are critical to averting disaster and avoiding costly detours on his quest. Being mentally swift and strong even in stressful circumstances is a good thing. Your husband is probably much more likely than you to be undeterred and undistracted by emotion in high-stakes situations and to sort through priorities with speed and precision.

How this plays out:

She: The girls at work are so catty...I can't take their gossip anymore. It hurts.

He: Ignore them. Eat lunch at your desk.

You can pout at him, shout at him, throw a punch at him, but it won't change the fact that he is solution-oriented. You gave him a problem; he fixed it.

Cliché: Men are workaholics. It is more important to them to be top dog at work than to be helpful at home.

You could also say that men are meant to have a career (or a passion of some sort) and to *work* it: to perform and accomplish great deeds to benefit the world as well as the family. Men's nature is to tackle tough jobs with the intent of excelling; they want to go out and conquer, to succeed at challenges despite other pressures. They are born generally with a natural aptitude for these things and with the ability to work hard and consistently through all of life's changes and challenges. Be grateful that your husband is competing for power outside of the home, rather than with you in the home. And remember that because he is biologically driven to achieve in the world, he becomes testy or depressed if focused solely on home matters.

How this plays out:

She: Why can't you wrap it up and come home early?

He: I have one more meeting. I'll get home as soon after that as possible.

You can yelp in his ear, remind him of past promises, hang up the phone without saying good-bye—but his biology dictates that he earn his worth before intimacy. He would go crazy without work and he is more loving at home when he feels accomplished.

Cliché: Men are Neanderthals when it comes to expressing emotion. They are obsessed with the physical and only want

one thing from a woman.

Men obviously create life and protect it, both of which require physicality. Not only is a man's quest ultimately fulfilled in passing on his legacy to posterity, but his need for a sexual connection binds him to his wife and opens him up to emotional intimacy; he will generally express or release his feelings through physicality rather than with language. This physicality also helps perpetuate the human race in that your man is ready to use his power as necessary to protect and ensure the survival of his kin. He can be a father with the bulk, strength, and aggressiveness to act as a living shield in dangerous situations and to provide for his family in perilous circumstances; he is often innately honing the skills (throwing, jumping, running; practicing speed and distance, testing his strength), and gathering the information that may be necessary to that end.

How this plays out:
She: You're going out to play ball with the guys again?
He: What's wrong with that?

She can mention the shopping, the broken fence, and the tall grass in the back, or she can call to mind that he is a physical creature who will see to those jobs better and more willingly after a good game of basketball; he biologically needs play to balance out his intense drive to work.

Or:
She: Do I look okay?
He: I thought you could tell how pretty you look by the way I look at you.
She: No, honey. I'm a girl. We need words.
He: You look gorgeous...beautiful...ravishing.
She: No, I mean like poetry. C'mon.
He: Thou *dost* look gorgeous...fabulous.

She can sulk, lecture him, or belittle him, but he is action-not language-oriented, and he expresses his admiration for her through their physical relationship.

Cliché: Men are easily manipulated by women.

It is men's ability to work in concert and cooperation with women that helps build society. Most men want women to draw upon their male strengths and virtues because pleasing, impressing, and responding to women is central to their quest (Chapter 4). In fact, your man is motivated to be the best he can be by the fact of *you*. He is inspired by the thought of impressing *you*. His greatest joy comes from *your* happiness. This is at the heart of everything he is, everything he wants to be.

Let me show you how this plays out by sharing a personal story.

My Dream Becomes His Quest

Nearly twenty years ago, I became enraptured with my family history, my paternal line in particular. A string of seafaring grandfathers had accumulated real life-and-death adventures the way most people collect books or postcards. My overactive imagination ignited, and I spent years seriously investigating not only their personal lives, but nautical history itself. Our home burst with papers, letters, model ships, fine art, seashells, and lighthouses. I painted everything ocean blue. We coated our Florida pool blue. Even the new carpet was blue. My aspiration to write a historical fiction based on one particular forefather filled my life with the sea. I traveled to all the American ports he had touched just to further my research, but without a trip to China or Scotland, I'd gone about as far as I could go. That is, until Sea Trek.

It took only a day or two after hearing about an upcoming

crossing of the Atlantic by two tall ships between Europe and the U.S. for my Honey to sign me on as crew. I still wonder where he got the money back then, but in his mind, that was not the issue. He was fixated on my dreams—an ideal I had not even specifically articulated; he just knew it, and he just did it. My man put me on a plane, duffle bag in hand, to catch up with the Sea Trek ships in Bermuda for the last leg, bound for New York City.

The year was 2001 and the month was October: twenty-five days after 9/11. My ship, the Norwegian liner *Statsraad Lehmkuhl*, all three masts and three hundred feet of her, would sail past a still smoking Ground Zero, and dock in the New York harbor—*if* they would let us.

We bulldozed our way through a one heck of an Atlantic storm, twenty-two sails straining to wrangle the breezes, propelled toward our open ending. I credit my imagination, which was in top form after years of books and photographs and movies, for the illustrious fact that I was the only one in the amateur crew of one hundred who could keep a meal down! (Or maybe I'm a Viking if you go far enough back.) Over and over, the crew put me on bow watch with a rotating partner. No one but me on my overnight watch could stomach that position for very long—the plunging and the rising of the ship was too dramatic.

The real drama, however, lay ahead of us. As we glided into New York Harbor, we realized we were the *only* ship allowed to do so; the tension-filled city distrusted all strangers. Our poignant night, alone in that vast harbor (usually one of the world's busiest), made us sad yet heady.

What else could we do but dance?

Long after midnight—after one last reverie to Neil Diamond's "Coming to America," while the lights of Manhattan glistened to starboard and Lady Liberty radiated port side—I finally fell asleep with my friends on deck. I dreamed of my Dale and how much I loved him for this.

Clearly, my husband considers it his life's mission, his delight, his passion, to do what he can to help my dreams come true. We have visited Athens, Barcelona, Brussels, Budapest, Munich, Stockholm, Salzburg, Tel Aviv, Tokyo, Glasgow, Honolulu, Antibes, and Paris. We actually lived in London. It is his work—a very hard-earned thirty-year career with tremendous and painful upheavals—that carries us to these fantastic places, but that is *why* he works: for *us*, for *me*, for our children, for our grandchildren, for dreams.

Norway was the most spectacular trip of all. It won't surprise you that I spent my free day in Oslo at the Viking Ship Museum, the Kon Tiki Museum, the Norwegian National Maritime Museum, and the Fram Museum (named for a famous polar vessel). After that, Dale was so keen on getting to Bergen (on the opposite coast) that we hopped buses, trains, and ferries through the fjords. Of course, it was raining when we arrived. (Big surprise: it rains 300 days a year there.) I didn't mind; I'm a Pacific North-westerner; venturing out into the puddles of Bergen, Norway, was fine with me as long as I could share an umbrella with Dale. He hurried me into my coat and boots, and, confiscating the biggest umbrella the hotel offered, led me through the rotating doors and out onto the wet streets. My man was on a mission. I had to step lively to keep my head dry.

With a twist here and a turn there, we at last emerged from the labyrinth of cobbled lanes leading to Bergen's picturesque harbor. Lined with yachts bundled up for winter, the misty scene made me step out from under the umbrella and cry heavier than Norwegian rain.

Straight ahead—towering over the wharf, over the boats, over the buildings, and even the mountains—in all her glory, in all her splendor, in all her majesty, in all my dreams—stood the *Statsraad Lehmkuhl.*

Dale had remembered that Bergen was her home and brought me to her.

I know I could have traveled to Europe alone. It is certainly possible for a woman to make her own dreams come true. But that experience turned into a Nordic fairy tale only when presented by my Intimate as a gift of love, the beautiful fruition of decades and decades of investment...in him.

When I made my choice thirty years earlier to be a Wife for Life, when I worked to become as strong as a Pioneer Woman and used my inherent creativity to master the art of marriage, when I decided the greatest talent of all was maintaining relationships, and that I would use my power to inspire my husband—not just accepting but embracing his maleness, his oppositeness—I was laying the groundwork, all along, for that day in Bergen.

World travel and Norway might have you thinking Dale is an unusually good and lucky guy, but you only know him *now*. I shake my head thinking how everyone in our early days—and I mean everyone—thought I should toss him! He was terribly "stupid" (his own word) about relationships *and* the future (even by his own admission)—which is true of many young men until their cause is found and their crusade underway. No one told me that, but I knew it somehow in an abstract and hopeful way, so I hung in there and tried to mature myself. It took a while, but eventually he landed a quest and thereafter, grew and grew and grew, and me too and too and too.

That kind of metamorphosis was only possible because as he sacrificed himself, *he found himself* and learned to love with a purpose. Now isn't *that* a twist on the outdated notion of a woman sacrificing herself to a man! We prickle at the suggestion of wifely surrender but swoon over *his* heroics. The idea of a man giving his all for the love of his life makes us melt. Want a real-life, close-to-home, earth-shattering example? Think about this: Your man would, if necessary, die for you.

Now *there's* male nature for you. Juxtapose that with the modern woman's idea that she has evolved past needing a man. He does not have the luxury of not needing you! His drive to impress you will never be extinguished. It is in his very cells, in his blood, in his brain, in his soul. A Nice Guy will work tirelessly—in his masculine style, not your feminine style—to make and keep you happy and to show you how much he loves and depends on you— if you help hone and honor his righteous quest (or the quest for a quest).

The stones of the Western Wall in Jerusalem are still standing because people have used their dreams to reinforce the ancient mortar: countless tiny papers, full of women's dreams. Millions more are filled with the quests of men. The essence of each prayer spirals up to heaven and, in my imagination, intertwines with the others like the braids of a rope. And when that rope reaches its destination, God grabs the line and lifts mankind.

Men and women need each other.

Part 2

HOW TO AVOID BECOMING
A DREAM BREAKER

6
Killing Him Softly

Many people are very surprised to find out what love can be like
underneath its charming exterior.
—*Mike Mason, writer*

I once had a nightmare that started out like a dream. Spring had
popped out of the ground and all over the trees in bright, unearthly
colors while the sun splayed warmth and light so intense, you
could hardly open your eyes. Four young women, all in their late
teens and early twenties, stood in the shade of the wraparound
porch, watching while I positioned myself and my camera in the
center of the road. I had bought each of my subjects brand-new
outfits of pure white—summer cloth that smelled and looked like
fresh linen on a clothesline. As the breeze ruffled their dresses and
teased their hair, I carefully set up the tripod and secured the
camera, playing with the lens to get it just right. These pictures had
to be perfect. I finally motioned to the first girl and told her to start
walking down the road away from the camera. "Go on! Go on!" I
urged. "All the way." With each step, the girl, like Wonderland-
Alice, shrunk in size until she fit like a dot in the center of the lens.

"Stop!" I called. "That's it!"

Click.

Next came Girl #2, then 3 and 4. With the push of a button, I
preserved each of them like pressed blossoms, the epitome of
innocence, beauty, and springtime: not at the end of the road, but at
the beginning, before summer, when they could breathe morning
air and believe in warm afternoons. Fall was far, far away and

winter would never come.

I waved at the girls and they waved back, all of us pleased as poppies. They began to chat happily, and I turned back to the camera, prepared to dismantle the tripod and pack up my bag.

I never got the chance.

The sun, which suddenly grew scalding hot, began to drip. It moved down and across the sky, then bloated and filled the opposite end of the street. Like a glob of paint pitched at an unsuspecting canvas, it drooped and then ran onto the rest of the landscape, overwhelming the pastels with oranges, reds, and browns. I watched helplessly as everything melted into the liquid goo. Even the girls dissolved one by one, their white dresses trailing with tenacity, sucked gradually into a whirlpool of grey.

I woke up sobbing, grieving.

What Happened to Spring?

As a wife, mother, mentor, counselor, advisor, leader, friend, daughter, aunt, and sister, I have known, and lost my heart to, many young women, and the four in my dream represent them all. Most recently, an especially beautiful thirty-something, an unmarried school teacher with a tall, slender figure, chestnut hair, and doe eyes became my friend. As we talked, she looked at me deeply and asked: "People are in love and are friends when they marry. Why doesn't it stay that way?" My heart slowed down. Every time I see fear of failure overpower hope and confidence, the vision of that ruined landscape makes me want to sob again.

It does happen. There is no denying it. Spring turns to summer and summer to fall and fall to winter, and winter can be very, very cold. You may have already been there, or perhaps you *are* there, or you have observed it in the lives of others, particularly family. For some, the ice creeps up over the decades until they find themselves frozen in a distorted version of marriage, or they decide somewhere along the line that waking up to shivers is no longer tolerable, so they separate after many years.

For others—actually, for most others, since the majority of divorces happen in the first seven years—an early frost catches them by surprise. The young couples, cultivators who have been diverting a lot of energy from the roots into creating leaves and flowers on their marriage tree, find they must invest more stored energy than they bargained for to produce a second flush of romance and happiness. Since it is still so early in the growing season, this is quite possible. However, there is also the potential that freezing temperatures will blight their springtime flowers to such an extent that the tree won't produce any more flowers that year, and they thus assume there will be no fruit come summer.

In order to grow and produce, a husband and wife have to reveal their vulnerabilities to one another; we have to put our thoughts, dreams, and emotions out there. Only the belief that we are accepted and loved *as is* gives us the trust and courage to let buds unfurl, exposing delicate leaves and petals to the air. If that spring air, which we depend on to be forgiving and gentle, turns harsh—if our partner responds to our emotional nakedness with insensitivity, treating our weaknesses or ignorance or good intentions with coolness, carelessness, contempt, or condescension —then there is a very strong probability that the freeze will damage whatever flowers of trust have formed and ruin the subsequent fruits.

The catastrophe in all of this, unfortunately, is that spring is not as capricious as she seems. She is not some imp drawing us irresponsibly into a fool's paradise, enticing us with artificial blue skies and plastic gardens. She does not tell us to fling open the windows just so she can douse us with rain. Newly formed marriages, like spring, are actually very predictable and thus survivable.

Mine was no exception.

When Dale and I jumped feet-first into the very deep water called marriage, our parents (and presumably everyone else who cared) watched us from the pool's edge to see how long before we came up for air. They knew that we did not fully comprehend what we were doing. No one told us that we had just surrendered personal autonomy; that we had given ourselves completely into each other's immature hands; that we had no strategy or defense or protection other than love, and that our love at that stage was more like a pool toy than a life preserver. They didn't tell us that once our souls were sealed, we would either sink or swim together, that we could *never* be altogether severed, that we would cause each other joy or remorse for the rest of our lives. In the giddy state that is newlywed bliss, we wouldn't have listened to that gibberish anyway. Like reckless French revolutionaries, we threatened to cut off the head of anything that opposed us. Our righteous romance seemed so invincible, in fact—so impervious to outside intimidation, so inevitable in the cosmic scheme of things—that it took a whole two or three months before we detected the leak. It was just a whistle of air to begin with, but the fizzle became a fissure, and soon we were losing air and taking on water faster than we could reinflate ourselves.

And really—should we? Reinflate? That was the question. Personally, I was out of breath. I didn't know if I could manage blowing up my plastic Superman every day for the rest of my life. He'd be leaking again within a day or two anyway. I gradually stopped patching up my ideals—as well as the person who was responsible for deflating them. My darling of a man became a major liability, and it got to the point that I could barely look at him. All the good, worthy aspects of his character and manhood, the things about him that had lifted me to ecstasy on our wedding day, were rapidly sinking in value, replaced by the rising importance of all the annoying, alarming aspects, things I was convinced he'd purposely kept hidden from me. What I didn't know, what I couldn't see, was that I had fallen in love with a potential, not a person.

Although my childhood was not a traumatic one, I came into

adulthood with my own plans (like every other human being), including some daydreams that I imagined would right my personal nightmares. And isn't that where many dreams begin? Emerging out of the perceived deficits in adolescence and childhood? ("When I grow up...") We can hardly resist the embedded influence of our youthful experiences, the way we were raised. Feeling victimized (often unconsciously), we look to others —especially our partners—to soothe the pain, to heal the ego, to fill the gaps, to fix the break, to restore the self, to repair the heart. Women especially can be susceptible to savior substitutes, and in those days, I considered Dale the universe. I expected said universe to revolve around me. Very much like the baby birds that appear every spring outside my living-room window, I acted perpetually dependent, always hungry. *Gimmegimmegimme*, the newborn says, mouth gaping, anxiously awaiting another morsel.

That was the pressure I put on Dale. With marriage, as opposed to dating or courtship, my expectations of him had obviously, and rather dramatically, changed. At first, I communicated those demands manipulatively. Then, when he didn't respond to my subtle calls for transformation, my hints began to sound more like commands. Of course, when that approach didn't work either, I resorted to ultimatums.

Poor guy. Because my appetite for attention was insatiable and because his execution was not up to my standards, his emotional and mental health began to deteriorate and his physical health was not far behind. I had no clue of the traumatic impact my attitude had on him or appreciation for the fact that, as a young man, he had been handed the controls with no experience or tutoring in how to fly a plane. We managed to take off on the wings of love— all very exciting, and what a view!—but neither of us knew how to keep our jumbo jet in the air.

Since a man lives with the incessant pressure to perform and bets his own self-worth on success, I want to emphasize how gutsy it was for Dale to climb into the cockpit called *commitment* in the first place. Because he is a good guy, a well-intentioned guy, he committed not only to the wedding day, but to a lifetime of co-living and co-giving. He compromised the precious independence that he, like all men, had fought so hard for since boyhood. He took on hefty responsibilities—not just for himself anymore—but for me and our future children, including promises to…

- please (always),
- provide (as much as possible),
- protect (when necessary),
- problem solve (as called upon), and
- procreate (as agreed upon).

Quite a checklist for a new co-pilot. Now that I appreciate how much courage it took for him even to taxi down the runway, I understand why men in general are slower to commit to marriage than women are. As clinical psychologists and coauthors Connell Cowan and Melvyn Kinder explain in *Women Men Love, Women Men Leave:* "Men today seem more afraid of commitment not because they don't want to marry or enter into life-long bonds, but precisely because they do and they are taking it seriously" (p. 174-175). And the five Ps should be taken seriously. The healthiest families need men who are willing and able to do all five. Even so, to a guy with no experience in family building, the Ps are very intimidating.

My groom, like most grooms, however, took confidence in the innate knowledge that pleasing, providing, protecting, problem-solving, and procreating were in his male nature. "And," he reasoned, "didn't she fall in love with me because I'm a man? Surely, she loves me enough to be patient as I master the five Ps, and I think she believes in me enough to help me become the man I want to be." When he was convinced that I actually, truly, genuinely, had faith in him, he mustered up the derring-do to say "I do." We looked at each other across the altar: he, at his fantasized version of me, and me, at my idealized version of him, and there was no doubt we could fly.

Then suddenly, before we knew it, within just a few months of takeoff—when the exhilaration had died down and the intoxication had worn off—we were looking at each other, not across an altar draped with the bridal bouquet, but across a bare kitchen table with a vase of wilted daffodils between us. I detailed how I felt in my personal journal:

I think I will burst with sadness. Dale played his guitar and sang "Blossom" for me tonight. Memories crashed forth, one on top of the other— and then the tears. I ran outside and while he talked to his parents who had called, and I cried and cried and cried and hugged myself. Dale of course was distressed and helpless. This has happened more than once. Last Sunday, I felt just as disordered, so unhappy. We sat in the car and waited. I waited for some sort of peace to calm me and Dale waited for some sort of understanding. My heart was breaking. I wondered amidst my flood of tears if our marriage was right—if I had been honest with myself. And though it is the most soul-rendering thing to admit, I don't feel like I have had a true burning in my soul that it is right. I try and brighten my mood by other means, but the light fades and so does my soul—empty indifference. And it hasn't happened all at once. I am in a panic. Can the whole thing be called off?

As Mike Mason describes in *The Mystery of Marriage*, "Marriage faces us squarely with the problem of what to do with love once we have finally caught it. Or rather, once it has caught us" (p. 65). That's how I saw it: I was caught, I was trapped, I was in trouble. And I was very, very frightened. *What had I ever seen in him?* Of course, I could not bear to look at myself, to see my part in the deterioration of our springtime. All I cared about was that he had failed me. I misinterpreted his insecurity as inability and that meant I couldn't respect him. And how could I live with a man I couldn't respect?

The truth was, as we will explore more in a later discussion; using the thematic paradigm offered by Emerson Eggerichs, Ph.D., in his book *Love and Respect, The Love She Most Desires, The Respect He Desperately Needs*, my lack of respect while demanding his love was actually hurtling us toward alienation.

I was the inadvertent catalyst. I had the power. Whenever someone hears that Dale and I were at divorce's door years ago, they inevitably ask me, straight up: What happened? Well, you haven't heard the worst of it.

Why Do We Hurt the Men We Love?

Whenever I recall the times I was hurtful to Dale, I remember one incident in particular. I don't know why this shameful day stands out in my mind more than any other, because there were plenty of days like it, but perhaps because it was a red-letter day.

It was a hot, sultry night and Dale was glad to escape to the cool of our basement bedroom after the baby was tucked away. I followed him down, but not to disrobe and lie near the fan. Sleep was the last thing on my mind. Outside, pranksters well-versed in pyrotechnics were celebrating the Fourth of July a couple of days early, and it infuriated me all the more. Like one of their firecrackers, I was about to explode. It took the tiniest friction— Dale asking, "What's eating you?"—to send me into the stratosphere.

My husband bolted upright in bed, back against the wall. I never left the bedroom doorway, intentionally blockading the only way out. With both barrels full, I bore down on him with a vengeance. Words spewed out of me like the nonstop rounds of a machine gun; I never took a breath. What I didn't know back then was that, as a woman, I had at least six cortical areas for language in both hemispheres of my brain, compared to his *one*, so I unfairly outgunned him. I also didn't comprehend how paralyzing or fearful it is to a man to be overwhelmed, or flooded, by intensely negative emotion. Truthfully, it probably wouldn't have made much difference if I had known. I was so riled up, I would only have pressed my advantage. Even seeing the visible effects of a splattered ego—for there might as well have been blood all over the room—did not give me pause. I kept at him with a merciless barrage of criticism and contempt for over an hour, ruthlessly sure of my mark, feeling all the while oh-so-vindicated. When at long last I ran out of steam, he slumped over lifeless.

I left the room and went upstairs. The big show was over, both inside and out. In the one a.m. stillness, I heard a whimper from the nursery and felt a twinge of guilt. Heading to the kitchen to grab a cup for myself and a bottle for the baby, I passed the family calendar, highlighted on an otherwise bare wall by the spill of a street lamp. There, around the number 4, just beneath the block letters J-U-L-Y, was a fat, red-marker circle: my reminder that I was about to menstruate. If a live orchestra had underscored my horror at that moment, the string section would have shrieked in dissonance.

I had killed a man for PMS.

We women go crazy for all kinds of reasons. And men drive us crazy in all kinds of ways. Every relationship is a delicate balance between attachment and autonomy, between her needs and his, between my will and yours. Like ice skaters who circle together then spin apart, we are a team, even as we are individuals. That's obvious. What is not so obvious is how to achieve just enough simultaneous oneness and otherness to keep the dance flowing. When the relationship is relatively new, it is especially start-and-stop frustrating. You can expect to step on toes and land on your butt more often than not. But that's no reason to quit! You're just warming up.

Or cooling down.

After my fireworks display, and after seeing the red-letter day on the calendar, I took care of the baby and went back downstairs. You won't believe it, but Dale was still sitting in bed. He hadn't moved an inch. His eyes were glazed and unblinking, and his face was white, but thank heaven, he was breathing. I stared at him from the doorway for a long while, summoning up the perfect expression of my heartfelt penitence. It finally came to me.

"You know everything I said before?"

He glanced at me wearily.

"You can forget it."

I don't know how long he stayed that way, but when I left to sleep on the couch, he was still sitting in bed, eyes glazed, mouth gaping.

I have learned a lot since then by studying expert wives and reading expert authors. Of course, I can vouch for the theoretical veracity of all the professionals because I am a professional wife: I have lived out a thirty-five-year marriage. Yes, we survived my attempt at cold-blooded murder. In fact, we survived several more near-death experiences, and the next few chapters will explain how. But before we get into that, we'll need to dig a little deeper into our feminine nature; a nature which sometimes resembles the classic *femme fatale.*

7
What Are We Afraid Of?

Excessive aggressive or passive behavior comes from the
same place of lacking genuine self-worth.
—*Debra Mandel, Ph.D., psychologist*

There is a quaint little fable, told originally by Aesop, about a traveler who…

> "…wearied from a long journey lay down, overcome with fatigue, on the very brink of a deep well. Just as he was about to fall into the water, Dame Fortune, it is said, appeared to him and waking him from his slumber thus addressed him: 'Good Sir, pray wake up: for if you fall into the well, the blame will be thrown on me, and I shall get an ill name among mortals; for I find that men are sure to impute their calamities to me, however much by their own folly they have really brought them on themselves'" (trans. George Fyler Townsend, p. 46).

Like most of us these days, I have known many women who fell down the well. Over and over, I have watched helplessly from a front row seat as two players I love act out their tragedy. If forced to take sides in the drama, in virtually every case, I sympathized with the woman as she demonized her man. Too bad I didn't know then what I know now. I would have offered more than a shoulder to my woman friends: I would have compassionately helped them consider their own part in the predicament. And that is precisely what I am going to do for you now—not because I don't sympathize (I've been there, remember), not to make you feel bad, and certainly not to imply that all men are inculpable or easy to live with. Like Dame Fortune, all I want is to rouse you before you fall into the well.

Since you are reading *Wife for Life*, I assume you dream of succeeding in a lifelong marriage because you love your man and you think he has the potential to cherish you. If I'm right about that, then you will not only be open to this discussion, but hungry for it, because you know as well as I do that too many women divorce their Mr. Right in hopes of a Mr. Better, only to find themselves playing out the same part in the same drama, but with a different leading man. Understanding the possible why behind these aborted attempts at love is just as important as understanding the certain why behind the successes—in fact, even more important. The destructive force has to be identified before the constructive can have a chance to work wonders.

So, don't let this chapter depress or offend you. It is, in fact, meant to churn up the soil in your heart, helping you unearth the little weeds that can potentially (and usually inadvertently) choke your relationship. Even if your spring blossoms have endured some frost already, juicy summer fruit is still possible. My own marriage is a testimony to that, as well as many others positively affected by *Wife for Life*. It just takes a woman to warm things up again; or rather, it takes a woman who believes in her power to effect change. That's ironic because the woman who leaves her man does so ultimately because she has given up on changing the situation. And if her guy is the one giving up, it's because he too has lost hope of change, or more likely, is tired of her attempts to change *him*. As a woman, you do have the power to change things, but you can't force *him* to change. If you try, the only thing that will change is how he feels about you...and it won't be pretty.

Since forcing your husband to change never ever works—if

there is any hope of resolving the crisis that is the crux of every story, you have to concentrate on the only character in the play you can rewrite: you. Granted, some rewrites take more effort than others. For instance, a woman may unintentionally replicate generational patterns (treating her husband the way Mom treated Dad), or she may be dealing with deeper psychological issues such as a fear of being controlled or dominated (perhaps as a result of childhood trauma). Women who have been hurt in the past may also blame men for their unhappiness, which affects their marital relationship. Such aspects of character may require serious professional editing: concentrated counseling, study, or spiritual help. Other rewrites however, are far simpler; in fact; most wifely revisions are just a question of self-editing: tweaking the dialogue, reassessing motivation, angling the plot toward a happy ending. Since most of us fall into this second category, the inadvertent *Crazy Lady* (whom we will later discuss in depth), I'm going to focus on *her whys* rather than on more serious issues. If you sense that your relationships with men are affected by troubling aspects of your past, I hope you will keep reading (and come to *ramonazabriskie.com* for support, mentoring, Wife for Life University, and inspiration); in addition, please seek out professional and spiritual guidance, along with books and materials by those with clinical training and experience.

Though your past or your personality may not warrant psychological counseling, no doubt you are nevertheless dealing with insecurities. We all have worries about measuring up. Self-esteem is not something we strive to achieve and then once we've got it, we've got it. A sense of worth is such a lofty goal that it always remains a goal—meaning that it's never quite arrived at to anyone's satisfaction. We women are especially frustrated by our deficiencies and limitations. The tank of self-worth (and it's a tank, not a bucket—it's that big) has to be refilled frequently—so frequently that we spend a virtual (if not a literal) fortune on products and programs that promise to pump up our tank. And this is where the man in our life comes in.

A husband pays for his wife's ravenous need for validation, one way or another. Living with a woman's fluctuating sense of self-worth must be confusing and sometimes demoralizing to a man. He sees us feeling strong and appealing one minute, and then weak and ugly the next. It distresses a well-intentioned man to see the woman he loves fluctuate this way because, remember, he feels an innate responsibility to protect and provide for her: to make her happy. His own sense of worth, in large part, comes from *your* self-esteem! When we tumble into the well, we yank him with us. What that boils down to is this: every time we mistreat him— every time we are manipulative, mean, critical, disrespectful, demanding, or contemptuous—the real culprit, the real antagonist, the real disrupter, is the other woman: the one inside you that suddenly goes crazy for validation. We all know her. I call this *other* woman the *Crazy Lady*. She can get the best of us in spite of ourselves. We are especially vulnerable to her when it feels like we cannot give another ounce, trust another inch, or be brave another day. In other words, depleted; in other words, overwhelmed, in other words, out of control; in other words, *stressed*.

You can prove this to yourself. The next time you feel a doozy of a tizzy coming on, when you feel like ripping into him, instead, ask him for a bear hug. Don't laugh. Go with me on this. Think of it as an experiment. Your Crazy Lady can be instantly calmed—subdued from a roaring lioness into a whimpering cub—by a man's loving arms. The sudden physicality of his love can often act like magic; the effect can be stunning (unless your animosity is long-standing and deep-seated, in which case you may need the professional help mentioned earlier.) The metamorphosis from lioness to lion cub is possible for most of us, because the truth is you're not so much upset with *him*, though you may feel sure that you are. What it's really about—deep, deep down—is insecurity: *your* insecurity. You crave validation at those super stressful moments because you are tired, hungry, angry, scared. Whining, worrying, fussing, or stewing—can make us rather unpleasant to live with, however. The worst is when we feel unlovable, unbeautiful, or undesirable. That dismal assessment of ourselves is often confirmed by our behavior, including the way we treat our partner. How strange that we should subconsciously set out to prove we are right about being so unattractive!

In my search for answers, I found it personally liberating, even uplifting, to unearth some of the baffling fears that we women hide under our soft skin, and I thought it very interesting that all those fears relate to our lovability quotient, our self-esteem. The more we let insecurities rule us apparently, the more difficult it is for us to love and to be loved. The more successful we are at dealing with these womanly anxieties, the freer we are to love, and to receive love, with all our heart.

However, before we can manage, let alone overcome, the sneaky fears that plague us—the anxieties that actually block the validation we crave—we have to know they exist. Women who don't recognize the real cause of their pain often end up blaming and hurting their husband. As Cowen and Kinder say in *Women Men Love*:

> "There is perhaps nothing so crippling as fear and nothing so maddening as being afraid when we are not sure what it is we are afraid of. Fear is perpetuated by old, repetitious experiences that reaffirm our darkest and gloomiest thoughts. The antidote to fear, the only real and effective one, is change. And change requires new experiences, not familiar old ones. Conquering fear requires facing it, opening the closet and letting the light shine in; if you keep the closet door sealed tight in hopes that somehow the dread will creep away, you will never conquer it" (p. 100).

I used to teach my children that every human being is more

complex than the astronomical universe and more intricate than the microscopic one. Obviously, we can barely comprehend ourselves, let alone anyone else. I only hope to shed a sliver of light on the cavern where you hide your insecurities; I leave it up to you to use that tiny beam to explore your own soul in more depth. If you want to go beyond this introductory discussion, there is a world of books and spiritual guides out there to help you. Then again, maybe this opening foray is all you need to eliminate a few cobwebs. Either way, I hope our talk will be helpful.

From our very first page together, you and I agreed that as women, we put a high premium on lasting romance. Let's begin then by uncovering one of our most poignant worries: *losing him.* I have often lain in my husband's arms and made him promise to never leave me. Though I know they are only words—because I understand intellectually he cannot name the time and place of our ultimate parting—I still want to be emotionally assured again and again that he is as intent on forever as I am. Lady Mary Pierrepont understood this. In a letter to her future husband, Edward Wortley Montagu, on the eve of their marriage in 1712, she wrote: "I tremble for what we are doing. Are you sure you shall love me forever? Shall we never repent? I fear and I hope" (*Love Letters: An Anthology of Passion*, p. 14).

A woman may become uncomfortable, disconcerted, even distressed, when her man is emotionally unavailable to her, and a woman in love can hardly bear the thought of finishing life without her husband if he died. But she is even more terrified of his indifference or rejection. Worse still is the prospect of abandonment. Once a man and woman are blended, the separation of souls is one of the, if not the, most painful of human experiences. It is no wonder that the dread of it motivates us for good or for ill.

Women also fear *disappointment.* We set very high expectations for ourselves and our families, sometimes basing too much of our self-worth on the actions and accomplishments of our husband and children. The romantic in us also naturally builds up fantasies, as we have already discussed. When things or people don't turn out the way we hoped (or tried to orchestrate), it's a bitter experience for a wife or mother. This unwanted reality, or the fear of it, if allowed to torment us for long, manifests itself in our relationships. I know I have had to recover and rebuild relationships after facing and overcoming my fear of disappointment.

The women's movement may very well have exposed, if not exacerbated, another of the fears that plague women. We have been taught to value our strength and independence, and rightfully so, but some of us, in a mistaken understanding of feminism, shun *interdependence*. Instead of prompting us to feel grateful for the better times we live in—liberating us to make the most of our modern marriage—history may have served to put us on perpetual guard duty. How can a couple develop a grand relationship if the wife is suspicious that her man will exploit her for the simple reason that he is a man and she is a woman? How can she cherish or be cherished if she is afraid that her identity will be lost, that her sense of self will be swallowed up in his? How can a wife ask for her husband's love if she's so afraid of needing a man that she pushes him away? This stealthy fear is a major roadblock to the oneness we long for with our husband.

And last but not least—and remember, this is not meant to be an exhaustive discussion; I cannot detail all the nuances of the feminine heart—there is one fear, maybe the most furtive of all, that undermines marriage like a termite eating away at the foundation of a house. It is the fear of *exposure*: the worry that our husband will somehow discover who we really are, what we really think, where we've really been—and that he won't like it. Strangely, this fear has a flip side: a woman can worry even more that she will be exposed to *his* imperfections and vulnerabilities— and that she won't be able to handle it. My woman friends get wide-eyed in agreement when I read them this quote from *Women*

Men Love:

"What women really want is for men to be more open and expressive about loving feelings toward them—not the entire spectrum of feelings. A woman is likely to be quite unnerved if a man becomes too open, too vulnerable. Exposed male vulnerability and pain trigger strong anxiety in most women" (p. 248).

Yikes! Whether we are terrified of revealing ourselves, or we dread knowing too much about our husband, we lose either way, because retreat, withdrawal, denial, and neglect stand in stark opposition to friendship and intimacy. Scary, isn't it: the revelation that secret thoughts and hidden attitudes like…

- the fear of losing him,
- the fear of being disappointed,
- the fear of interdependence, or
- the fear of exposure,

…can drag us kicking and screaming toward our greatest fear—*alienation?*

But don't let this discussion of wifely fears push you over the edge. I bring a message of hope! There is one fact that can arrest a woman's slide down the well if she is brave enough to reach out of her comfort zone and grab hold of it: the scariest, the freakiest, the most frightening revelation of all.

Ready?

He is just as afraid as you are.

8
What Are Husbands Afraid Of?

In the old days, Birdie would have pumped up his ego, assured him that it would all work out in the end, that he was destined for greatness. But she'd grown tired in the past few years; they both had. And he'd failed to land so many jobs over the years, no wonder she'd stopped believing in him.
—*Kristin Hannah, Distant Shores: A Novel*

It was many years ago, during a season of unemployment, that I first glimpsed a facet of my husband that I had no clue existed before that day.

A guy wearing a tool belt had just delivered a certified threat from the electric company. With deep foreboding, I took the envelope to Dale at his desk. He slit it open and stared at the contents. The red print bled through so that I could make out the numbers, even from the other side of the desk. Our eyes met. He looked at me intently, in a peculiar way, as though he was torn between crushing me to his chest or hiding behind his desk.

Then, the strangest thing happened.

My husband fell forward; his forehead to his arms, and wept. He wept and wept and wept.

Good heavens! My big, burly, confident, fix-anything, know-everything-man is scared! He's really, really scared!

All of a sudden I comprehended, like never before, the immense burden my husband carried—just by being a man.

That eye-opener (after I got over the scare) established a new empathetic undergirding in my relationships with men—especially my husband, of course. It also spurred me into another of my research projects: what are men afraid of? I wanted to understand that vulnerable part of him, a part I knew he would never, could never, verbalize to me. What I learned was truly surprising. What I figured out in my own head turned my heart upside down.

As we have already touched on, men have an innate fear of not measuring up. On a primitive, biological level, as Michael Gurian explains, "[a man] is driven to show his worth constantly" because "he does not feel he has inherent worth" (*What Could He Be Thinking,* p. 126). From boyhood on, a guy is challenged by the world to prove himself, and Mother Nature instills in him the determination to perform so as to power his quest. Consequentially, the yearning for success and recognition is so deep-seated, so biologically and culturally ingrained, that a man's sense of self is completely tied up in demonstrations of strength, physical or mental. The drive to be brave and to win is so obvious, so historically ubiquitous; it's become a male stereotype. What's not so observable is just how delicate men's own ambitions make them.

Proving yourself involves risk: any contest of strength is potentially hazardous to the ego because the possibility of failure is a real and present danger. And men are positively terrified of failure. In the Academy Award–winning film, *The King's Speech* (The Weinstein Co., 2010), when Bertie breaks down and sobs to his wife, Elizabeth, "I'm not a king!" he is, in a sense, articulating the fear of every man. Behind all the bravado, you can bet there is a boy who cringes when he's laughed at, trembles when he's bullied, and shrivels when he's scolded. Without enough male mentors and exemplars of success, some men spin their wheels in young adulthood, paralyzed by this fear.

That dread of inadequacy, when combined with another fear, *relinquishing independence,* keeps many men from progressing in relationships, from growing up and committing to one woman. It is a real concern to the average guy that someday, somehow, he might become dominated by a demanding woman and she will pressure, use, or intimidate him—power that can only be wielded by someone he really cares about.

Experts say that the specter of control and dependency is especially fearsome for a young man who may still be separating psychologically from his mother. His natural fear may also be intensified by a disturbing parental example or family pattern. To break free and stay free, independence is a crucial form of confidence—a belief in himself that he's fought hard for: *that he can and will be just exactly who he is or who he wants to be,* no matter who or what is against him. This conviction is central to finding and achieving his quest, which, as you know, is central to his manhood. To replace that precious autonomy and courage with the prospect of confinement and cowardice at the hands of a woman, especially the woman he loves, is abhorrent to him. Honoré de Balzac, the famous French writer, expressed this fear in a letter to his future bride in 1833: "Good heavens; I am terrified to see how much my life is yours!" (*Love Letters*, p.14).

That being said, this next masculine worry made me shake my bridal curls in bewilderment. As much as my groom seemed to shun over-attachment, he was also scared to death of *feeling alone.* It's true! Men— particularly young men—paradoxically need and fear emotional connectedness.

Though I, as a new wife, thrived on connections, my husband took pride in self-sufficiency. It surprised him then that he felt uncomfortable whenever I focused on a person or project other than him for any significant period of time. The sense that he was neglected blindsided him. If he continued to observe that I was unavailable or drifting from him, anxiety set in because he felt he had no recourse. Unlike a woman, a man cannot easily communicate his neediness without feeling ashamed of it. Thus his cues for attention come across subtly at best; the busy wife can easily miss or misinterpret, discount, or disparage, what's really going on in her husband's heart. I wince thinking how insensitive I was to this as a young wife. Unexpressed loneliness is just as painful to men as it is to women.

Closely associated with feeling neglected, a man may feel unneeded. Next to failure, this is perhaps his gravest fear. His compulsion to prove himself plays into his hunger to be useful and needed; it helps us to understand his long hours at work, his relish for solving problems, his extensive projects at home or in the community. Your man is saying to everyone, but especially to you, *do you still need me?* When he contributes, and his contribution is acknowledged as worthy, he is reassured that the answer is yes, and his fear of uselessness is alleviated. His craving for the respect of his wife, family, and associates is also fulfilled. However, if he thinks the answer is no, a man will (as John Gray observes in *Venus on Fire, Mars on Ice: Hormonal Balance—the Key to Life, Love, and Energy*) lose emotional and spiritual momentum, becoming increasingly passive and depressed.

While volunteering as the house manager for an acting company many years ago, I held open the doors of the theater while audiences exited each night. For the most part, people acknowledged the courtesy and said something positive about the production. There was one show, though, that elicited a very different response. It was Arthur Miller's renowned *Death of a Salesman*, the story of a middle-aged man whose family and career disintegrates all at once. As the audience exited, the women pleasantly complimented the play and wished me goodnight, but every single man—and there were hundreds during the course of the run—passed by me either stony-faced and silent, or sore-eyed and sniffling. Some continued to weep openly, trailing distractedly behind their chatty wives or girlfriends. I was truly amazed and did not understand what was happening—but I do now. The fate of the salesman, Willie Loman, stirs up men's worst fears. His story represents the ultimate tragedy in a man's mind: *uselessness.*

I hope it doesn't scare you too much to know how frightened your man really is; that he...

- needs to be needed (he is afraid of uselessness).
- loathes feeling neglected (he is afraid of your indifference or unavailability).
- must protect his independence (he is afraid of becoming dependent).
- has to succeed (he can hardly bear the idea of failure).

Killing Him Softly

Understanding the pieces of your man's heart that may have puzzled you in the past, should help you feel stronger, even empowered; your natural empathy is in high gear. At his next sign of self-doubt, you will be less disturbed or perturbed by it, and that is a very good thing. But don't leap from your chair into his arms just yet. And for heaven's sake, don't start a running dialogue about his fears or needs, or prod him to open up, just so you can feel closer to him, or help him, or merely validate what I'm telling you. You are not his psychotherapist. And neither am I. Please do not make me responsible for torturing a man—because that is exactly how he will perceive your pressure to discuss his emotions.

No matter how solid your relationship, if your husband is like most guys, he is afraid somewhere deep inside of being overwhelmed by your emotional demands. I call it *killing him softly.*

It may seem strange or unfortunate or irritating to you, but most men are not comfortable with emotion in the same way women are. Neither are they insensitive brutes. Your man feels things very deeply; it is just that he is wired to respond to emotion differently from you. Experts Gurian and Gray note that a man can actually be neurally stressed (biological brain reactions) by the same emotions that give a woman pleasure—and the stress skyrockets in the face of intense emotions associated with negativity. Psychotherapist Mary Jo Rapini, LPC, posits that women verbalize emotion, while men's emotional language is physical—that is, a man needs to physically release the emotion that a woman would express in words. And neuroscientist, Reuben Gur, Ph.D., Director of the Brain Behavior Laboratory and the Center for Neuroimaging in Psychiatry at the University of Pennsylvania, in Philadelphia, who has conducted a number of studies on sex differences in emotion, confirmed to me personally that emotions go way beyond estrogen or testosterone. His research has found that men are indeed wired *to act* during times of high emotion. As he explained via email to me:

> "Male brains are optimized to carry information from the perceiving to the acting part within each hemisphere, while female brains are optimized to communicate between the two hemispheres. We can conclude that male brains are more active in all limbic regions below the callosum, which process emotion through action, while female brains are more active in the cingulate region, where emotions are processed symbolically and which is closer to the language areas."

What that means is that while you as a woman are wired to talk about your feelings, he is programed by Mother Nature *to do* something about them. That biological directive is the most overwhelming during intense emotion; in fact, a Nice Guy will shut off, quit talking, or withdraw, rather than *act* in a way that he is afraid would be harmful or hurtful to you.

Dr. Gur's findings support my earlier contention that men are designed to stay levelheaded and focused, processing logically and rationally rather than emotionally; they are wired to arrive at a solution from a take-action paradigm. When you push a man too aggressively or too persistently into expressing emotion, his natural response is to retreat from the conversation in order to protect himself, keep his head clear, and protect *you* if things get hot. After an intense encounter, his blood pressure and immune system will take far longer than yours to stabilize. Minutes after you've brushed off the incident, he may very well go on raging, crying, or quivering; but it won't be in any audible or visible manner, except on rare occasion. This may be for your good. He wants to keep you safe, and he instinctively believes that you respect and rely on his mental and emotional strength. And the truth is, dear woman, you do.

Just think of it: all that pressure on your Nice Guy to perform and to handle his fears in a masculine way. He lives every day under massive expectations, stalked by a host of ghosts, just because he was born male. Many of his most intense thoughts and feelings have played out on a stage with no audience; he may hardly be able to identify them himself. But now that you've had a peek from the wings, there ought to be at least one person who sympathizes with his personal drama.

Obviously, I am prone to theatrical metaphors. Much of my early life was on stage—in fact, Dale and I became acquainted (and experienced our first kiss) while performing as opposite romantic leads in a musical. The show, *Guys and Dolls*, was wacky fun, a parody that captures the essence of this discussion. I played Sergeant Sarah Brown, leader of the Save-a-Soul Mission (based on the Salvation Army), a woman full of self-righteousness and high expectations—just like young me at the time. Beneath her stiff uniform, however, as beneath my cloak of virtue, Sarah felt a little insecure and a lot romantic. "For I've imagined every bit of him, from his strong moral fiber, to the wisdom in his head, to the homey aroma of his pipe," she daydreams.

But when bad boy Sky Masterson, the devilishly handsome, suave gambler, (a.k.a. my boyfriend, Dale) tries to seduce her into letting her hair down, she eventually capitulates. Now it's his turn to worry, because he didn't bank on falling in love. His independence is threatened by her dependence. So what's a leading man to do? Give in, of course! Sarah and I acted triumphant when, in the finale, Dale—as Sky—entered dressed in a uniform like hers with a bass drum strapped around his neck, assimilated into marriage and the Mission street-band. While the women in the audience clapped and laughed appreciatively, it seemed to me that the men looked chagrined.

Reflecting on that silly show all these years later, I can now project that Sky and Sarah Masterson's happy ending probably did not last long. It's the same reason Dale and I almost lost our *forever*: with her head full of fantasies and fears, Sarah had, right from the start, unintentionally set herself up to *un*love Sky. Beneath her confidant, charming exterior, sweet Sarah Brown must have, over time, morphed into the consummate *Crazy Lady.*

9
The Crazy Ladies

Consider how hard it is to change yourself and you'll understand
what little chance you have of trying to change others.
—*Jacob M. Braude, American judge and humorist*

I hope I've made it clear by now that I cannot empower you by concentrating on *him*, which is why our discussion will continue to focus on your choices and behaviors, not his. *Wife for Life* is about *your* power to succeed in marriage, *your* power to love, *your* power to change, *your* power to grow as a wife and as a person. It is not about fate. It is not about victimization. It is not about regretting your choice in a husband or blaming him for your unhappiness. That kind of thinking gets you nowhere close to intimacy—and far, far from forever. The repercussions of alienation and divorce are simply beyond imagination. You have to focus on moving from spring blossoms to summer fruits; you want to appreciate the diversity of autumn; and you have to endure the winters that blow your way so that you can achieve a grand, lifelong marriage. You are a Pioneer Woman. You are a Creator. You have the Talent, and I'm going to teach you how to be a Dream Maker. It is all about cherishing the man in your life and feeling cherished by him. But in order to absorb the *whats* in that process, I have to warn you about the *what-nots:* the specific behaviors that will repulse instead of attract him. You see, by the time a woman gets to the point that she sees her Nice Guy as the fount of all frustration and she cannot imagine what she has done to deserve this life of indifference or discord, it's pretty certain she is repulsing him; she has somehow become his Dream *Breaker* rather than Dream Maker.

And what exactly is a Dream Breaker? Let's define "dreams" to begin with. As John M. Gottman, Ph.D., and Nan Silver, coauthors of *The Seven Principles for Making Marriage Work*, describe, dreams are "the hopes, aspirations, and wishes that are part of your identity [which] give purpose and meaning to your life" (p. 218). Dreams are our guides in life. Like an unseen force, we are compelled one way or another, through every little choice, by these inner compasses. Hopes, aspirations, and wishes take up so much room in our soul, in fact, that we sometimes have little room left over for anyone else's dreams. We tend to hoard and protect our prized plans, thinking that they will one day materialize if we can keep them uncontaminated. "Unrequited dreams," says Dr. Gottman, "are at the core of every gridlocked conflict" (p. 133). When our dreams are frustrated or threatened, we may go into a panic that instigates disrespectful behavior; we are likely to pull up the drawbridge and roll out the cannons, ready to defend our personal cache to the death.

High on a rocky plateau, presiding over one of the most ancient cities of the world, sit the ruins of the temple of Athena, the goddess of ancient Greece who symbolized a veritable litany of virtues: wisdom, courage, inspiration, civilization, law and justice, strength, and skill. When I first laid eyes on the Parthenon, I felt unsettled by the juxtaposition of its broken columns and disintegrating portico with the grimy cement buildings and crumbling government of Athens. I am a fourth generation Greek-American and I had come to Greece expecting magnificent civilization as well as architecture. Where was my Hellenistic heritage?

I found it literally in pieces—atop the Acropolis.

What remains today of one of the world's most recognizable monuments are fragments of ancient dreams—hunks and chunks of the people who constructed it in 487 B.C. As the centuries rolled on, Christians, Ottomans, and Venetians each played a successive role in changing its face and purpose. But it was Thomas Bruce, seventh earl of Elgin, who, from 1801 to 1812, disassembled and relocated about half of the surviving sculpture from the Parthenon, including columns, friezes, panels, and statues. This incredible collection is on display today, not inside the Acropolis Visitors Center and Museum at the foot of the mountain, but 1500 miles away in the Elgin room of the British Museum. Elgin thought of himself as the rescuer of these marbles, but the Greeks tend to see him as a vandal.

Like the Greeks, we naturally worry that our personal Parthenon, the treasury of dreams we have built up over a lifetime, will be raided or ruined, stolen piece by piece, never to be reassembled. I know I became increasingly distressed when I realized that my dream of going to church as a family every week (something I sorely missed as a child) was threatened by Dale's penchant for cozy Sunday mornings (something he enjoyed as a child). In the first year of our marriage, as he slept in and relished his brunch, he became in my mind an immoral treasure hunter, stealing jewels from my sacred temple of dreams to build his own. In hyper-defensive mode, I naturally began operating out of fear of disappointment, instead of patience and faith, defaulting to weapons like self-pity, humiliation, and blame in an attempt to defend my dream. Of course, forcing life to go the way I thought it should only drove my husband into the enemy camp. A war began, not only between the two of us, but inside his heart. Like any man in that position, he knew he needed me, but he felt I was using that very dependency against him. He wanted to please me by getting up and going to church, but felt demoralized by my moral superiority and threatened by my emotional attacks. How could he even *want* to make my dreams of becoming a church-going family come true when all I gave him was grief about it? Since I wasn't even satisfied when he *did* go to church (because I felt like he had merely acquiesced to my demands instead of leading us there), the man couldn't win. I see now why he preferred staying under the covers.

Sometimes, as you defend your dreams, what you are really doing is acting on your fears. In this example, I thought I was righteously defending my dream of going to church as a family, but on a deeper level, I was motivated by my fear of disappointment. The result was that Dale's fear of inadequacy as a man and as a husband was fanned to life. He felt I was disregarding his dreams and disrespecting him as a man, which disqualified him from becoming my Dream Maker. In other words, *when a wife defends her dreams by acting inappropriately on her insecurities, she exacerbates her husband's self-doubts, which is the opposite of inspiring him.* And if an inspiring wife is cherished by her husband, how do you suppose he feels about the Crazy Ladies?

Introducing the Crazy Ladies

Now don't be tempted to skip this part, even if you've been married for years and years and feel confident that the way you treat your husband is entirely positive and you couldn't possibly be a Crazy Lady. Or maybe you feel like the beautiful unmarried thirty-something who reacted to my presentation on the Crazy Ladies with, "I would *never* do or say those things!" Either way, I urge you to reconsider. A mature woman, married for decades, approached me after another one of my presentations and admitted that she had started the evening feeling cocky, but ended up stunned when she saw herself all over the Crazy-Lady map. Another left me this note: "I have been married for forty years and have four sons. I did not think I needed this presentation. I was wrong." Comments like these pile up on my desk and accumulate in my inbox.

So brace yourself. We are going to take a brief look now (maybe a hard look for some of us) at the specific *whats* that nudge, or sometimes shove, a man down the road to alienation. We will scrutinize five incarnations of the Crazy Lady and list some of her behaviors. As we do, keep in mind that we are trying to think about this from his point of view rather than yours. Though of course there are two sides to every story, my purpose is to help raise your awareness of his side of the coin. With that knowledge, you can effect change in your marriage, but it will not initially be through him; it will be through you and your approach to the relationship. Rather than break down the door like a SWAT team, provoking or intimidating him with assault tactics, you will learn how to patiently and subtly appear in his sweetest dreams through the back door: the entrance to his heart that's kept private just for you.

Except when you're one of the Crazy Ladies. Ashamlee, Stupidia, Irreleva, Betraya, and Depressa will never ever be allowed in that secret door. Care to know why?

Crazy Lady #1: Ashamlee

- Shows she is disappointed with his job or the income he provides. Cries about things the family cannot afford.
- Reminds him that his education is inadequate or that hers is superior.
- Teases him about (or ridicules) his body.
- Communicates contempt for his masculine nature.
- Accuses him of not being loving or attentive or supportive enough.
- Laughs *at* him about anything.
- Questions his decisions in front of others (including the children).
- Sends him the message that his fathering is inadequate.
- Makes disparaging comments about him (or their marriage) in public.

- Speaks disrespectfully of him to, or in front of, the children.
- Complains about his partnership or leadership in the home.

Ashamlee sometimes acts on her fear of disappointment, which triggers her husband's fear of not measuring up. What she ends up communicating is: You are disappointing. You are inadequate. You are ridiculous.

Crazy Lady #2: Stupidia
- Treats him as a non-entity in the company of others.
- Interrupts him before he has time to formulate his thoughts or express himself.
- Makes fun of him (teasingly, she says) in front of others, including referring to him as another one of her children.
- Barrages him verbally.
- Corrects, makes demands of, or hands out ultimatums to him as if he were a child.
- Directs, criticizes, or questions his driving.
- Gives unsolicited advice or takes over a problem he is working on.
- Questions, demeans, or otherwise second-guesses his decisions.
- Downplays or belittles his worries or problems.
- Snubs his choice of activity and insists on alternative plans.
- Scolds him for forgetting things she's told him in the past.
- Berates him for not taking care of the children to her exact specifications.
- Frames a request for help as a demand or expectation.

Stupida sometimes acts on her fear of being exploited, which stirs up her husband's fear of becoming subservient and losing his independence. What she ends up communicating is: You are inept. You are foolish. You are obtuse.

Crazy Lady #3: Irreleva
- Is apathetic about his interests or accomplishments.
- Often chooses her own pursuits over his.
- Spends more time and energy on others than on him.
- Turns to others for help with her challenges rather than to him.
- Makes important personal and family decisions without him.
- Carelessly or purposely leaves him out of the children's lives.
- Discounts his attempts to please her and seldom shows gratitude.
- Puts his requests at the bottom of her to-do list.
- Makes little to no attempt to do the things that please him.
- Takes charge of their plans and time together.
- Fails to acknowledge or admire his successes publicly.
- Implies that physical intimacy is unimportant or distasteful.
- Consistently prioritizes her children's needs over his and depends on the children to meet her emotional needs.
- Sends the message that the family doesn't really need him.

Irreleva sometimes acts on her fear of losing her identity or of exploitation, which ignites her husband's fear of uselessness. What she ends up communicating is: You are boring. You are useless. You are repulsive.

Crazy Lady #4: Betraya
- Finds other projects more worthy, or pressing, or interesting than her marriage.
- Neglects his needs in order to take care of other people's needs.
- Compares him to other men or speaks glowingly of other men.
- Communicates with, or spends time with, other men recreationally.
- Flirts obviously with other men at social occasions.
- Talks (or blogs, tweets, or Facebooks) to others about her marriage in a sarcastic way or shares intimate aspects of her married life.
- Doesn't bother to make herself attractive to him, yet obsesses over whether other men find her attractive.
- Spends the family income with little or no thought of partnership, responsibility, or appreciation.
- Is apathetic about his interests, for which she probably showed enthusiasm during courtship.
- Refuses physical intimacy to manipulate or punish him.

Betraya sometimes acts on her fear of inadequacy, exposure, intimacy, or of getting hurt, which stirs up her husband's fear of neglect or loneliness. What she ends up communicating is: You are not as good as... or as important as.... or as fascinating as...

Crazy Lady #5: Depressa
- Whines and complains.
- Thinks of his responsibilities outside the relationship as competition.

- Overlooks the importance of his work and downplays his worries.
- Begrudges the space and time he biologically *needs* to recharge.
- Insists on spending every moment and doing every activity together.
- Resents that he can't read her mind.
- Rarely states clearly what she really needs or wants, but acts like a martyr when things don't go her way.
- Uses silence, pouting, or tears to manipulate or punish him.
- Initiates conversations about feelings in which she expects him to open up.
- Pries into or needles him about his feelings when he's down or distant.
- Wants to discuss their relationship when she is emotional.
- Acts perpetually upbeat and positive, even when he seems sad or hurt.
- Frequently expects him to take full care of the children and household chores when he is home, in addition to his employment.
- Acts disappointed over his lackluster spiritual or family leadership.
- Conveys in a hundred ways, subtle and not-so subtle, that he is a failure.

Depressa sometimes acts on her fear of abandonment, loss, or disappointment, which fans her husband's fear of being overwhelmed by emotional demands. What she ends up communicating is: You don't meet my needs. You don't care enough. You don't matter as much as I do.

No doubt a hundred personal examples ran through your mind

as you perused the list of Crazy Ladies. Let me share one of my own, when I threw a bucket of ice on what could have been a steamy getaway.

Depressa Gets Her Way (or in the Way)

Though it meant missing the Royal Wedding in London, our home at the time, I had opted to accompany Dale on a business trip to Munich, Germany. His company assignments in Europe had him in a plane, train, hotel room, or cab, week after week. The only way I could get out of the flat was by hoofing and red-busing it all over London in my work as the leader of a big, busy organization. I was bone-tired; I craved nurturing from Dale, and I sorely needed a personal holiday. Munich promised both.

The morning after we arrived then, I thought I had won the lottery when Dale told me over a European breakfast that every one of his Munich appointments had just cancelled. There was no option, he said, but to stay in Munich for the planned five days since his next presentation was in Stockholm, and all the travel and hotel arrangements were settled. I suddenly had my hard-working husband all to myself for five whole days!

At the surprising news, I did what any loving wife would do: I jumped out of my chair and gave him a noisy kiss on the cheek. "Wunderbar!" I cried. "What fate! What an opportunity! *What's wrong with you?*"

He just sat there, poking his fish with a fork. "I was looking forward to working this week," he said.

Now, if I'd been in better form that day, I would have gently sat back down and taken a minute to think about what he meant in the context of the male drive to achieve and the male fear of uselessness behind it. I would have reached for his hand and said something sympathetic. I would have given him an hour or two (or however long it took) to process his disappointment without forcing him to justify it to me, without trying to fix it for him, and without trying to jolly him out of his gloom with cheerfulness. I would have just let him be. I would have graciously let him retreat into his mental cave, knowing he would come out of it all the sooner, taut and strong and ready to spring into romance.

But I didn't. Instead of kissing him lightly and asking what he wanted to do next—the Crazy Lady Depressa emerged...in full swing. She used every tactic in her arsenal to defend her dream of a romantic week together, to lay on the guilt, to bury him in her hurt. *Why*, I wondered, *would he grieve the loss of a few days of work when I was right there, totally available to him? What about my needs? Why wasn't he as excited about this unexpected gift as I was! Doesn't he want to be with me?!* That train of thought (or emotion) all looks pretty rational on paper, but believe me, I was anything but rational when it came out in huffs, sobs, and stonewalling over the next twenty-four hours. He could have been all mine, heart and soul, within two hours, maybe less, if I'd resisted the Crazy Lady. Instead, I sent him to the far corner to wait out my tantrum with fear and trembling, and the entire rest of the week, though we both apologized and forgave, felt off kilter. We ended up watching the televised royal wedding taking place that week back in London, in glum silence.

Thankfully, Depressa rarely makes an appearance these days, but I still have to stay on my toes to keep her at bay. She may be your nemesis too, or perhaps Stupida or Irreleva daily challenge your sanity. Just remember, your Crazy Lady comes out of your internal woodwork—like a poltergeist trying to possess your normally loving, composed, rational self, when you are feeling overwhelmed, tired, hungry, insecure, grouchy, or afraid. It is so vital to keep this fact about your womanly self on the front burner that I'm going to say it again and hope you highlight it in orange or write it on a sticky note. (I don't suppose you'd hang it on the fridge?)

We are especially vulnerable to the Crazy Ladies when it feels like we cannot give another ounce, trust another inch, or be brave another day. In other words: depleted. In other words: overwhelmed. In other words: feeling stressed.

"Oh, great," I hear you saying. "That's me 24/7."

And it's true, of course. Stress is always with us. Life, for women, has become complex. Everyone knows it. In today's demanding world, we are too often—despite our best efforts—fraying badly at the edges. Some of us, frankly, are coming unraveled. Knitting ourselves back together again is a necessary daily ritual, but we often can't even find the basket of yarn we need in order to do it. And therein lies the great paradox, the dramatic irony, the absolute absurdity of that madwoman we call the Crazy Lady: *she's* the one hiding the basket.

10
A Castle Built For Two

The door to the human heart can only be opened from the inside.
—*Spanish proverb*

It took only a day or two after moving to England before I swore I would never in a million miles drive a car there. Instigating a fourteen-Mini pileup on one of those jumbo roundabouts was not on my American-in-London agenda. Instead, I put my money (or Oyster card) on Britain's public transportation system, which had little chance of wrecking anything—except my sense of competency. I am, by nature, directionally challenged; standing in a tube, train, or bus station, surrounded by hundreds of others who know exactly what they are doing, leaves me completely, utterly, hopelessly discombobulated. I stare at reader boards announcing arrivals and departures the way tummy-growler midnight-prowlers stare into fridges expecting the contents to rearrange themselves into a casserole.

Luckily, my daughter was also living in England for a time, on an internship, and luckily, she inherited her father's GPS genes, so with her help I was able to travel the hundred and fifty miles from London to the county of Shropshire to explore a little family history. Though the train ride turned out pleasant enough, I sighed with relief as we emerged from the station onto the streets of medieval Shrewsbury. Just as we hoped, the county turned out to have enough parish churches, archives, and graveyards to keep us busy for days. Our favorite stop, though, was Ludlow Castle, a ruin perched above a winding river and rolling green countryside with a vista so picturesque, you would swear a master landscaper had designed it, down to the last hedge, grove, and cottage roof.

As we toured the stone rooms, stairwells, and turrets of Ludlow Castle, I thought of what I'd recently learned from a book called *The Medieval Castle in England and Wales* by N. J. G. Pounds:

- A castle is both a home and a fortress.
- A castle, though different from every other castle, is always built, as the book puts it, "according to certain clear principles."
- A castle is always part of a community; it never stands in isolation.
- A castle, though it may exist inside a town, must be able to cut off everything outside its walls with the closing of a gate or the raising of a drawbridge.

Exploring castles, though exhilarating, exhausted me. Back at Reading Station, as we dodged the mobs and dragged our luggage, I nearly broke down. The ruckus of the station ruined me by the time we were descending the escalator.

And then—through all the moving bodies on the floor below— I saw him: transcending the commotion, his face full of calm anticipation, riveted on mine—so solid, so sure, so still. I did, of course, melt the instant I reached him. My honey is a big man, and his arms supported (as much as comforted) me. As we kissed, I began to cry.

Here, I thought, is my fortress: *my very own castle.*

The truth—despite what the sarcastic or cynical may say—is that a husband is meant to be your *castle*; he should be your best and first line of defense. A loving, devoted man can serve as your greatest ally, your biggest help, your sweetest soother and most reliable problem solver. He can be both a home and a fortress. He should even be your confidant and best friend and you may ultimately become his Intimate. Like a castle-built-for-two, you are part of a greater community of friends, family, children, and coworkers, but when necessary, he rolls out the cannons, pulls up the drawbridge, and majestically seals out everything except him and you, if he is built right that is, on "certain clear principles", over time.

Laying a solid foundation for your castle begins by treating your husband with respect and understanding as consistently as possible from day one. You build him up, stone by stone, over the days, weeks, months, years, decades, until by the time you are old people together, nothing can destroy his love for you—not even you! By then, both of you will have become so loving, flexible, forgiving, and resilient that what might have seemed like grounds for divorce in year one will do little more than turn up the corners of your mouth in year fifty. However, if you allow your Crazy Ladies to take over too often, your man will never become the tower of strength and compassion you dream of. The Crazy Ladies are not in the business of constructing castles. They are frustrated Dream Breakers (impatient and short-sighted)—not imaginative Dream Makers. And building a man is building a dream is building a castle: each an enterprise that takes patience and imagination.

Think of it this way: you need him on occasion to take over with the kids, to do more for you around the house, to say just the right thing when you have absolutely had it—right? You need him to show you affection, to tell you you're beautiful; to say "I love you," to take your side against the world. *You need him to be your castle.* Well, then, if that is what you need, here is your first brick: banish the Crazy Ladies, send them into exile and do your best to keep them there. What that means in no uncertain terms (as my mom used to say), is taking responsibility for *First* Respect—as opposed to *reserving* your respect until you've decided he's earned it. This principle is at the heart of *Love & Respect* by Emerson Eggerichs, Ph.D. He points out that a woman who has no problem with the concept of unconditional *love* may, however, bristle at the idea of *respecting* her husband "unconditionally":

> "To [women], the words unconditional love aren't contradictory at all, and when they don't receive love from their husbands, they let them know it. Women are much more...apt to show how they feel, while men shut down. Men don't know how to deal with the fact that they aren't respected, and they can't put a voice to their feelings. The husbands think, Well, if that's the way she feels, there's nothing I can do....When the wife flatly says her husband will have to earn her respect before she gives him any, she leaves the husband in a lose-lose situation....Is it any wonder he shuts down in the face of all that?" (*Love and Respect*, p. 44).

Since the last thing we need as stressed-out women is for the man in our life to shut down, to give up on relationship-building, and since the first thing we need is an ally and friend in our husband, then we have to think in terms of giving him what I call *First* Respect. First Respect requires that you treat him as an equal consistently, beginning *now*. In short, it means that you relate to him not as a mother relates to a child, or a boss to an employee, or a coach to a student, but as an equal; treat him not as if you were judge, jury, and hangman, but as an equal; view him not as an extension of yourself who automatically thinks and reacts exactly as you do, but as an equal; regard him not as someone who can read your thoughts and anticipate your needs, but as an equal. Then and only then, when you see him as a valid *other*—an individual with the right to be himself, exactly as he is—then you will finally (no more ifs, ands, buts, commas, or semicolons) be on your way to building your castle!

- First Respect is necessary to help him feel he can be your castle.

114

- First Respect motivates him to want to be your castle.
- First Respect grants him the time he needs to learn how to be your castle.

First Respect is your best hope of staying together, of overcoming his male fears and your female insecurities. First Respect is the first step to reaching your dreams and achieving his quest. And again, you have to start now. Waiting to give him respect until he becomes your dream guy, living up to certain standards or expectations, will never produce results. *You can't wait for a tree to grow before you water it.*

Do you see now what I mean about the Crazy Ladies hiding the basket of yarn? They discount, disrespect, and thereby alienate the person who is potentially your best source of love and comfort. Let the Crazy Ladies try to get any kind of sweetness from him, and he will simply pull up the drawbridge to protect himself from the battering rams. And there you are: standing at the gatehouse, pounding on a door that will never yield; stressed, unraveling, fraying at the edges. Your beauty is melting in a puddle of tears. Of course, you can turn to other remedies for stress, other ways of knitting yourself back together (you should have multiple remedies, actually), but if he is locked in and you are locked out, I promise, all the solutions in the world put together won't end the siege. When a woman's marriage is unhappy, she comes apart at the seams.

You, dear lady of the twenty-first century, need a *knight* who knows how to *knit*.

11
Teaching A Knight To Knit

On whom shall I lean, if not you?
—*Gustave Flaubert, French writer*

They are not as rare a breed as you think. If you sort through your friends, you will probably think of one who has a husband who brings her coffee in bed, who reads to the children at night, who forsakes an evening out with the guys because she needs him. Or maybe the guy takes the brakes in for inspection before they squeak, or automatically leaves his muddy boots on the porch. You may even have heard of a husband and wife who do the dishes together and then dance in the kitchen. And until now, you might have presumed that women with husbands like that are just plain blessed. *Sally is sooo lucky! Did you hear what Joe gave her for her birthday? or, Jenny said she and Brian sat up all night talking! Can you believe it?*

As much as we admire wives who have husbands who are handy with the knitting needles—men who nimbly pick up their wife's dangling strings and tuck them in—there is no need to envy them. Luck has nothing to do with it: you too can have a knight who knows how to knit. The trick, (and it's all wrapped up in First Respect) is accepting the basic fact that, in most cases, it takes time and a concerted effort for a husband to learn to purl.

In *Project Happily Ever After: Saving your Marriage When the Fairytale Falters,* journalist Alisa Bowman relates in down-to-earth, no-sacred-ground detail how she went from fantasizing about her husband's death to this confession: "I would never have...expected to feel such a deep, unwavering, strong love for my husband. Now, whenever I allow myself to think about that funeral, tears come to my eyes and an ache comes to my heart. No, he's not allowed to die...not the one person in the world who understands me and loves me anyway" (p. 230).

What is significant about Alisa's account in the context of *Wife for Life* is that she was the one who went on red alert. Though her husband, Mark, seemed oblivious, Alisa knew something was not right in their marriage. She took responsibility for researching the topic and putting together a plan she called, "Project Happily Ever After," in which she introduced her husband to marriage-saving principles, piece by piece, until today they were well on their way to a beautiful marriage. Alisa also discovered her power to create the marriage of her dreams by reorienting *herself*. She began to appreciate and respect her husband's quest (he had opened a store) and to see his behavior, which seemed unforgivable during the dark days, from his male perspective. She practiced approaching and responding to him, and to stressful situations, more effectively. She learned to forgive and to desire him again. And Mark is, from Alisa's description of him, very much her castle.

From my point of view, all that positive change came about when Alisa honed one critical skill, a talent the Crazy Ladies will never possess. In fact, we're talking about it now because this one skill may diminish and even eliminate the Crazy Ladies, helping to arrest that downward slide toward alienation. As you master it, you will drastically reduce the stress and insecurity you feel, the fears that foster disrespect. I call it *teaching a knight to knit*.

When I was a little girl, my great-grandmother Lela, the Pioneer Woman, in addition to pressing shirts, taught me how to knit and crochet. I have small hands, even as an adult, so as an eight-year-old I found it a challenge to hold those big needles. Manipulating them with unsteady fingers made me self-conscious, but I kept at it. It helped me that Gammy exuded patience. She knew it didn't come naturally to me, and that she had way more experience than I did. But she also believed I could and wanted to do it, so she kept the basket of yarn on hand and, at appropriate intervals, pleasantly enticed me to try, try again. I'm sure that if she had expected too much too soon or forced me to sit down and loop when I wanted to leap, I would never ever have finished that doily.

Nice Guys aren't so different from that. They really want to learn how to make you happy. Remember: for a married man, all roads lead to his wife. He wants desperately to succeed with you. A shot of feel-good testosterone shoots through his veins and enlarges his heart every time you light up. But knowing what to do or how to do it comes about as naturally to most guys as fumbling with big knitting needles does to a child. For example, to expect our good guy just to sit quietly and listen while we process verbally, validating our feelings, letting us clean out toxic emotions, resisting Mother Nature's call to action—which is the inborn male compulsion to fix things—stretches him to the limits. When his damsel is in distress, more often than not, a guy's inclination is to take it personally, even if she's not blaming or criticizing him. She whines, she whimpers, she weeps. The knight on horseback feels restless. He is a hero, after all (or deep down wants to be), and a hero—obviously—either *is* the answer or *has* all the answers. As the moat fills with her tears, his options are:

- get defensive,
- get depressed,
- get away, or
- get to work on solving her problem.

And how do we frequently respond when he chooses to charge and champion—to offer a solution that makes sense to him? *You don't understand!* More weeping. *You're not helping at all!* Gone are the days when any nice fella who could zing a bull's-eye, slay a dragon, and charm in the bedchamber (provide, protect, and procreate) was a shoo-in for Lady Marian.

One of the roles your knight probably did not anticipate when he showed up in shining armor on your wedding day, was that of psychotherapist. Listening to, validating, and supporting a wife emotionally is a strange new world for a man of action. Your job may be to gently persuade your Nice Guy that letting you spill emotion and just sit there takes just as much courage as life in the camps. However, as relationship expert John Lund, Ph.D., cautions in *For All Eternity: A Four-Talk Set to Strengthen your Marriage* (Covenant Audio), it helps your knight if you keep those let-me-just-spill-it talks to an agreed-upon amount of time. Men like exits, says Dr. Lund. For instance, tell your man you need to talk for fifteen minutes and then keep to that fifteen minutes.

I checked out the suggestion. "Honey," I said to my husband, "can I talk to you about something?"

"Suuurrre," he said (read: not so sure).

I mentioned Dr. Lund's comment about men and exits, and asked him what he thought. He agreed completely.

"So why did you hesitate when I asked if I could talk to you?" I said.

He could not say. He knew I was not going to criticize him. He knew I wasn't upset. Yet even after thirty-five years, he automatically reacted defensively to "Can we talk?" I didn't have to do a lot of scientific research to find out why. Remember his fear of being overwhelmed with emotion? Remember his need to protect his independence? Remember his drive to succeed? All three are on the line when you say those four little words, "Honey, can we talk..."

That doesn't mean he can't or won't support you emotionally. He wants to. And he can learn. Some men are better at it than others, depending on their background, personality, or stage of life. My own darling of a man was awkward about it at first, but over the years he has become very good at listening and counseling me appropriately when I'm stressed. Dale does a crackerjack job of knitting me back together. He is also the king of jumping in to help with the kids or the house or any of my zillion zany projects, and of finding opportunities (especially romantic ones) to get my oxytocin (the feel-good hormone) flowing like a river.

But I have to ask.

Nearly always.

And that is the fulcrum where the Crazy Ladies and the Dream Makers wrestle for control of the seesaw. The Crazy Ladies push off with, "He should know that I need him without my saying so! If he really loved me, he would innately understand, sympathize, and run to my rescue," while the Dream Makers counter, "Since he is an independent person who processes information differently from the way I do, he cannot know what I need unless I communicate it to him nice and clear and friendly-like."

Of course, the Dream Maker is right. Of course, he is totally different from you. Of course, he grew up with a completely different family and in a different environment. Of course, he is a man and you are a woman, thus your brains function, well, differently! He honestly, truthfully, no bones about it, does not automatically perceive when you are overwhelmed, overworked, tired, resentful, and about to throw yourself out of the turret and into the moat.

The fact is, a knight, to be a knight, needs an explicit mission —and *you* have to give it to him.

12
A Mission For A Knight

In peace there's nothing so becomes a man / As modest stillness and humility /
But when the blast of war blows in our ears / Then imitate the action of the tiger.
—*William Shakespeare, Henry V* (III.i.3-6)

A mission for a knight can begin by outlining his charge—the task
of helping you—in "the language of request and respect," as Dr.
Lund puts it:

"It would mean a lot to me if..."

"I would appreciate it if..."

Drop "you should," "you must," and "you ought" from your
vocabulary. They don't work. Any superiority or disapproval in
your voice ("Why didn't you...?" "How could you...?"), pushes
him away and you won't get anything worth having in response. In
fact, you are likely to start an argument. Remember, this man is
your equal and these phrases reek of Stupidia.

John Gray, in *Venus on Fire*, observes that men respond much
more readily to requests beginning with the word *will* or *would*,
instead of the word we women usually default to, *can*. To
illuminate the difference in effect, he asks us to imagine a man
proposing with, "Can you marry me?"

Again, I have proof of this concept from my own marriage. It
does work! Can you try it? I mean, *will* you try it? Just switching
out the more polite-sounding *can* for *will* makes it much easier for
your knight to respond definitively (and of his own free *will*) to
your request. Here are some other ways of framing your needs as a

mission for your knight:

- "It makes me happy me when you notice my hair. Do you like the new cut as much as I do?"
- "I heard it's a great movie. A date night would mean a lot to me. Will you get tickets and reservations for dinner?"
- "The kids and I are going to work in the garden this weekend. It's gonna be fun. Will you be our heavy-lifter?"
- "I would so appreciate one of your big, bear hugs right now. I'm feeling nervous and it soothes me to bury my face in your chest."
- "John needs help with his homework and the baby's soaking wet. I can't do both. Would you change her diaper or would you rather help out John?"
- "The situation at work still has me steaming inside. It would help me if you just sat by me and did nothing but listen. No problem solving please. Will you just listen?"
- "I appreciate your need to play with the guys, but it would mean a lot to me if you spent the afternoon with us at home on Saturday. Will you?"
- "Honey, it makes me happy when the kitchen is shiny clean. I so appreciate your help with the dishes. Will you sweep also before you're finished?"
- "I am in the middle of a recipe and need more eggs. Would you run to the store for me?"
- "When we go to bed at the same time, I fall asleep so much deeper and faster. It helps me feel secure. Will you come to bed with me now?"
- "I'm late for my meeting and the kids are late for school. Would you drop them on your way?"
- "I know you love me, but it makes me so happy to

hear it. As a woman, I crave the *words*. Will you melt me with that beautiful voice and say 'I love you'?"

Do you see how taking responsibility for expressing your desires in calm, direct statements actually gives you power? There's even more power in keeping those statements brief. My husband prefers that I make a request by stating what I want *right upfront*; he calls it "talking to the big dog" (a reference to a way of doing business). To his great exasperation, I have a tendency, like most women, to justify a simple request with a long, sometimes contorted exposition that winds into the finale: "So, I need..." or "So, will you..."

Laying out the background information makes sense to me, but the fact is, his natural response is to get antsy, tune me out, or jump to the wrong conclusion—all of which are extremely aggravating to a wife who needs his attention and sympathy. All I have to do to avoid that is make my case (in most instances) by stating my objective at the start: *"Honey, will you watch the kids on Wednesday night so I can do the shopping?"* I do not have to spell out that I haven't gone shopping yet because our old neighbor called complaining again and the kids broke a jar of peanut butter and what the dog didn't lick up I had to get on my knees and scrub right then and there because I already have permanent strawberry jam footprints on the new living room carpet from last week and I'm still not sure I got up all the glass slivers from the peanut butter jar and I would have gone shopping after Scouts on Tuesday but Billy's teacher sent home a ridiculous assignment and now I need to get to the store before Grandma and Grandpa come for dinner on Thursday. (*Breathe.*) He really just needs the basics: "Honey, I would so appreciate it if you would watch the kids tomorrow night for a bit while I run to the store. Will you do that for me?"

If his eyebrows go up, *then* he's asking for the strawberry footprints. If I tell him the jam-and-peanut-butter story *after* I get the eyebrow signal, he can listen to it in *context* because I have stated my objective upfront. If I don't ask for what I want at the beginning of the conversation however, chances are he will interpret my request as a tirade of complaints. And as Dr. Lund explains, complaining is the language of a child to a parent, not of communication between equals.

It all comes down to this: If I need my husband to help lighten my daily burdens, to understand my anxieties, to comfort me when I'm down, to bolster me when I feel inadequate, to be romantic when I need it most—then *why, oh, why* add to my tension and his confusion by harboring secret expectations of him, making both of us resentful? How frustrating is that! And how mentally exhausting to hint or manipulate him into action. That's crazy! I hope it will surprise you how easy it is to simply verbalize what he can do to mitigate your stress, and how happy he is to oblige.

And even if he hesitates or disagrees with you on occasion, I agree with Alisa Bowman's advice: "Tell him what you want, but be okay with not always getting what you want. You'll feel more loved if he understands your needs—even if he doesn't necessarily agree with them—than if he doesn't understand you at all but does your bidding because he's too exhausted to stand up for himself" (*Project Happily Ever After*, p. 160).

Taking the Sting Out Of a "Smartie"

Teaching a knight to knit also means articulating certain kind of hurts once in a great while—things he repeatedly says or does that pain you—but bringing up offenses like this must be done with great compassion and maturity. In the long ago past, for instance, my jovial husband occasionally revealed something that embarrassed me in front of others. How was I to handle it? Michael Gurian suggests you say (when you're alone, obviously), "You couldn't see it, but that really hurt me when you said..." (*What Could He Be Thinking?*, p. 167). This approach maintains husband-respect as well as self-respect, while alerting him to what I call a "smartie": something he does or says that really smarts—and I mean *smarts* (genuinely hurts my feelings as opposed to just annoying me). Remember: chances are he did not *mean* to hurt you. Picture those big, hairy hands fumbling with a pair of knitting needles and remind yourself that his relationship skills are evolving, that he is trying to master the ins and outs of life with a wife. The whole point is to draw him closer, not push him away. Please don't be guilty, as I once was, of Crazy Lady manslaughter. Be merciful. Be sparing. Be infrequent. And be direct. A *smartie* only stings for a moment, like an insect bite on your ego—so you can restrain your tongue briefly until the swelling goes down. Remind yourself that he is acutely sensitive to disapproval and afraid of your overwhelming him with emotion. Piles of words will only smother his ability to understand. Teaching a knight to knit means choosing instead to be very clear, very succinct, and very respectful when you gently bring up an offense and convey your need: *You couldn't see it, but it really hurt me when you said..."* then follow up with, *"it would mean a lot to me if you tried to see it from my point of view..."* or *"A hug and a kiss and a little apology would do wonders for me..."* and conclude with *"If the situation comes up again, I would be so grateful if you did this...."*

In all probability, he will still react defensively by instinct, but he won't be nearly so vehement as if you laid on the blame and criticism; and if you are expecting a little push back, his bristling won't bother you so much. If he doesn't melt into an apology, simply let it lie and give him time. Model what *you* need— patience, sympathy, and good listening—and chances are he will remember your example. Next time, he will try to handle himself with a little more grace, and you will feel better for informing him of the smartie in a kind, rational, forgiving way. Over time, this approach toward teaching a knight to knit *sensitively* can pay big dividends.

Time and Space

There are a lot of other dynamics in the husband-wife-communication-of-needs that we do not have the space to go into, but I strongly recommend reading up on the subject (in the back of this book, as well as in Chapter 17, you will find a list of works I've found helpful). Though their approaches may vary, all of them will tell you one way or another that one of the most critical aspect of effective communication is timing, which involves respecting a man's need for independence. Give him space: room and time (physically and emotionally) for him to be alone and to problem-solve or to process or to do whatever he wants. Let him suit up again in his chain-mail before you send out the next distress signal. If he were at your beck and call 24/7, fulfilling your never-ending to-do list, your man would drop dead. Science now tells us that he is different from you in that he must, biologically and hormonally, shut down after almost any kind of concentrated action (including conversation). His heart and his hormones are designed to act, rest, restore; then act, rest, and restore again; he doesn't go-go-go nonstop the way you and I do. If you let him disappear into his office, vanish into the garage, escape on a run, or yes, dissolve into an easy chair after work, or following a conversation, or when he has accomplished something you have asked of him, he will come out of mental hibernation sooner and stronger. Refreshed and ready because he feels confident that he has succeeded, and grateful that you supported his need to regroup, he will literally live longer and love better.

Just remember: your man is trying. A hero's life is exhausting. Outside your home and relationship, the world is senseless and insensitive. Imagine facing that world with a partner like Ashamlee, Stupidia, Irreleva, Betraya, or Depressa, who humiliate, demean, ignore, control, demand, pressure, blame, or whine to get what they want or need. Wouldn't you respond just a little more gallantly to a clear, straightforward request? First Respect makes a difference at any point in any relationship, but if you adopt these simple approaches early and make them a habit, both of you will benefit immensely and almost immediately for the rest of your lives.

Let me show you *teaching a knight to knit* in action. A wife I mentored found it a tough sale when she tried repeatedly to convince her husband that she could not tolerate frequent late-night get-togethers with friends. Hanging out well past midnight was a tradition with him, but the wife (who normally loved social fun) had to be at work early the next morning, and she knew she was a guaranteed basket-case without a certain amount of sleep. Wife would hint as much when the clock struck ten. Husband would say, "Just a minute," and act a bit annoyed. By eleven, Wife was whimpering on the couch. Eventually, reluctantly, Husband got their coats, but good-byes took another thirty minutes.

This routine went on for months until Wife despaired. She wrote to me with bags under her eyes. I asked her first of all to explain the situation to me from his point of view, which she did rather well. She honestly respected her husband and loved their friends as much as he did, so she decided she would again pleasantly, but clearly, express her needs ahead of time: kindly, succinctly, matter-of-factly, and then stick by her guns at the get-togethers. Gently, but firmly, she repeated her request on those nights with a sweet, "Honey, I'm turning into a pumpkin. Will you take me home now please?" and showed sincere appreciation when he responded— even if it was a little slower than she hoped for. Of course, you can guess what happened over time. As he came to comprehend her sincerity and her dependence on him, he began not only to respond more quickly, but to anticipate her needs. Eventually, they were out of the house and on their way home without her having to say anything. He now consistently, tenderly, takes care of her in this situation—and in many others.

Building a castle may take weeks, months, years, or even a few decades (the physical ones sometimes took centuries), depending on you and your man and the subtleties of your particular relationship, but it's worth it. The Crazy Ladies will never know what it feels like to be wrapped in a partner's devotion, to feel so safe that all the fear in your heart dissipates. Allowing him to do more for you, by asking him kindly and sensitively, enhances not only your feminine power but his masculine pride as well. As Dr. Gray notes, "A man will always love a woman more when she's getting what she needs" (*Venus on Fire*, K. 2206-2209). When you help your man feel successful in his partnership role, you will both be oriented toward *forever*.

13
Dream Breaker Road

Then [Emma's] ideas would gradually settle, and, sitting on the grassy turf,
digging into it with little thrusts of the tip of her parasol, Emma would ask
herself again and again: "Oh, dear God! Why did I ever marry?"
—*Gustave Flaubert, Madame Bovary*

On our first night in Honolulu (we'd been married five years), we had dinner at an outdoor table at a Waikiki Beach restaurant. The same breeze that ruffled our hair sent pink clouds chasing across an amber sky. Flaming torches lit our faces, which occasionally broke from concentrating on each other, to look out over the violet sea; ships and sails silhouetted against a glorious sunset.

It was the beginning—and the end—of a dream come true.

The next day, a blistering tropical sun scorched us from top to bottom. Alarmed, we hurried to the hotel and hobbled to our sanctuary, but even the crisp bed sheets hurt. The pool, on the other hand, felt good—until we began to pucker up like sun-dried tomatoes, and chlorine infected Dale's enraged epidermis.

By sunrise, he had a rocketing fever and throbbing pain inside both ears. The hospital emergency room confirmed our own diagnosis: infection caused by entrapped water. Sensitive to the touch and yowling in agony, all Dale could do for the next several days was to take medicine every two hours and watch all-night reruns of *Hawaii Five-O*.

Sooner or later (and usually sooner), every marriage will feel like a

Hawaiian holiday gone awry. Relationships, like travel plans, rarely go as planned. In fact, if there is one thing I can guarantee each and every bride it's that nothing will turn out quite the way you think it will. Here are some of the questions or worries posed to me by real women:

"I did not expect to feel so lonely."

"Why don't we talk like we did when we were dating?"

"I didn't know it would be years before we could afford a house."

"He doesn't pay attention to me like he used to."

"I can't believe how long it's taking him to get through school."

"It feels like we hardly see each other."

"No one told me how much the baby would change things."

"We got along so well before we got married. Now we can't agree on anything."

"I thought two incomes would be enough."

"He said he knew where he was going, but he's changed directions four times."

"I never dreamed I'd live so far from my parents."

"How come everything is more stressful than before we were married?"

"Why didn't anyone tell me it would be so hard?"

I try to console these women by admitting that I was thinking the same things as a new wife. Disillusionment hits every marriage square in the face at some time to some degree. Like the waves that nearly swept me off of my feet when I stood in the Pacific Ocean as a child, life has a way of breaking on us, and it can break us if we're unprepared. Balancing in the shifting surf, I remember panicking as the sand ran out from between my toes. Only the hand of someone more experienced and surer than me helped me stay upright.

I want to be that person for you.

So, even though writing about the Crazy Ladies is making me a little loopy (I'd much rather talk more about building your castle), we can't turn around and head toward *forever* quite yet. Hold my hand and hold your ground. You need the big picture, which means we have to face the salt and the spray and go all the way—all the way down Dream Breaker Road. After you are familiar with what happens between disillusionment and alienation, and after you know how to manage the conflicts in marriage, you will find it easier to recognize and rectify your predicament when you start to get off track. You can also better appreciate and apply the principles in "Becoming His Intimate" (Chapter 19) and "Becoming His Inspiration" (Chapter 24) because you will be aware of the alternative. Thus, dear sister, in this discussion I will attempt to finish the answer to my young friend's question from Chapter 6: "People are in love and are friends when they marry. Why doesn't it stay that way?"

The Moment Of Truth

There are so many nuances of circumstance, experience, and personality that go into anything human; it would be ridiculous to claim there is one track or one reason or one person responsible when a marriage falls apart. There is, however, a commonality in the way a woman reacts to her man following the honeymoon period that can have a significant impact on the marriage. For instance, when a bride turns into a wife, she has to make a number of critical choices, including how she will respond when she realizes for the first time that:

- his dreams might conflict with hers (the fear of interdependence)
- she is no longer the sole focus of his life (the fear of losing him)

- he cannot always understand or support her the way she thought he would (the need for validation)
- he doesn't seem content with her emotional or physical availability (the fear of exposure)
- he isn't as sure, strong, selfless, or ambitious as she originally perceived him to be (the fear of disappointment).

It is at *that* moment that a woman has great power to affect her future. Will she focus on becoming a Dream Maker for herself and her husband, patiently managing her fears, sympathizing with his, expressing her needs and her feelings in a way that he will respond positively to, buffering the natural conflicts in their partnership? Or will she set the stage for unhappiness by letting her insecurities get the better of her? Will she react to her sense of disillusionment by allowing the Crazy Ladies to come home to stay?

We can rightly call this tipping point the proverbial *moment of truth* because what we are talking about is the realization of the truth of things as they are, not as we fantasized them to be. It is important to make this distinction between truth and fiction not only because it affects your marriage, but also because it's a step forward or backward in your own maturation. In *We: Understanding the Psychology of Love*, Dr. Johnson speaks beautifully to this stage in personal development:

"...this is the main distinction between human love and romantic love: Romance must, by its very nature, deteriorate into egotism. For romance is not a love that is directed at another human being; the passion of romance is always directed at our own projections, our own expectations, our own fantasies. In a very real sense, it is a love not of another person, but of ourselves... When we are focused on our projections, we are focused on ourselves. And the passion and love we feel for our projections is a reflexive, circular love that is directed inevitably back to ourselves" (p. 92).

Love, as Dr. Johnson further explains, cannot be a "mutual religious adoration of such overwhelming intensity that we feel all of heaven and earth revealed" (p. 72) in it. How could a couple keep a house, pay bills, or raise children that way? Men especially, but women too, would feel the emotional pressure so acutely on top of all the other anxieties of life that it could not be tolerated for long. Relationships would waste away in short order—and many do of course, for this precise reason. One partner or the other (usually the woman), falls deeper and deeper into disillusionment, punishing herself and her husband for the loss she feels. Because she cannot foresee the consequences of her behavior, she may even believe she is acting in the best interests of the marriage as she morphs into Ashamlee, Stupidia, or Irreleva.

The ultimate tragedy takes place when a wife lets her ability to respect and trust her husband wear away completely. Dismayed and fearful as he grows ever more distant, she complains, lashes out, pushes too hard, or clams up, when all she really wants is love. Instinctively (and understandably) she craves validation, but the way she is trying to get it will not turn the *Castle Closed* sign around. Both husband and wife languish for want of true human understanding, and the marriage dies a slow, painful death.

An equally tragic scenario occurs when the wife keeps the disillusionment to herself. Perhaps she feels ashamed or uncomfortable bringing it up, or maybe she fears exposure or interdependence, or it could be that she can't quite articulate the source of her discontent. She may even think that things will magically change somehow and that she ought to save face or keep her options open by not fessing up just yet. A woman may also send mixed messages (though clear to her) that confuse a man or don't sink in at all. Regardless; such indirectness, silence, miscommunication, or pretense allows her man to believe that all is well, setting him up for a shocking finale when she turns apathetic, distant, or disdainful.

The nuances of individual relationships vary, of course, sometimes significantly, and no one has discovered a predictable timetable for the demise of a marriage. However, it's safe to say that for most unhappy women, disillusionment advances like a glacier—very slowly, very subtly, growing more intense and more immense by the year. The mass of heavy ice, carrying rock and debris from the past, gradually deforms the landscape. We clearly don't want that to happen to you, so let's take a blunt look, in the plainest terms, at how the downfall begins and progresses.

Dream Breaker Road originates with:
- *idealizing* him ("You are perfect for me");
- then moves to *disillusionment* ("You are not meeting my needs the way I thought you would");
- to trying to *change* him ("I want you to be more like I think you should be");
- to getting *frustrated* with him ("I am disappointed that you are not meeting my expectations");
- to *confusing* him ("I want to trust you but I do not respect you");
- to *antagonizing* him ("I cannot support you");
- to *disdaining* him ("You will never succeed");
- to *sabotaging* the relationship ("I do not need you and I can act without you");
- to finally *alienating* him ("There is a better life or man for me").

I have deeply reflected on my own marriage, as well as those of many others, including the many women I have mentored. I have plowed through piles of books and studies written by respected professionals and academics, yet I think Dream-Breaker Road is most clearly illustrated in Gustave Flaubert's 1856 classic,

Madame Bovary (translated below by Lydia Davis). In this story of illusions causing disillusion—though Emma Rouault does not personify all women—an unhappy wife's romantic self-deception and where it leads her are still instructive.

Madame Bovary

Nearly any woman can relate to newlywed Emma's picturesque vision of the honeymoon: "As the sun goes down, you stand together on the shore of some bay, inhaling the fragrance of the lemon trees; then, at night, alone on the terrace of a villa, your fingers intertwined, you gaze at the stars and make plans" (K. 996-98).

Not long after the ceremony, Emma first detects her discontent: "Before her marriage, she had believed that what she was experiencing was love; but since the happiness that should have resulted from that love had not come, she thought she must have been mistaken. And Emma tried to find out just what was meant, in life, by the words "bliss," "passion," and "intoxication," which had seemed so beautiful to her in books" (K. 910-12).

Assuming it is her husband's fault for not romancing her, Emma overlooks the man's devotion and focuses instead on his deficits, including the annoying fact that he is happy just being a country doctor: "But shouldn't a man know everything, excel at a host of different activities, initiate you into the intensities of passion, the refinements of life, all its mysteries? Yet this man taught her nothing, knew nothing, wished for nothing. He thought she was happy; and she resented him for that settled calm, that ponderous serenity, that very happiness which she herself brought him" (K. 1009-11).

We know that wishing, manipulating, or forcing a man to change never works, and so Emma enters the frustration stage: "Meanwhile, acting upon theories that she believed to be sound, she kept trying to experience love...[but] Charles seemed neither more loving or more deeply moved. When in this way she had made some attempt to strike the tinder against her heart without causing a single spark to fly from it...she easily persuaded herself that Charles's passion was no longer extraordinary" (K. 1050-51).

Emma's frustration eventually sours their lives as she carelessly, and sometimes purposely, begins to antagonize and confuse her husband: "What was more, she no longer hid her scorn for anything, or anyone; and she would sometimes express singular opinions, condemning what was generally approved, and commending perverse or immoral things: which made her husband stare at her wide-eyed" (K. 1417-20).

When even her daring disrespect fails to change things, Madame Bovary begins to look at her husband with disdain and contempt: "'What a pathetic man! What a pathetic man!' she said softly, biting her lips...With age, he was developing coarse habits; at dessert, he would cut up the corks of the empty bottles; after eating, he would run his tongue over his teeth; when swallowing his soup, he would make a gurgling sound with each mouthful; and because he was beginning to grow stout, his eyes, already small, seemed to have been pushed up toward his temples by the swelling of his cheeks" (K. 1339-43).

At this point (several years down the line); Emma is ripe for the last push into alienation. She begins to sabotage her own marriage by dwelling on what might have been: "And through what lamentable folly had she spoiled her life this way, with one sacrifice after another? She recalled all her natural fondness for luxury, all the privations of her soul, the sordid details of marriage, housekeeping, her dreams falling in the mud like wounded swallows, everything she had desired, everything she had denied herself, everything she could have had! And for what! For what!" (K. 1060-62).

She basically finishes the job as she fantasizes foolishly about other men: "She would wonder whether there hadn't been some way, through other chance combinations, of meeting a different man; and she would try to imagine those events that had not taken place, that different life, that husband whom she did not know. All of them, in fact, were unlike this one" (K. 1062-64).

It won't surprise you that poor Emma is easily enticed at this point into an affair with a man who takes advantage of her vulnerability. Of course, she will get hurt again because the new relationship is based on the same flimsy notions as her marriage, except this time, the man is far less worthy. She tells the lover who secretly intends to leave her: "What harm can come to me, after all? There's not a desert, not a precipice, not an ocean that I wouldn't cross with you. When we're living together, our life will be like an embrace that becomes closer and more complete every day! There'll be nothing to bother us, no worries, nothing in our way! We'll be alone together, we'll be everything to each other, forever . . . Say something, answer me" (K. 3628-30).

Emma's tumble into alienation begins because she "could not convince herself that the calm life she was living was the happiness of which she had dreamed" (K. 990). In other words, she could not get past false expectations. This is the mentality Dr. Johnson describes in *WE*:

> "...the cult of love...that seeks to spiritualize relationships into a very perpetual and superhuman intensity... these inherited ideals cause us to seek passion and intensity for their own sake; they plant a perpetual discontent that can never find the perfections it seeks. This discontent grays over every modern relationship... [it] holds an unattainable ideal before our eyes that blinds us perpetually to the delight and beauty of the here-and-now world" (p. 47).

I still remember, with a pang of regret, the days I let my dissatisfaction get the better of me; blinded to the sweetness of what could be, I made my heart sick and my husband miserable with my negativity. When I think how narrowly I escaped careening all the way down Dream Breaker Road early in marriage —how I might have ended up in alienation instead of in a grand marriage—it sends a shiver down my spine and a tear down my cheek—literally. It's why I'm writing this book: so you can avoid that same close call.

Keep reading.

I want to strengthen your resolve with yet another perspective: your husband's.

14

Why Did The Husband Cross The Road?

Intention is a close friend of commitment. Without commitment and intention, the Princess would still be alone, and the Prince would be sunning himself on a lily pad. To begin with, the spellbound prince carried a strong intention to be free of his frog suit, and toward that end, pursued his goal of the liberating kiss.
—Sue Patton Thoele, expert on women's emotional health

I'm going to tell you a love story that is as old as time. Of course, it begins with a Nice Guy who meets a Nice Girl. Nice Guy is attracted to Nice Girl and spends time with her. Nice Guy wants *more* time with Nice Girl. So Mother Nature, the matchmaker of all matchmakers, flips the *on* switch. He is suddenly able, thanks to an influx of subtle but powerful chemicals (pheromones) to set aside his normal tendencies in favor of much more romantic behaviors. His stimulated cortex and limbic system (the part of the brain that handles emotional and sensory responses) are now concentrating on verbal communication, eye contact, and close listening. He is, in two words, open and expressive. The magician, Mother Nature, has transformed Just-a-Nice-Guy into very appealing Really-Romantic-Guy. Girl loves it and she loves him. End of story—at least, in the movies.

In real life, the adventure is just beginning—for him. Nice Guy is now complete in a way he's never felt before, with a new reason for living and loving. Mother Nature declares this mission accomplished and preps his brain and body for the next stage of life. Yanking away the carpet he was soaring on, she forces him back to earth, where his limbic system can now concentrate not only on his partner, but on all the other things a man has to worry about: making a living, raising children, distinguishing himself, pursuing a quest.

With Groom's attention diverted from romance, and with his biology helping him focus on other responsibilities, Bride suddenly feels like her adventure is ending, not beginning. And who can blame her? He seemed so perfect during courtship: loving, supportive, believing. It was easy to love Groom while she was the center of his universe, but now, she wonders, is he really as devoted as she thought?

Bride's worry and neediness confuses and distresses Groom: his actions seem perfectly natural to him. Though he doesn't feel biologically prompted to romance her in quite the same way he used to, or to express himself quite as freely without that shot of pheromones, he still *wants* to succeed with her desperately. He believes that all that he is doing (or not doing) *is for her.* But, Just-a-Nice-Guy's need to be needed while protecting his independence has kicked into high gear, and his fear of being overwhelmed by emotion has replaced Really-Romantic-Guy.

A few months after her wedding, I told this love story to my daughter. She in turn, shared it with her married sister-in-law who reportedly exclaimed, "Well, *that* would have been nice to know!"

I couldn't agree more. If only science had known in 1977 what science knows today, someone else might have written this book, and I might have understood my husband instead of resenting him. Because I could not figure out what in the world was going on, negativity took over my perception of things, and I responded to this natural adjustment in our relationship like a major fall, breaking my heart—and crushing his—on dangerous Dream Breaker Road.

That's not to say that Nice Guys don't do dumb stuff. Mine did. He had a lot to learn about nurturing relationships in those early days, but so did I. I believe we were magically brought together to help each other learn to love, and in the process, create a family. Mother Nature equipped each of us with talents, tendencies, intelligence, and skills that would eventually mesh into one, cohesive unit.

At least, that was her plan.

Until someone did something that caused someone some pain and it suddenly seemed something surely was wrong. But what? And who? Here is how Dream Breaker Road looks from his point of view in many cases:

- It begins with *fantasizing* her ("You are perfect for me");
- moves on to *disillusionment* ("I thought I made you happy");
- to *trying to please* her ("I need you to be happy");
- to getting *frustrated* with her ("I need your respect");
- and ultimately to *despairing* of her ("I'm tired of failing you")

Now, don't fly off the handle thinking I am portraying women as solely responsible for every unhappy ending. *I am not.* As I've said before, I have dearly loved and sympathized with women of all ages and from all walks of life as they have gone through the terrible ordeal of divorce. Yet in the context of the norm (the Nice Guys), it's worth considering a University of Michigan Institute for Social Research long-term study called the Early Years of Marriage project, which found that far more women blame their husbands in a divorce than men blame ex-wives. In fact, 80 percent of women blame their husbands, while only 4 percent of women blame themselves, and the majority of men simply accept their ex's view of the break-up. Could that have anything to do with a man's weary state of mind at the end of Dream Breaker Road ("I'm tired of failing you")? The truth is, the road too frequently traveled has two sides.

In the hundreds of conversations I have had with women about their troubled marriages through the years, the other side of the road is predictably underrepresented. So, in the interest of the big picture, I want to share with you a very personal male perspective garnered from individual interviews with ten divorced men: former husbands who fit our definition of Nice Guys in that—for all their faults—they never purposely set out to hurt their wife. These guys and their stories were not scientifically selected or categorized, except that none of the marriages involved serious anger issues, personality or mental disorders, toxic upbringings, or emotional or physical abuse—which I've said repeatedly is outside the scope of this book. So, I'm not trying to represent this as any kind of definitive study. The men I interviewed all dealt with common stressors like finances, employment, housing, children, in-laws, and health issues, but never perceived or expected their marriage to be in dire straits; each man believed he and his wife had lived pretty well, and each one meant very well.

Our one-on-one conversations began with this invitation: "Tell me about your marriage experience." Without any other prompting, these men willingly opened up to expose their pain. Why, you may wonder, would they share so freely with me when men generally dread emotional overload? In almost word-perfect unison, each one said with deep sincerity: "I'll do anything to help save anyone from going through what I went through."

These men used words like "horrendous," "anguish," "brutal," "horrific," "gut-wrenching," and "broken." A Marine compared his divorce to a dangerously stressful stint in Afghanistan. Another spoke of a dark period in the months after their split, when he isolated himself from the entire world (literally no one knew where he lived) and thought of nothing but taking his own life. One man looked deep into my eyes and with sober shame said, "If, on my wedding day, I could have wound the clock forward, I have to say, though it kills me to admit it, that even having my beautiful kids, who I love with all my heart and cannot imagine life without, does not make up for the torture I've been through. The joy does not outweigh the pain."

And then he wept.

He wasn't the only one. Each man cried while telling his story. And I cried with them. How could I not? Their stories, though the specifics varied, ripped me up because they were so much alike. Of all the common denominators, the most disturbing was the fact that each and every one of those men is still bewildered about what *really* happened. In all honesty, these men remained troubled— long after counseling, legal proceedings, and the final decree—by what they did or did not do that changed their wife's attitude towards them. Tracing the evolution of heartbreak was virtually impossible; each of these guys thought he was doing his part when his wife's dissatisfaction became more and more apparent.

From the specific incidents they related, it became obvious to me that each woman confused her husband by camouflaging her desperate call for *connection* with *disrespect*, though it was interesting that none of the husbands used that word—they clearly avoided it. Admitting they were disrespected, even in the context of a candid interview, was too painful. One man said he felt like he'd had a "knife through the heart," which is exactly what it feels like to a man of good intentions when a woman communicates, "You have failed me." When a woman's misleading bid for affection misfires, things can get progressively worse and worse, until the relationship collapses under the weight of mutual frustration.

Now we all know this goes both ways. A disillusioned husband can send the same demoralizing message to his wife: "You are inadequate." This is just as injurious, and my next book will speak directly to *him*. But this book is for *you*, the aspiring Dream Maker, and if you are going to achieve a beautiful lifelong marriage, you have got to understand and sympathize with what goes on in his heart as well as your own. Defensiveness will never empower you;

in fact, it is a sure sign that you feel out of control. I want to put you back in control, in the powerful position of creator and keeper of the relationship; but to get you there, you have to be open to a husband's point of view. For instance, can you imagine...

- ...receiving a Father's Day card from your bride, with a sweet message about your future children together? A week later you find all your clothes packed and sitting on the front porch.
- ...looking forward to your wife nuzzling your neck every night as you climb into bed with her after your late shift at work? Then, six months into your marriage, she inexplicably stays on her side of the bed and never nuzzles again.
- ...getting a loving anniversary letter from your wife that closes with: "I can't wait to see what the next eleven years will bring." Eleven months later she's suing for divorce.
- ...your wife of twenty years telling you how much she loves and needs you one night and the next morning presenting you with a spreadsheet detailing how your debts and assets are about to be divided?

That's really, truly, precisely what happened to our guys, only they're not clear why!

A random comment I came across on a relationship blog sums up a man's disorienting journey down Dream Breaker Road: "After fifteen years together—which held many, many 'I love you so much!' moments—she recently told me that she didn't love me and perhaps she never really had. She's moving out tomorrow. I'm still working through the hurt and anger, but I don't think I'll ever get over the bafflement."

Are we getting the big picture yet? Maybe this statistic, as reported by anthropologist Helen Fisher, Ph.D., in *First Sex* will help: "Men are roughly 25 percent more likely to abase themselves to keep a marriage going, giving way to a wife's requests and making elaborate promises to change" (p. 276). She goes on to confirm what we already know—that far fewer men than women initiate divorce.

Another researcher, Terri Orbach, Ph.D., professor at the Institute for Social Research at the University of Michigan and lead investigator on the University of Michigan study mentioned earlier in the chapter found that a couple is almost twice as likely to divorce when a husband reports that his wife doesn't show him love and affection, as when a man says he feels cared for and appreciated. Not a big surprise. Everyone wants to feel cared for and appreciated. But hold your horses (or your husband)—here's the wow factor: the reverse does not hold true! Even if the woman feels a lack of affection, the couple is not more likely to divorce. What does that mean? It means, concludes Dr. Orbach that men seem to need nonsexual affirmation from their spouses even more than women do! She explains why that is in her book, *Finding Love Again: 6 Simple Steps to a New and Happy Relationship*. Most women, she says, receive regular affirmation from many people or multiple sources, while their men have no one giving them the shoulder rub, the hug, the touch, saying "good job" or "you can do it," but their wives (p. 227-28). Just let that sink into your heart... He is absolutely dependent on you (and probably you alone) to positively affirm his worth and value. Do you really want to casually toss life-saving, dream-making affirmation out the window by dwelling on *why can't he? why won't he?* or *why isn't he?*—which, by the way, are all telltale signs that you are balanced precariously on the precipice of Disillusionment Drop-off.

If a woman doesn't want to fall off that precipice—if she wants to mature with a man into old age—then she has to let go of those kinds of thoughts and love her Nice Guy in the here and now. It may be a hard habit to break for some of us, but as Cinderella's fairy godmother would say: it's possible! A woman can appreciate her ordinary man for the ordinary things he does for her (thereby saving her marriage from disillusionment) if she...

- differentiates between what's really important in their relationship and what is not.
- realizes that what she thought were personal weaknesses are actually part of his biology.
- gives him the time and space he needs to mature.
- makes allowance for plain old imperfection, just as he must for her.

And that, my friends, is what being a Wife for Life is all about.

Okay, okay, I admit that staying content in an imperfect relationship with an imperfect person is not always easy and that you can't help wishing for a miracle once in a while, but believe me, you really don't need a fairy godmother to brighten things up. You can be your own fairy godmother.

Want to know how?

15
The Pioneer Woman Challenge

No matter how good your marriage, you will go through times of drought.
Your husband was never meant to completely satisfy you, nor you him.
—*Juliana Slattery, clinical psychologist*

Before we move on to fairy godmother territory, I just want to clarify one thing: there is nothing in the whole wide world wrong with falling in love—that is, becoming enchanted with another human being. As music, literature, and *The Princess Bride's* Miracle Max remind us: "...true love is the greatest thing in the world— next to a nice MLT—mutton, lettuce and tomato sandwich." (Act III Communications, 1987). Believe me, the last thing I want to do is deter you from romance by talking about disillusionment. I believe the intense aspirations of a man and woman's earliest days together—those snapshots of pure anticipation before disillusionment threatens—can act like the photos and postcards one treasures from a beautiful visit to an exotic place. If you pull them out and look at them often enough, they serve as reminders of your noblest ideals and purest dreams, which in turn can lift you up and over disenchantment. How many counselors advise stale or unhappy partners to think about why they fell in love in the first place? Re-enchantment starts with remembering happy yesterdays—every day.

But remembering your original yardstick is just one tactic in what must become a whole way of life for the Dream Maker. *Wife for Life* is full of ideas that can be summarized into one big philosophy: *the objectives and actions of a Dream Maker are the results of thinking proactively.* What that boils down to is *responding* to your loved one (considered, thoughtful action) instead of *reacting* to him (letting the first thought or feeling that comes to mind determine how you treat him).

Let me give you an example. I recently observed the interaction of a newly married young husband and wife that greatly impressed me. During a lull in the group conversation, the wife turned to her husband, who was absorbed in something on his reading device.

"Hey honey," she said—"whatcha reading?"

He swiftly shut down the device. "Nothing."

"No, really, come on. What is it?"

"I said nothing."

Worry flitted across her face. I worried, too. A reply like that would certainly get a reaction from most women.

"Oh"—she hesitated for a second, then with a genuine smile said—"You were just starting a book, weren't you? I'm sorry to interrupt."

She moved over to him and took his hand; his face instantly relaxed into a grateful smile, and I had to close my gaping mouth.

Obviously, the husband did not want a group conversation about whatever he was reading, nor did he wish to call attention to the fact that he was reading while everyone else was socializing. He wasn't sure how to get out of it, thus he answered abruptly. I expected this young wife to interpret his action as defiant secrecy and to react out of her own insecurity with something like, "Why won't you tell us? What are you hiding?" (Betraya), or, "Fine, then! Who cares?" (Irreleva), or, "You shouldn't be reading—we're guests, remember?" (Stupidia), or (to the group), "He never tells me anything" (Ashamlee), or worst of all, "So, what's her name?" (Depressa).

But, no; she tempered her instinctive reaction and instead *responded* by proactively taking charge of the situation in the most positive way possible. With extraordinary deftness, she sidestepped an uncomfortable situation and saved all of us—especially her husband. That kind of deferential on-your-feet response deserves a plaque in the Dream Maker Hall of Fame and the endearment of her husband (which was evident for the rest of the night). From the skill of her dignified decision, I knew exactly what she was made of: my new heroine was a Pioneer Woman.

Like Lela Avis Pollan Schroeder (Chapter 1), this young wife was, at a very deep level, confident in and satisfied with herself—otherwise, she could not have responded to her husband in such a big-hearted way. If she were any less solid inside, her insecurities —the fear of losing him, of disappointment, of dependence, of exposure, or of compromised dreams—would have become instantly inflamed by this teeny-tiny tension, this split-second of stress.

As I tried to show you through my great-grandmother's life, building beautiful relationships requires a woman of pioneer proportions: courageous, pliant, resilient, centered, and most of all, self-reliant. In order to preserve and cultivate her stake—her man and their family—a Pioneer Woman takes care of herself. This is the only way she can give from abundance (from a full heart and with a strong body) and receive with confidence (from a deep-seated belief that she deserves nurturing and attention). She is also able to make and stick with difficult choices and live from the heart (the Talent). Last—and perhaps most importantly—she believes in her own objectives, but finds a way to meld them with the hopes of others, particularly those of her husband (the Dream Maker).

So there she is, the Pioneer Woman—eyes riveted on the horizon, face to the sun, defying the wind. Kind of takes your breath away, doesn't it? Are you sighing with admiration, or hyperventilating with anxiety? The Pioneer Woman *is* epic, but don't let that intimidate you. It's not as hard as you may think to become her—to survive, if not by-pass, Disillusionment Drop-off.

You too can become impervious to just about everything Mother Nature throws your way and protect your claim on the Road to Forever if you will follow the principles in *Wife for Life*, including the one simple piece of advice in this chapter: the exercise that I call "The Pioneer Woman Challenge". I promise that it's not as strenuous as plowing a prairie or as distasteful as plucking a chicken. Any woman can do it. Any woman will love it.

All you have to do to execute The Pioneer Woman Challenge is *romance your own heart.*

Be your own fairy godmother.

Go get happiness—by yourself and for yourself.

Thrill yourself. Fill yourself.

Do not, I repeat, do not depend solely on his attention, his love, to make your world glitter. If you do, you will end up like the main character in Kristin Hannah's *Distant Shores: A Novel*. As a middle-aged woman, Elizabeth Shore recognizes her responsibility to herself almost too late to save her marriage.

> "Years ago, he'd tried to tell her that all her happiness shouldn't depend on him. He'd watched as she'd given up more and more of herself. He couldn't stop it, or didn't stop it, but somehow it had become all his fault. He was sick to death of it" (p. 11).

It's not until Elizabeth is on the brink of alienation that a friend, a divorce lawyer by profession, gives her this blunt advice:

> "Look, Birdie, women come into my office every day, saying they're not happy. I write down the words that will tear their families apart and break a lot of hearts. And you know what? Most of them end up wishing they'd tried harder, loved better. They end up trading their homes, their savings, their lifestyle, for a nine-to-five job and a stack of bills...So, here's a million dollars' worth of advice from

your best friend and divorce attorney: If you're empty, it's not Jack's fault, or even his problem, and leaving him won't solve it. It's your job to make Elizabeth Shore happy" (p. 6).

Not very pretty, and rather harsh, but she is right about one thing: It *is* your job.

Husbands learn soon enough (and to their dismay) that a wife's craving for time, affirmation, validation, and appreciation are rarely satisfied. We women snatch up every tidbit of affection like a child who has just discovered candy. The sweetness fuels our yearning for more, more, more. If he said "I love you" or "You are beautiful" once an hour for the next fifty years, it wouldn't be enough.

My own need for external reassurance came home to me many birthdays ago. I decided to test everyone (especially Honey) by making no reference to my personal holiday during the entire month of January. The results were devastating. Not a single soul —parent, child, sister, friend, husband (*gasp*)—remembered. The red-letter day came and went without a whimper. Now, before you scream "Revolution!" (which I came close to doing at the time) let me add this: Honey was under huge pressure at work, serving tirelessly at church, and acutely worried over finances. He comforted, cuddled, and counseled with tenderness. It's just that his calendar was off.

When I realized that accusation would never produce a bottle of perfume, the truth hit me like a whiff of cheap cologne: I had been thinking for too long that it was my husband's primary job in life to make me feel good, to heal all my wounds, to spend every possible minute with me, to be emotionally available and responsive 24/7, to always want what I want. I had set myself up for disillusionment.

Thankfully, I wised up and made a course correction which stuck. I call it the *Pioneer Woman Challenge*. My birthday is now advertised far and wide and way in advance. I am responsible to ask for and inspire special attention on January 27. As for the other 364 days of the year, I try to savor his expressions of love (a look, a touch, a thoughtful comment) like expensive chocolates. I rev up just thinking about his last kiss and relish romantic journal entries like éclairs on peanut-butter days. Healthy, balanced doses of giving and receiving from family, friends, God, and myself, keeps my tank full. His three little words ("I love you") then top me off and overflow into a puddle at our feet.

And that's the secret. *Fill your own tank by taking responsibility for your own happiness.* Romance your own heart, and then he can top you off!

There is a simple way to get started, or continue, in the Pioneer Woman habit of filling your own tank so that you can avoid Disillusionment Drop-off and give from abundance while receiving with confidence. I don't mean to make it sound easy— we are talking about the greatest challenge of a woman's life, the seesaw between nurturing herself and nurturing others—but I know you can do it. Get out your journal. Let's get to work.

Step One in the Pioneer Woman Challenge is to make a list of three things that you do, or can do, or would like to do, that *dazzle* your heart—that is, three of your greatest *passions*. My own personal list starts with writing a book. Yours will include your own dreams, projects, and long-term goals. Maybe you have been nurturing your passions for a long time, maybe you are well on your way to achieving them, or maybe you have to dig a little to even think of something that really excites you. It doesn't matter. It doesn't even have to be practical. It's your list. Explore your soul and have fun with it.

Step Two in the Pioneer Woman Challenge requires another list, this one an inventory of at least ten things— the longer, the better —you do, or can do, or would like to do, that *delight* your heart—

that is, ten ordinary, everyday things that make you feel good. You want a lot of simple, feel-good activities so that you can choose one or two or more *every day*—no matter how busy you are. Do you like to sit at the piano for a few minutes? Shop at your favorite store? Get your hair and nails done? Go for a run? Maybe you enjoy calling a friend, talking to Mom, or meeting your girlfriends for lunch (girlfriends are a must). Or perhaps your delight comes from your job or from volunteering. Then again, you may like to take pictures, draw, watch TV, plant flowers, or write letters. I also love walking outdoors, singing out loud, and dancing to the radio. Rocking a sleeping baby puts me blissfully to sleep. A piece of costume jewelry does wonders, and fresh pillowcases or a new kitchen towel make the world beautiful again. Lots of women read, meditate, do yoga, journal, or blog. These may be little things, but that is what delighting your heart is about: ordinary things that take minor effort, time, and money. Finding ways to nurture yourself will psychologically and physiologically boost your sense of self-esteem, well-being, and emotional independence.

Delighting your own heart relieves everyone in the family from the impossible responsibility of making or keeping you happy from day to day. It frees your heart to spend less energy on stress and self-pity, and far more energy on those you love. *Dazzling* your heart can bring you joy and thrill your family as well—as long as you don't take on too much and neglect *them* in the process. Do not go overboard: romancing your own heart is not a license to become selfish and insensitive. I remember an actress friend who came to me, not really for advice but for validation. Her conscience was pricked because she saw her husband and children minutes a day at best, and regularly spent weeks or even months away on location. "I know I'm a better wife and mother," she said of her self-indulgence, "because I'm doing what I love."

Her husband and children did not agree.

To make sure you do not slip into Irreleva or Betraya territory while taking the Pioneer Woman Challenge, ask yourself as honestly as possible and as frequently as necessary, "Is the challenge helping me to *respond* to my family with love, generosity, and intelligence? Or am I still *reacting* to situations because I feel more stressed than ever?" Just as romancing your own heart can help you become a Pioneer Woman, its counterfeit, self-indulgence, brings out the Crazy Ladies.

You can avoid such self-deception by pursuing your passions in a measured, patient, inclusive way. Draw your husband and children (as much as possible and as much as they are interested) into your passions. Prioritize their well-being over that of everyone else in your world (see "The Last Talent Left Standing," Chapter 2), so they never have to question your why, your availability, or your love. Give their passions just as much enthusiasm as you give yours. If you can do that while you romance your own heart, then:

- You will feel better and better about yourself, stronger and stronger at heart.
- Your mental, emotional, and spiritual self-reliance will increase so that disillusionment cannot get a foothold, either in early marriage or in mid-life, when many women discover they have given to the point of exhaustion.
- Confidence in and satisfaction with yourself will undergird all your relationships, especially your marriage. You will have more love to give.
- Romance and reality can merge into a union of heart and mind. Because you have more patience, you won't be offended so easily, you'll forgive more readily, and you will have more fun and more romance.

And here's the best part: if you do it right, just the way I've told you, romancing your own heart will make you irresistible.

Your inner contentment reassures your man. Your genuine cheerfulness draws him to you, especially when he is troubled. Your Nice Guy will absolutely love his Pioneer Woman—so long as you communicate your passions openly, respectfully, and enthusiastically. Explain, if necessary, why you feel that pursuing this passion will actually enhance your relationship. If you treat him as your castle, he can help you discover a pursuit if you don't already have one. This doesn't mean you have to get his approval before you make the slightest move toward your own happiness. What it does mean is that you must employ the Wife for Life principle of First Respect when it comes to plans that involve him or the whole family in some way. Do your best to make a plan together. Dale has truly helped me balance my passions with our family life, and it's wonderful to have a partner who can help me discover myself.

On the other hand, if he takes exception to your proposal or suggests modifications, remember that he may legitimately question increased demands on him, the family, the budget, or most of all, on you! Listen with an open heart. You may need to re-think pursuing a particular passion at a particular moment in time. Everything has a time and a season. On the other hand, perhaps all your husband needs is reassurance of your love, a sincere reminder that the marriage is your number-one priority. Never, ever forget: *you only have so much time and so much energy.* To become his Intimate, you must be oh-so-wise in how you spend both. Romancing your own heart is about becoming more beautiful to yourself *and* your family, not more distant. It's about strengthening your sense of self-worth, not diminishing theirs.

Minerva Teichert, a passionate, larger-than-life artist (quite literally, she painted murals), is a beautiful example of this delicate balance. After classically training with the great teachers of the day, she returned home to her beloved American West in the 1930s to marry cowboy Herman Teichert, "a man more nearly meant for me than anyone else in the world," according to biographer J.U.

Pinborough ("Minerva Kohlhepp Teichert: With a Bold Brush", Ensign, April [1989]: 34). For over forty years, she directed her household from their isolated Cokeville, Wyoming, ranch—while painting hundreds of works using the walls of her living room as a giant canvass. They say she could stir supper on the wood-burning stove while touching up a mural on the wall! Minerva's American West and religious art is justly admired today, and though I will go anywhere to see it exhibited, what I most stand in awe of is her talent for romancing her *own* heart as she *responded* to her loved ones. She was able to meld her passions ("I have to paint," she said), with the hopes of others, particularly her husband's quest as a rancher. He supported and cherished her for it.

My favorite of Minerva's impressionistic watercolors is *Handcart Pioneers*, in which a woman wearing a prairie dress stands on her toes, raises her arm, and lifts her chin, as if to salute the company following her as she and her husband crest a mountain pass. Though the pioneer's enthusiastic gesture bespeaks her joy in accomplishment, it's the red paisley shawl fluttering round her neck that grabs the viewer. Minerva, an outspoken advocate of women's rights, purposely and repeatedly chose paisley—a bold, colorful fabric—for her female subjects because to her, the cloth represented *powerful women*.

Minerva's paisley fabric then, epitomizes a Wife for Life, a Dream Maker, a Pioneer Woman. Because she has taken responsibility to manage her fears and cultivate her courage, resilience, and self-reliance, the Paisley Shawl Woman has the power to *respond* rather than *react* to her loved one. As keeper of the relationship, a Pioneer Woman has the strength, talent, self-assurance, and fortitude to wave her marriage forward—no matter the height or depth or number of mountains and valleys (or natural disasters) on the road ahead...

16
Preventing Earthquakes

Was that an earthquake, or did you just rock my world?
—*Classic pick-up line*

Queen Victoria, the longest-reigning female monarch of all time (1837-1901), came to greatness by all three of Shakespeare's criteria: she was born in line to the throne, and thrust into that eminent position at eighteen; her *achieved* greatness came when she married a man whose name became forever linked with hers: Francis Albert Augustus Charles Emmanuel, or, as officially titled, Prince Albert of Saxe-Coburg and Gotha. Their reign and romance are considered a zenith in Great Britain history and their love affair makes becoming a queen seem a doable, if not an enviable objective. On her wedding night, Queen Victoria wrote in her diary:

> "I NEVER, NEVER spent such an evening!!! MY DEAREST DEAREST DEAR Albert...his excessive love & affection gave me feelings of heavenly love & happiness I never could have hoped to have felt before! He clasped me in his arms, & we kissed each other again & again! His beauty, his sweetness & gentleness –really how can I ever be thankful enough to have such a Husband!" (*Queen Victoria: A Personal History*, p.123).

But lovers and legends are two different things, as we know from

Gillian Gill's account of the royal marriage in *We Two: Victoria and Albert: Rulers, Partners, Rivals* (p. 184):

SLAM!
Albert locks the door behind him.
POUND-POUND-POUND!
Victoria: "Let me in! We have to talk!"
"Who is there?"
"The Queen of England!"
No response.
Another knock.
"Who is there?"
"Your wife, Albert."
Door opens.

I dare say that such a scene, witnessed more than once at Buckingham Palace, has played out in every household in America. Husbands and wives, even happy ones, disagree once in a while and get a little hot, if not a little haughty, under their royal robes. That's right. There will be conflict in *every* marriage. Surprise! Even if you perfectly applied all the Dream Maker principles we have discussed, the result would be *im*perfect. And what's wrong with that, really? No one would read a love story that didn't have a little push-back, a little wrinkle, a little shudder in it. If lovers are identically matched—in the sense that there is nothing to develop or overcome or resolve between them—what growth or depth can there be in their union? Picture-perfect marriages, the ones that have a husband and wife who enthusiastically agree on everything all the time are obviously a myth.

Thank goodness.

Conflict between partners—if minimized and managed—can actually be soul stretching. It helps us see things from a different point of view and it teaches us how to accommodate others. You can be sure that your loved one needs to challenge your solo perspective once in a while or you would end up a selfish creature with a boring, lifeless marriage. That's because love is not about pandering to our egotistical prejudices. Love is about expanding our perspective.

In *The Mystery of Marriage*, Mike Mason offers a beautiful explanation of how dethroning the ego, painful as it may seem, is actually one of the benefits of loving and living with another human being:

> "It is no small thing to open our hearts and our arms and allow another to enter there, to grant to another person the same worth, the same consequence, the same existential gravity that we take for granted in ourselves. The fact is that our natural tendency is to treat people as if they were not 'others' at all, but merely aspects of ourselves....For truly to open our hearts to other people is to invite them into our own throne room and to sit them down on our very own throne, on the seat normally warmed by no one but ourselves. And to do that is to have the throne, the seat of the ego, rocked right off its foundations. Love is an earthquake that relocates the center of the universe" (p. 49).

Love may make the world go round, but it also shakes things up.

Disagreements between husband and wife have to be expected and prepared for—just like a natural disaster.

No one plans a disagreement, of course, just as no one goes looking for an earthquake, but those who know how to minimize its effects and pick up the pieces will have the best chance of becoming stronger than ever.

In order to thrive, a marriage has to survive, and while Part Three is all about *thriving*, this part, Part Two, is about *surviving*. Obviously, many marriages do not survive the earthquakes that result from natural conflict. Husband and wife behave like a couple of tectonic plates, pushing each other around, jockeying for position, causing so much friction that everything based on their union is shaken, smashed, or ripped apart. But disagreement doesn't have to be devastating if you equip your emergency kit with the skills that will help you:

- prevent unnecessary conflict,
- protect your marriage during conflict, and
- persevere despite unresolvable conflict.

Pay attention. Your life as a wife may depend on it.

Preventing Hurtful Conflict

I am not a therapist any more than I am a geologist, but I know that a rupture, whether it happens deep in a marriage or deep in the earth, is caused by a sudden release of energy that has been gathering tension beneath the surface. Events that are truly seismic don't just shake the ground, but go on to trigger landslides, tsunamis, even volcanic eruptions. Intense quakes can level the landscape in seconds, but even tremors of a lesser magnitude over a longer period of time can cause significant damage.

Clearly, no matter the kind of quake, there's a good chance of getting hurt. And the damage affects not just you, but all the people around you. Arguments are no different. Anger, the potent epicenter of serious contention, causes the buildup and release of negative energy, which releases an avalanche of physiological reactions that hurt the heart—in every sense of the word. Our most vital organ begins to race and the panic hormone, adrenaline, starts pumping. Consequentially, our mental processes go haywire. (Gives a whole new meaning to the term Crazy Ladies, doesn't it?) Creativity and humor go out the window as oxygen in the blood is reduced, and blood supply to nonessential parts of the body decreases. A whole horde of physiological ramifications puts us in a primitive state of defensiveness. We physically cannot, when angry, absorb information. And if we're not thinking clearly, where does that leave communication, affection, and sympathy?

Anger obviously impairs any human heart and mind—but I want to remind you that a man experiences an extra jolt in a heated argument, a series of aftershocks that a woman does not feel in the same way. You may have a sad and heavy heart, but it's actually beating at a normal rate. His is not. Research shows that men are more likely than women to become *flooded*, mentally and physically overwhelmed. This very intense reaction takes much longer to ebb away; your man cannot return to a normal state as fast as you do. As we learned earlier, minutes after you've brushed off the incident, he may very well go on raging, crying, or quivering— though not in front of you or in any audible or visible manner, except on rare occasion. A Nice Guy in most cases will instinctively shut down in order to protect both of you.

Does that sound like something a Dream Maker wants to be a part of? Of course not; intimates may disagree, become annoyed, and even overtly contradict one another, but they do not contribute to a 9.5-magnitude argument. It's worth every proactive effort you can make to prevent that from happening.

And there are ways.

First of all, though most arguments seem to be about nothing and to appear out of nowhere, every earthquake has an initial hypocenter, or rupture point, just below the angry epicenter. This is where it all begins, under the surface, and there are numerous professionals out there who help people locate and resolve their focus (another name for the hypocenter). If you are already troubled by earthquakes of alarming severity and regularity, you may need counseling. On the other hand, if you are a newbie at marriage, the strategies involved in understanding fears and gender differences, as outlined in the concepts of building your castle, teaching a knight to knit, First Respect, the Pioneer Woman, the

Talent, the Creator, and the Dream Maker, are all powerful preventives against serious conflict. In fact, if you continually review and practice what we've discussed so far (because that's what it takes to make a grand, lifelong marriage) as well as assimilate all the really fun stuff we are saving for Part Three, such as companionship and the Laws of Attraction, you will have a foundation so solid and so deep that whatever tremors do come along won't damage your marriage in the long run. As Dr. Gottman puts it, a "profound friendship will be a powerful shield against conflict. It may not forestall every argument, but it can prevent your differences of opinion from overwhelming your relationship" (*Seven Principles*, p. 96). The living truth of this tenet is evident every day in my life with Dale.

Because I am his Intimate and his companion (the subject of Part Three), and because we trust one another so completely (a product of many years' effort), we see conflict for what it really is: incidental, a scribble of a squabble that fades like disappearing ink. In fact, I can't even recount a recent disagreement (say, one that's happened in the past week), not because we haven't disagreed during that time—I'm pretty sure we did, at least once a day—but because I can't remember the details. That's not an aging memory, that's a maturing marriage. Which brings me to the first brick we must reinforce in your castle if we are to secure your marriage from unnecessary conflict: How often, and in how many ways, do you say: "I'm here for you, sweetheart"?

I credit Dr. Gottman's most recent book, *The Science of Trust: Emotional Attunement for Couples*, for this insight. His research shows how critical it is for your partner to know you *are there* for them. If you are one of those lucky women with a blessed marriage, you know what I mean; in fact, you might even take it for granted. But it's not luck or angels that deserve the credit. Your husband is entitled to a face full of kisses for it. You see, the only way to give someone that kind of security, which is the cornerstone in the foundation of your marriage, is through what Dr. Gottman calls *turning toward* him (p. 138). If you trust your husband, it's because he treats you with kindness. You know he is there for you; it's obviously your job to be there for him. And if you don't yet feel that you can trust your Nice Guy to be there for you, it's still your job to turn toward him, to pay real, enthusiastic attention to him as consistently as possible. Though it may take time for him to respond in kind if you have both slipped into turning away more often than turning *toward*, you nevertheless have to keep trying. If you reward him with immediate appreciation every time he turns toward you—however irregularly or infrequently—his desire to turn toward you will increase.

In the unlikely event that you have consistently turned toward him over a significant period of time and he has not responded, employ the principles of teaching a knight to knit and gently, respectfully talk to him about it. In most cases, unless there are deep wounds to heal or personality disorders to be reckoned with, human nature is such that the more you turn toward your partner, the more likely he is to respond in kind—with time. Remember the Dream-Maker mantra: it's all about how you *respond* to him. *Turning toward* is not about *doing* more for him; it's about lighting up when he makes the slightest bid for your attention. Let me give you some examples that illustrate the difference in responding by turning *toward* intimacy, or *away* from it, or *against* it:

He walks in the door with the classic, "I'm home!"
Toward intimacy: "Hurray! So glad! How was your day?"
Away from intimacy: (delayed reaction) "In here. I'm busy."
Against intimacy: "Finally! Geez. I'm dying here."

He suggests doing something together:
Toward: "Sounds great. What do you want to do?"
Away: "Ah...hmmm. How about [new idea] instead?"
Against: "Are you kidding?"

He asks you to do him a favor:
Toward him: "You bet. Is this afternoon okay?" (And you do it.)
Away: "I'll try." (And you forget.)
Against: "Do it yourself."

He says he's worried:
Toward: "What is it, baby?"
Away: "Tell me later."
Against: "You never ask if I'm worried and I've got lots more to worry about than you."

He comments on something on TV while you're on the computer:
Toward: (looks up) "Interesting. Why do you say that?"
Away: Grunt.
Against: "Can't you see I'm working here?"

He finishes a fix-it job you asked for:
Toward: "Fantastic, honey! How did you do it?"
Away: "Finally."
Against: "I hope you didn't make it worse again."

He calls with good news about a promotion at work:
Toward: "I knew you could do it! Tell me more."
Away: "That's nice. Gotta go."
Against: "They picked you? Why you?"

He wants to be physically intimate in bed:
Toward: [Fill in the blank.]
Away: "Maybe tomorrow."
Against: "No way."

Every one of your responses to his desire for your attention and affirmation either reinforces or chips away at your foundation. Isn't it amazing how these pocket-size opportunities are so minor in time and effort, yet so major in consequence?

These few examples may be enough to get you thinking and responding like a Dream Maker, but if you're still a bit shaky on how important or feasible these teeny opportunities are, let me quiet your *buts* with a rock-solid statistic. In his landmark study of newlyweds, Dr. Gottman's researchers found that those who divorced within six years after the wedding had, as newlyweds in the lab, turned toward their partners 33 percent of the time; the couples who were still married six years later had turned toward their partners *86 percent* of the time. The couples who remained married had responded positively even to trivial requests, satisfying each other over and over with, "Yes! I am here for you" (The *Science of Trust*, p. 199).

There's just no arguing the point. Sustaining anger causes you to lose your head *and* your intimacy, while becoming attentive saves both. As Willard F. Harley, Ph.D., notes in *Fall in Love, Stay in Love,* anger is indeed a "love-buster" that seeks to punish (p. 106). You cannot handle a disagreement constructively while in an angry frame of mind; your heart constricts too much, physically and spiritually. There is just no graceful way out of an outrage once you're in one. Remember my Fourth-of-July Crazy Lady all those years ago in Chapter 6? The best exit line I could come up with was "Forget it." I couldn't even put together an intelligent apology, let alone an empathetic response!

No, the best way to prevent an earthquake is to build a foundation of friendship, to become his Intimate and his Dream Maker, to secure your love with ties of trust by turning toward intimacy at every opportunity possible. Then, when tremors come your way—as they will, even on the Road to Forever—it will be just a china cup, a feeling or two, that gets rattled. With a stable, reinforced foundation, nothing breaks.

No one has to get hurt.

17
Protecting The Relationship

Never misjudge the heart of your beloved.
—*Ludwig van Beethoven*

I love the following personal insight, from Nancy Reagan's memoirs, into her relationship with Ronald Reagan:

> "Fortunately, our fights don't last very long. Years ago, when we were on vacation with my parents at the Arizona Biltmore in Phoenix, Mother described a pair of newlyweds she had overheard at the pool. The bride was crying, and her husband swam over to see what the problem was. 'You were cool to me in the pool,' she said. Somehow, that line stuck. Whenever something isn't quite right between Ronnie and me, one of us will say, "You were cool in the pool." That's a signal that we have some repair work to do, to fix whatever small problem has come up before it has time to grow into a large one" (*My Turn*, pp. 121-22).

Not only did the marriage of President and Nancy Reagan endure over five decades together, the First Couple represent one of the greatest partnerships America has ever known. Can we attribute their happiness and longevity to "You were cool in the pool"? In part, of course we certainly can!

Protecting your marriage during conflict is the next best thing to preventing conflict in the first place, and an early repair is an incredibly useful tool in the Wife-for-Life-emergency-kit. It also helps to know the early warning signs of a quake, to have a plan for when to drop, cover, and hold on to something sturdy if things begin to shake. If you are going to protect your relationship during conflict—making the safety of your marriage your priority—it's a good idea to identify and deal with potential perils before 1.5 turns into 9.5. Like the Reagans, you want to fix problems when they are small.

Which brings me to oatmeal.

I have prepared hot cereal for my daughter, Ashley, every morning for decades. Her diet, because of her disabilities, is limited and specific. I'm embarrassed to admit it, but it took sticky oatmeal boiling over and messing up my stove not once, but many, many times, before I got the hang of keeping the pot at a simmer. Though now I could win a world-class oatmeal competition (I wonder if there is one?), I still occasionally let my guard down. Rushing to the rescue of a bubbling pot a second before it spews is quite a trick in and of itself.

A Wife for Life must develop this skill—not with a pot full of oatmeal, but with a man full of self-will. Keeping things cooking at a nice, steady simmer is optimal, but if neglect or a misunderstanding causes a regrettable incident, a Dream Maker gets there in time to minimize the damage.

Responding to impending conflict before it turns into war requires a strong woman. If you are feeling weak, you risk defaulting to one of the Crazy Ladies. But if you've been teaching your knight to knit and taking the Pioneer Woman Challenge, you will very likely have the presence of mind to resolve problems before they shake things up too badly.

Let's begin by imagining a stressful situation in your marriage coming up rather unexpectedly; you're about to boil over. Perhaps the man in your life—your castle—has made an unfortunate choice. Nice Guys do mess up. At that kind of moment, it is the supreme challenge of the Dream Maker to stand strong and not let a wave of disappointment, hurt, or frustration suck her under. In our surviving-an-earthquake-guide, that means taking a step back to process or evaluate before acting on your feelings. We'll call it *drop and cover*: dropping back (taking time to identify your feelings and to process them before expressing them) in order to *protect* the relationship.

Drop and cover is always necessary when you are on the brink of violating First Respect. Since nearly every day will present you with the temptation to ignore First Respect, you will also have a daily need for drop and cover. Most of those First-Respect challenges will be minor and incidental, while others will be perpetual trials, including a particular one that more and more women are dealing with: Wife makes more money than Husband.

Because women today have just as much education and opportunity as the men in their lives, in many families the woman outstrips her husband in earning potential. An article in the *Wall Street Journal* (July 21, 2012) quotes statistics from the U.S. Bureau of Labor showing that 40 percent of American women are the breadwinners for their families. Nothing wrong with that, of course, unless as the breadwinner, you start seeing yourself as having superior judgment. If you are tempted to focus on making the right decisions instead of building the right relationship, as Juliana Slattery, Psy.D., puts it in *Finding the Hero in Your Husband*, you will be in violation of First Respect (p. 55). And when First Respect is repeatedly disregarded, your husband's confidence in himself and his trust in you will inevitably deteriorate. Crazy-Lady Alert: Stupidia and Irreleva on the prowl. This is a classic call for drop and cover.

Another kind of power struggle that can threaten First Respect surfaces when your loved one has made a poor decision regarding family or work. It may be obviously detrimental or merely a choice you just don't agree with. Whichever it is, and no matter how sure you are of his wrongness and your rightness, it's time to drop and cover. Think hard about his male drives and insecurities before you respond. Remember, he is mortified of failure, especially of failing you. (Imagine that baby chick from Chapter 4 in the palm of your hand.) What you say and do next will either draw him to you ("Help me understand, baby") or push him away ("How could you!"). The latter reaction will obviously start a rumble. Crazy Lady Alert: Ashamlee is chomping at the bit.

A Dream Maker will do her best to drop and cover in the midst of an earthquake in order to avoid forsaking First Respect. As we've discussed throughout Part Two, your response must be as measured and as rational as possible, free of all condescension, contempt, criticism, and contention. Your Nice Guy (though you may not see him that way when things shake, rattle, and roll) is an individual with the right to *respect*—just as you expect him to give you *love* when you fail, frustrate, or disappoint. When the breaker hits the rocks, First Respect is the hand you must hold to keep the relationship from going underwater. It is your sturdy table in an earthquake.

Here is another example of drop and cover in action. Suppose I realize that Honey is going to be late to an event that I thought he understood was important—something the children and I have been counting on. I'm ready to blast into Crazy-Lady territory as I look at the letdown in my children's eyes. Honey-man has made a very poor decision by my way of thinking.

"Off with his head!" screams Depressa, the queen of fairness and feelings. She has no trouble rounding up a posse: every hurt from the past comes running.

But wait! Just as they're stringing the rope—*ta-da*! Dream Maker to the rescue! She stands dauntless in front of the mob, begging them to think before they lynch! "Drop and cover!" she cries. Take a breath. Ask yourself, *"Have I ever done that? Have I ever disappointed or frustrated someone? Have I ever had to break a promise?"*

Ahhh, shoot. Well, of course I have. Everything I want to accuse him of in my righteous indignation, I myself have done in some way, to some degree, in some respect, at some time. An honest evaluation of my own faults is a sure-fire way of squelching the volcano: a great example of drop and cover. My team member, Brooke, calls this tactic "go to the mirror." What she means is, taking a look at *yourself*, either literally or figuratively, will right your perspective and keep that teapot from shrieking.

I have also learned the value of not reacting to the first piece of information I get (sage wedding-day advice from my father-in-law). Instead, I drop and cover by reminding myself that what *I* know about the situation represents a *small* piece of information. If I want to protect our relationship during conflict, I have to withhold judgment. There's even more safety in taking it a step further and judging optimistically, as in, maybe he's late because of a flat tire, or an important phone call, or a state patrolman!

Let me clarify here that drop and cover does not mean you are always agreeable or instantly submissive. No way. A woman absolutely needs to assert herself in conflict once in a while. Expressing yourself, getting your frustration out, often serves to keep you healthy and the relationship growing. Believe me, I am not advocating stuffing it! Rather I am advising that when you take on issues, avoid doing it immediately, harshly, or based on initial reactions. *Let your emotions be guides to needs, not dictators of action.* Though you might think you will feel better for blowing off steam, the heat will burn him deeply and his physiological recovery will probably take far longer than yours—if he can fully recover at all. As Mark Chamberlain, Ph.D. and Geoff Steurer, MS, LMFT describe it in their excellent book, *Love You, Hate the Porn*: "His world goes bleak, the wind is out of his sails, he feels defeated and deflated" (K 1637-1638). Withdrawal, defensiveness, resentment, impatience, acting out, even harshness, are common, lingering reactions when a man's "world goes bleak", when he feels hurt, insecure, attacked, or riled up.

Practicing drop and cover gives you the opportunity to think through what you want to say and how you will say it to avoid or minimize those kinds of unpleasant reactions. You don't need to pour on the lava to make your point, if it *needs* to be made. For instance, you might decide to say what you need to say by writing it. This can be a super way of venting privately—harmlessly, perhaps healthily—*just to yourself.* It can also help you communicate with your husband sans the emotion. Or maybe you can convey your point by *doing* something. This is especially effective when you feel like you've been repeating yourself on an issue with no result. It can actually be fun, as long as you are creative rather than mean-spirited.

Most often, however, you will just say exactly what you mean to say without a harsh or condescending start-up, at an appropriate time and place. You might even schedule or agree on a *time* to talk, although it helps to tell him upfront how long you want to talk and what you want to talk about (Chapters 11 & 12). Then again, scheduling might not be necessary if the two of you are in the conversation-habit. Dale and I are always looking for chances to talk. In fact, the more frequently you converse about all kinds of things, the less chance of a minor tremor turning into an earthquake. In a grand marriage, life together is, as poet Robert Louis Stevenson described it, "one long conversation, chequered by disputes."

Dream Makers take note of (even memorize) this one key principle: *though you need communication to feel close to him; he needs to feel close to you before he's willing to communicate.*

Specific ideas on how to discuss what you want or need from your man are outlined in "Teaching a Knight to Knit" (Chapters 11 & 12) and "First Respect" (Chapter 10). Know these well before you initiate potentially tense conversations. I also recommend the expert advice about negotiating with your partner in *Fall in Love, Stay in Love*, by Willard F. Harley Jr., Ph.D., and Michelle Weiner-Davis's suggestions in *Divorce Busting*. As I've said, Chamberlain and Steurer's *Love You, Hate the Porn*, is also extremely insightful. John Lund, Ph.D., has fantastic guidelines for offering and taking criticism in his set of tapes, *For All Eternity*, and of course, John Gottman's *The Seven Principles for Making Marriage Work* is invaluable. One of Dr. Gottman's key pieces of advice is encapsulated in a little proverb I first heard in England: *How it starts is how it finishes.* The most important tactic in initiating a difficult discussion is to start it softly, kindly, rationally.

All of these approaches, however, hinge on taking care of things whenever possible *before* they get hot. Distancing yourself mentally (and physically, if necessary) allows you to process intelligently and creatively. The Dream Maker rule of thumb for managing conflict: *before you tackle touchy issues, wait until you can focus on protecting the relationship.* That means waiting until your husband is calm, too. Letting him have a chance to lower his heart rate makes all the difference when you resume the dialogue.

And that brings us to the other person involved in the conflict, your husband. "Okay," I hear you saying, "I'll do my best to drop and cover, but what about him? There's nothing I can do if he's going to get upset."

Is there?

Well, actually...incredibly...wonderfully...yes! There is! As the keeper of the relationship, you have more power than you know—even in conflict. A study conducted by a team of Iowa State researchers, published in the Journal of Counseling Psychology (JCP, 54.2 [2007]: 165-77), found that wives, on average, exhibit greater situational power than their husbands during "problem-solving" discussions. And Dr. Gottman's research shows that a woman is able to influence the course of an argument—she can de-escalate an earthquake from a 5 on the Richter scale to a 1—by introducing one of these soothers (*The Science of Trust*, p. 71):

- *Empathy*: tune into his feelings. Let him know that you see, or at least want to see, into his heart: "I understand, honey," or "Help me understand what you're saying."

- *Affection*: even one sympathetic touch, look, or endearment does wonders: "Poor baby."
- *Accountability*: accept and state your contribution to the conflict. This takes a real Pioneer Woman, but is the most powerful soother of all: "I did it and I'm sorry."
- *Humor*: toss some fun into the heat of the moment, like water on flames. I'm talking about a funny face, a silly voice, a giggle, shimmy, or sexy pose. I don't care how ridiculous this sounds, as long as it doesn't come across as insensitive, it really works: "Come on honey, smile."
- If worse comes to worst, I'm sure Nancy Reagan won't mind your borrowing, "You were cool in the pool."

Dousing a volcano is only possible, however, if it hasn't completely erupted—get to your man before he boils over. The principles of companionship will help a lot with this (Part Three), but for now, let's just say that asking him questions and listening to the answers is everything. Avoid letting tension between the two of you escalate into anger since it is very harmful to his brain, body, and emotions. Clear reasoning goes out the window and the heart turns cold. By the time a little friction has worked itself into a major earthquake; he is completely absorbed in it; his male fears are awakened and his trust in you is leveled. Feminine soothers are truly powerful, but you must use them early in the conflict or they may not work. If he's puffing like a runaway train, your best option is always to drop and cover: "Let's just take a break and talk about this later after we've cooled down and thought it through." (Once again, if he has a serious recurring anger issue, professional help may be required.)

Let me add just one more thing about soothers: if your husband makes any attempt to appease or pacify you during a skirmish, let him! When he takes the initiative to calm you down or when he's the one smart enough to drop and cover, don't keep rumbling just because you're not finished! Thank God for a Nice Guy who cares and has the presence of mind to rescue your relationship in a heated moment. Imagine the hero whisking his love out of harm's way just in time. Accept his attempt to fix things, no matter how awkward or unsatisfying it may be. Turn toward intimacy. Your marriage will be instantly stronger for it. Make it clear that you are not avoiding the issue; you are not running away from it; you will come back to the problem later, if necessary, when your head is clear. In the meantime, follow his lead. Drop and cover. Forget about who started an argument; be the one who ends it—with respect. I once heard a speaker say, "It takes two to contend, and I won't be one of them." Good stuff.

And with that handy rule of thumb in our emergency kit, we are ready to wrap up our discussion with a practice session. Here are some examples of everyday conflicts that can benefit from drop and cover. Can you see yourself wanting to react and then remembering to respond with drop and cover?

You start to react: "You've blown it again! I'll just have to take over."
Drop and cover: Remember First Respect.
He'll be hurt if I act superior. There's probably a kinder way to approach this.

You start to react: "That is just about the stupidest thing you've ever done!" Drop and cover: Reflect on your own faults.
I've done stupid things, too. Guess I ought to cut him some slack.

You start to react: "How could you be so insensitive?"
Drop and cover: Withhold judgment.
I wonder if I understood it right. What is he afraid of?

You start to react: "Not again! You did it again!"
Drop and cover: Take a break.
"How about we discuss this later, after the kids are in bed?" and later, *"It's just that when you do that, honey, I feel so frustrated."*

He says, "Come on! I've had it! What do you want from me!"
Drop and cover: use a soother, such as, "My bad. That wasn't nice of me."

He says, "I've got something to say!"
Drop and Cover: Listen; then say, "Go ahead. I want to understand. I'll try not to be defensive."

You say, "You make me so mad!"
He responds, "Come on honey, I didn't mean it that way. Let's cuddle and watch TV in bed."
Drop and cover: Accept his soother with humor, "All right, but I get the remote."

Of course, these are generic examples. There are a hundred million variables, so there is no way to anticipate every possible conflict between you and your husband. Should managing conflict be a real issue for you, I strongly recommend that you read about it in the books I've mentioned, and that you visit me often at *ramonazabriskie.com*. You can also look for a personal mentor among your friends and family, or seek professional help. I'm well aware that the ground shakes for all kinds of reasons, and it doesn't always stop trembling when you want it to. Nevertheless, we are talking about feelings here, and feelings not only come and go, they can often be controlled with the right mindset. Let emotions guide you as you *diagnose* a problem; but don't let them *dictate* your actions. That's what a Dream Maker is all about. She sees things from a Wife for Life's perspective and then *responds*. She uses her power to prevent conflict when possible and healthy. And during an earthquake, she tries to protect the relationship by using appropriate, proactive approaches like drop and cover.

In a letter to his wife, American author John Steinbeck wrote, "Darling, you want to know what I want of you. Many things of course but chiefly these: I want you to keep this thing we have inviolate and waiting—the person who is neither I nor you but us" (*Love Letters*, p. 37). In conflict, you would be wise to put that entity— the relationship—*first*.

18
Persevering and Mountaineering

Maybe it is our imperfections that make us so perfect for one another.
—*George Knightly, in the 1996 Miramax Films motion picture Emma*

If you could stand on the deck facing our backyard between June and September, you would be awestruck by the two-hundred-foot firs, and you would be tickled by the little stream running through them. If you could stand on the deck facing our backyard between October and November, you would be enchanted by golden maples and delighted by the sound of a brook. But if you stood on the deck facing our backyard between December and May, you would see a swollen river running so close to the house that you'd want to evacuate.

I'd give anything to tame that creek.

Who knew when we bought the house that such a beautiful forest property could turn into a raging tributary of the Columbia River Basin? And a protected one at that! Our land is a legally protected watershed, which means basically that there is no way we can drain or deter that stream to landscape the backyard. Ever. A garden? Out. A playground? Out. A gazebo? Out. Aw, come on. Just a patch of grass, *pleeeease?* No. Out. Out. Out. Impossible. Unsolvable.

And that's the word I want you to remember: *unsolvable.*

Can you guess what I'm driving at? It's the big pill you don't want to swallow—the one that, despite growing up, never gets easier—the one you have to gulp down whole for your own good.

Unsolvables are the troubling issues in your marriage that will *never* be fixed: the ones that run so deep you cannot reach them. Some pieces of your loved one's property are protected, even from you.

Remember our discussion about dreams in Chapter 9? How it is natural to worry that the treasury we have built up over a lifetime will be raided or ruined, stolen piece by piece, never to be reassembled? Well, naturally, your husband feels the same way. There are some aspects to his upbringing, his heredity, his gene pool, his unique experience in this world, that have spawned deep dreams—convictions about the way life should be and personality traits or habits that are just not going to change.

No matter how hard they are to live with.

And here's the kicker. You have your own off-limits stuff that he has to live with when he'd really rather not. Maybe it's religion. Maybe it's politics. Maybe it's the way he brushes his teeth. You may never agree on the kind of house you want to live in or how it's kept up. He wants to spend holidays with family and you have always dreamed of Christmas in Hawaii. I like to be alone and he likes to be with people. Who knows? People are people and you are two people who have vowed to love each other—*in spite of the unsolvables.* Every marriage has them, a dynamic pointed out by Dr. Gottman in *The Seven Principles.* I have watched many couples wrestle with deep-seated differences and have learned from them that union is still possible. Each of these couples worked it out by concentrating on these five things:

- Talking talking talking about feelings, life stories, dreams.
- Empathizing and understanding.
- Accepting.
- Compromising.
- Sticking it out.

What a concept! If prime ministers and presidents could master it, we'd have world peace! Needless to say, it's easier written into a formula than done. As a Wife for Life myself, I am well aware that enduring in spite of unsolvables is the biggest challenge in marriage, the hardest part about living with another person. Your partner's contradictory dreams, views, and habits are ever-present, eternally in your face. Like the squeaky knee I couldn't get rid of whilst going up and down the stairs of London, certain conflicts just won't go away. One clue that you may be stuck with an unsolvable is that you repeatedly find yourselves debating the same thing without getting anywhere. Even so, *un*solvable does not have to mean *un*happiness! It will take time to figure out how to deal with the unsolvables in a positive way, but, not only can it be done; it can also be one of the most interesting jobs in marriage. It's certainly one of the most rewarding aspects of becoming his Intimate. When a man senses how sincere you are about understanding and accepting him, and that you are willing to work on compromises with good humor and intent, he will become your castle.

Don't let an unsolvable make you unlovable.

If you persist in defending your dreams and attacking his, without attempting to at least respect them...well, there are plenty of folks like that sitting by themselves at the end of Dream Breaker Road. The issue-that-would-not-budge became more important than their mutual dreams, even their happiness.

Which brings me to Budapest.

I fell in love with this European capital because it is populated with survivors. Even the buildings have outlived the ravages of war. Ottomans, Catholics, Protestants, Communists, and Nazis have competed, confronted, and crusaded against—but never crushed—this city. As I stood on our hotel balcony one evening, gaping at the panorama rising above the Danube, I realized that Budapest, colored at that moment by the most fantastic sunset, was more alive and exciting than ever in its history, primarily because

Hungarians well know how to *tough it out*.

One day in Budapest, I received a text from a wife back in London who was ready to leave her husband. "HE'S NOT WORTH IT," she screamed in capital letters. "Ever since I married this terrible man, I have been miserable!"

"Are you saying that every day of your whole marriage has been totally unhappy?" My fingers flew in panic.

"No," she admitted. "There have been good days and great ones too —" (I waited for the *but...*)—"but there have been terrible ones like today!" Then rapidly and back to all capitals: "It's UP AND DOWN and it's the same things OVER and OVER and I CAN'T TAKE IT ANYMORE!"

Now I knew for a fact (having spent hours and hours in her home over many months) that her husband was far from terrible and that she had been far from miserable. But there is something about an earthquake that makes things seem oh-so-much-worse than they really are—especially if you are young.

While in Budapest, we walked with our personal guide, Peter Polczman. He told us they'd moved all the statues of toppled Communist elites to a park where they have no one to preach to but each other. He pointed out a building that used to be Gestapo Headquarters and is now a museum. He led us down a residential street where old people sit on benches, watching young people hurry by.

"My grandmother," he said, as we rested on a stone wall (the ruins of some empire or another), "has seen it all."

"How did she survive?" I had to know.

"She just didn't get worked up over things." I must have looked surprised. He grinned. "She knew everything would pass."

His answer reminded me of the study mentioned in *The Case for Marriage: Why Married People Are Happier, Healthier, and Better Off Financially*, which interviewed, among others, people who described themselves as unhappily married. When the subjects were reinterviewed just five years later, researchers found that those who stuck it out rated what they had formerly called an "unhappy marriage" as either "quite happy" or "very happy." In fact, the worst marriages showed the most dramatic turnarounds (p. 148). I wish I had been able to use more than a text message to convince my London friend of that. She and her husband are now as far apart as they could be, in full-scale alienation.

I know as well as anyone that surviving—despite earthquakes, tornados, and fire—takes guts. But it isn't always the kind of courage that requires you to "screw courage to the sticking place," as Lady Macbeth would say. Sometimes it's the kind of fortitude that bobs buoy-like, up and down, anchored in place. After decades of family life, I would have to agree with Peter Polczman's Hungarian grandmother: most of what we get worked up over is not worth it; most of it is not here to stay. And even if it is here to stay, unsolvables often lose significance with time. In the actual scheme of things, events are rarely catastrophic. We just need to grab onto something, or someone, sturdy—and hold on.

The shaking will eventually stop, and when it does, the last step is *recovery*.

Recovering From an Earthquake

It's the graduate school of relationships. The smartest, most spiritual, most mature people on earth grapple with ascending this Mt. Everest, but those who make it to the top of Mt. Forgiveness say the view is worth it.

Standing at the summit, with the crystal breeze blowing in my face, I think I can say that to be just about perfect, and therefore to have a just-about-perfect marriage, we have to master only two things: *requesting forgiveness and extending forgiveness.*

At that precise moment, I start feeling mighty fine about my progress on both counts. The sky is clear, no clouds on the horizon. I feel fairly acclimated to the rarefied atmosphere. As my boots dig into the ice and I plant the flag triumphantly, it seems my membership in the elite club of Superior Spouses is secure.

Then...*crrrraaaaaccccck.*

Thunder rolls out of nowhere, the earth begins to shake, the mountain opens up, and suddenly I am in a familiar crevasse–not far, actually, from base camp (my wedding day). I have to choose again: to ascend or not to ascend; to apologize or not to apologize; to forgive or not to forgive; to repent or not to repent; to love or not to love. I have to choose again. And again. And again. And again.

And so does he.

Thankfully, forgiveness is not an emotion; it's a choice. And I can make a choice. So, I scrounge through my backpack of mountain-climbing paraphernalia and pull out three tools that have worked for me time and time again over the years. These steps—so perfectly articulated in *Becoming One Emotionally, Spiritually, Sexually,* by Joe Beam, Psy.D. (p. 119)—are my best hope for getting out of here and into the sunlight.

- Step 1: **Assign my loved one value again**. He's not a monster chomping at the bit to toss me over the edge; in fact, he's in his own crevasse right now, dreading hypothermia as much as I am.
- Step 2: **Decide not to take vengeance on him**. Put away the ice axe and screws.
- Step 3: **Restore our relationship**. This is a snow bridge that may take time and careful testing. Important: get an early start. Slick slopes are easier to cross on the morning of an incident (i.e., soon after). As the day (or weeks, months, years) wears on, the path gets intimidatingly mushy.

Restoring the relationship sometimes means I have to request forgiveness. It may be simple to acknowledge my part, but a real apology requires more than that. To ask for forgiveness, I have to recognize and admit my responsibility, not just my contribution.

Confession mixed with justification or accusation does little to relieve pressure on the relationship; it's a poor substitute for an honest, thoughtful, humble apology. No buts about it. And there are a number of ways to apologize. Here are just a few:

"I feel so foolish that I made such a fuss last week. I still have a long way to grow."

"I really feel bad about the pain I've caused recently. I only want your happiness."

"I ask your forgiveness for my mistakes and misjudgments of the past year, and especially for the hurt and anxiety I've caused this past week. I know you approach our partnership with a very even temper. You seem to take the whining and the occasional attacks as calmly as you accept my giddiness, optimism, and praise. I know I must try your patience to the extreme."

"Please, dear friend, forgive anything I said that might have wounded you. I ache at the thought. It is completely contrary to the promises I have made, to the bonds of trust and friendship we cherish, and to the manner in which you treat me. If you can forgive me and love me again, I know my pain is great enough to guarantee my promise to never be so hurtful again."

"I feel awful about our conversation this morning. I don't feel I told you enough how much I love and appreciate you."

"I can't leave you this morning without expressing my love and sorrow about last night. I awoke in the middle of the night, and vaguely remembering the circumstances that left me on the couch, I thought at first that they were only a dream. As I moved into our bed and put my arms around you, I realized I'd actually said and done those things and I wanted immediately to erase them. I felt like, *What was that?! Who was that?!* I am so sorry. Please forgive."

Those are all real requests for forgiveness, offered over many years, and they were all written by the same person: me. Like Anne Shirley in *Anne of Green Gables*, you could say I've had "lots of practice in making apologies." On learning more about the history of Dale and Ramona, a never-married woman said to me, "I had no idea so much failure went into a successful marriage!"

All the trouble I've caused and all the trouble I've forgiven, however, has made me increasingly expert at reading the weather and sidestepping falling rock. I spend less energy crawling out of crevasses these days and more time enjoying the summit. Thankfully, Dale and I have survived this thing called marriage— unquestionably the most daring undertaking in the human experience—because we did our best to:

- Prevent unnecessary conflict (turn towards intimacy).
- Protect the relationship during conflict (drop and cover).
- Persevere despite unsolvable conflict (hold on).
- Recover after a conflict (request and extend forgiveness).

So, fellow adventurers: no need to fear! Though you may not always like being tied to the same rope as your partner, as long as it's a line fixed on conquering together and anchored in forgiveness, you can avoid being buried alive by avalanches of pride. Remember, marriage is not about who's right and who's wrong or competing for the summit, but about spiritual collaboration and emotional teamwork. Though it may feel risky, the brave act of turning toward each other, instead of against each other, will renew you individually and reunite you as a couple. Once you reach the summit, the fresh breeze will dissipate your hurt, and the cloudless sky will fill you with hope. Forgiveness is a spectacular accomplishment.

Part 3

WHAT TO DO TO MAKE DREAMS COME TRUE

19
Becoming His Intimate

Give him one friend who can understand him, who will not leave him, who will always be accessible day and night—one friend, one kindly listener, just one, and the whole universe is changed.
—*Woodrow Wilson, U.S. President, 1913-1921*

I have been doing my own nails for, well, fifty-three years. Not long ago, however, while visiting my kids in Orlando and finding myself with a little too much time and sunshine on my hands, I found the gumption (and the funds) to dip into a spa pedicure. It turned out just as I feared—I *loved* it!

Exiting the place, I almost landed on my face while admiring my feet. Self-indulgence is splendid, but expensive, and I wondered all the way home how in the world I was going to justify a whole sixty minutes and twenty dollars every few weeks for the rest of my life.

One thing I felt good about: no manicure. I defied that particular extravagance and continued doing my own fingernails for months. Such was my intent the last time I pulled up to Perfect Nails for a pedicure. Little did I know the owners had set me up for the big fall that day by giving me Tina: the sweetest, gentlest non-English-speaking operator in the group. Her genuine care and consideration as she rubbed my feet with warm stones and massaged my calves with lotion exfoliated away any resistance, so that by the time she finished the pedicure, I was as gooey as a mud wrap.

Taking my hands in hers and nodding excitedly at a wall of

shimmering bottles, her whole pitch consisted of three whispers:

"Sparkle? Beauty! *Try!*"

Yes, *pleeeeease!*

Plunking first one hand and then the other into the warm hydro basin of bubbling love, I marveled. And leaving the parking lot, I almost mutilated a mailbox while admiring my manicure. How had that sweet-natured, lovely woman so bewitched me?

That thought reminded me of *Yentl* (United Artists, 1983), the film musical starring Barbara Streisand, in which a young nineteenth-century girl discovers the power of feminine attention. Frustrated at not having the same opportunities as the men in her Polish-Jewish community, Yentl leaves home when her father dies, disguised as a boy, to join the ranks of male Talmud scholar-students. Complications ensue, and Yentl ends up in the middle of a relationship between her best friend (and secret love), Avigdor, and his betrothed, Haddas. Avigdor's ardor for Haddas pains Yentl, yet—thanks to Yentl's masculine disguise—she begins to see Haddas' allure from the male perspective. As the plot thickens, Yentl becomes the new object of Haddas' lavish kindness. Without giving away the involved, improbable conclusion, let's just say that when all is revealed and resolved, Yentl embraces her unique identity as well as the best parts of her femininity: sympathy and tenderness. Though the story takes place in another culture and time, when women did not have the societal privileges they do today, an attentive woman still had the power, as Yentl realized, to stir a man's soul, just as *you* do today.

My married daughter was recently approached by a teenage girl. "I hope," the girl said, "that I can find a man like yours. He obviously adores you, the way he talks about you and treats you." Hannah agreed with her, but on reflection, wished she had answered, "It's all in how you treat him."

Think back to our discussion in Chapters 4 & 5 about the male quest and the male brain and our talk in Chapter 8 about male fears. And I hope you won't soon forget the Crazy Ladies or

Dream-Breaker Road. Hopefully you can now appreciate why men are wounded and repulsed by all forms of disrespect, and why they are conversely so receptive to the thoughtful poise and sincere concern of the Dream Maker. Of course you can! You too love feeling understood, and you too crave the nurturing touch. Another part of you reacts positively to respect and honor and optimism. Sympathetic, loving attention draws us out and we become naturally more pliable and accommodating, just as I felt that day in the spa.

Nice Guys obviously react to selflessness too. In fact, a man's insecurities—including his secret fear of failure, his longing to be needed, and his struggle between independence and loneliness—makes a Nice Guy especially responsive to generous, genuine consideration. A good man's mind is far more receptive to charity than to criticism. He cannot resist responding positively to the consistently sincere attention of his wife.

In *For All Eternity*, Dr. John Lund points out that 50 percent of husbands, on average, have no intimate—that is, someone they talk to about personal matters—*other* than their wives. Forty percent have *one* other close friend they can talk to, while only 10 percent have two or more. Wow! What a stark contrast to you and me. We women are something like the female elephants of Amboseli National Park in Kenya, who spend a great deal of time with other female elephants in a sort of matriarchal gang. Men, on the other hand, are like the young bulls that are kicked out of the herd and roam alone most of the time. It's not that men don't want and need the benefits of friendship. Of course they do. In the nineteenth century, for instance, deep male bonding and mutual support—of the sort we hardly see anywhere but in the military or the locker room anymore—was the norm. Today's society has dramatically eroded the number of friends and confidants in a man's life, and men's emotional isolation is steadily increasing. A husband naturally longs for his wife to fill that need, preferring her companionship above anyone else's—and most wives would love nothing more! Why, oh why then, do so many women complain about not feeling close to their husbands? What's up with that?

The Easy-Open Jar

Since a recent onset of arthritis, I've had a devil of a time opening things. Jars, boxes, and the most evil contrivance of all—prescription bottles—defy my fingers. The common twist-and-lift lid makes me wince if not gasp out loud in pain. Hearing me on the edge of swearing—*ta-da*—my Shining Knight rides to the rescue!...when he's around. Shining Knights have a lot of other people to save, too. In his absence, I have had to come up with all kinds of creative methods, short of dynamite, for cracking open cranky containers; some more effective than others.

Opening a man is something like opening a stubborn jelly jar: it's a sticky business. It's hard to believe that, when the only practical solution to loosening the lid is running warm water over it, so many women think a bundle of TNT is necessary.

Here's the gist of it: most men are comfortable with conversation as long as it's a simple exchange of information. This isn't to say that they don't have feelings they long to talk about. Remember, they are deeply emotional—some researchers say they are more sensitive than women, actually—and we know how all-consuming their quest is. But conditions have to be just right before they are willing to go there, to risk exposure. If they fear arctic conditions, for example, the gloves and parka stay on. Or if a husband suspects a pie in the face, you won't get him into the spotlight. Also, if he is under the impression that *he* is the source of your distress or frustration (even if he has nothing to do with it)—he will purposefully distance himself (not comprehending that you actually crave connection). And lastly of course, no man will open up to a partner who finds fault with the way he does things, big and small. *Don't put that glass on the coffee table! Now, dear, tell me your deepest dreams.*

Consider: would you show all your cards to a spouse who questions your decisions, belittles your worries, or laughs at your mistakes? Would you reveal your inner self to a partner who needles and pries or picks and prods? Or to a wife who clings like a vine and whines on a dime, or to a know-it-all that finishes your sentences? Not if you're a man, you won't. Dynamite never opens the jar; it just blows up in your face.

There are obvious reasons why Crazy-Lady tactics don't work. According to an e-zine article by Brett and Kate McKay, "The History and Nature of Man Friendships" at their blog *The Art of Manliness*, from the male perspective, true friends have three distinct qualities. One is the ability to be *nonjudgmental*, an attitude inherent in First Respect. And we know how important First Respect is to building your castle, becoming his Intimate, and filling the role of Dream Maker.

The second quality a man needs in a friendship, according the McKays, is *loyalty*. Here's where the trust issue really comes in. One of the main reasons husbands are reticent to reveal themselves, according to Dr. Lund, is that they know just how gregarious their wives are. They have seen us gossip with the girls and are concerned, often justly, that in the course of our conversations, we may accidentally, or even purposely, share their secrets. They worry too about the way we women let emotion build up until we erupt, explode, or disintegrate (as I did on that red-letter 4th of July).

The third quality men appreciate in a friend is the decision to be *straightforward*. A straightforward mate deals with issues in a clear, timely, unemotional manner: the very principles outlined in "Teaching a Knight to Knit."

So, as we inch our way toward becoming his Intimate, two elementary tenets are: cut the contempt and criticism, and treat him with First Respect (another way of saying, be nonjudgmental, loyal, straightforward).

Once a man feels inherently respected, the companionship and sharing he longs for with his wife, as his friend, are much more likely to happen. You can help your conversations become pleasant and bonding in nature by encouraging him in a specific way. Start talking about anything: casual stuff, but stick to the facts, ma'am; most men enjoy communicating about or teaching information. Then, let him give you casual information in exchange (whether it's his work or world events). Give him the same kind of attention you want from him: 100 percent. It will take him a while to warm up, but when he does, you can nudge him gently away from just-the-facts with a no-pressure, "And how do you feel about that?" Careful! No loaded questions. Your intent must simply be to get information, not to judge or manipulate him into the answer you are looking for. In other words: no agenda, because that would be Crazy. I fight a natural tendency to judge (or feel threatened by) his responses, opinions, and dreams, which I try to avert by thinking, and occasionally even saying this one magic word: *"Interesting!"*

If he really opens up emotionally and exposes difficult feelings (anger, sadness, fear), be prepared to feel unsettled (as discussed in Chapter 7) since most women inherently expect their man to be strong. Don't overreact, take it personally, or try to fix him. Look instead at his confessions in what the experts call an "emotion-coaching" frame of reference. For instance, you can view anger as a lack of control, or better, as *frustration* over a blocked goal. Some would consider ongoing sadness an emotional disorder, but actually, it is an indication of something *missing* in life. Try not to think of fear as a sign of cowardice, but rather as an indication of *insecurity*. As Chamberlain and Steurer write: "Pain, whether emotional or physical, is designed to direct our attention to something that needs to be addressed" (*Love You*, K. 1876). Choosing to listen, understand, and sympathize with the less-than-positive emotions in your man instead of dismissing them as unimportant, weak, or threatening, is critical to encouraging closeness between the two of you. Any other reaction will drive him away.

Remember the phrase (I have used so often): "Help me understand, sweetheart."

Perhaps the hardest part for me in all this is to be satisfied with whatever my husband feels comfortable sharing. Like Oliver Twist, I want to beg, "Please, sir, I want some more." But if I am grateful for what he confides in me, and I give him the most authentically affirmative response my heart can muster, I encourage more verbal sharing in the future.

Now, if your objective is to become his Intimate, keep in mind that friends can find solace in just being together. As a woman, you may bond verbally, but your husband can bond with you just by sharing a space with you. Ever notice how pleased he seems when you watch him engage in some activity, such as playing a sport or working on the car? He also likes it when you simply sit beside him in quiet contentment. This mode of bonding is sometimes referred to as shoulder-to-shoulder communication, and men generally love it. Even though most women prefer face-to-face bonding, mastery of this type of communication is possible, even pleasant. The outcome is certainly worth it. Listen to this beautiful tribute—posted recently on my blog by a young husband—to his wife of six years:

> "It is easy, as a man, to get going too fast in our efforts to build a successful tomorrow while battling back the silent fear of what lies ahead. At times, it can make life seem like jumping through a wave in the ocean: you know eventually you will get to the calm sea, but in the meantime all you can do is breathe and dive. I am so thankful for a wife who helps me turn off my brain. We take walks, go out to eat, or just sit. She is okay if I am quiet and checked out, and she does her very best to engage me in topics that help me relax. During our toughest times, she reassures me that love is all we ever needed. She probably thinks I don't notice, but I do."

See what I mean? Follow this sweet little formula for befriending your man...

- cut the contempt and criticism,
- treat him with First Respect (loyal, trustworthy, straightforward),
- encourage and enjoy informational conversation,
- enquire about his feelings on the subject (no pressure, no agenda, no judgment, just "Interesting!"),
- view and treat strong feelings from him in an emotion-coaching frame of mind ("Help me understand"),
- be satisfied with how much he shares,
- bond with him "shoulder-to-shoulder" on occasion (which may include silence)...

...and chances are that by and by, little by little, his lid will wiggle; his reticence to open up will lessen, and he may actually learn to tune into his feelings better as you gently draw him out into a safe place. It's worked nearly 100 percent of the time with my Dale, and we've enjoyed very healthy, mutually satisfying results. Running now for over three decades, our husband-wife conversation is part practical, part pleasure, part daydream, part counsel, part observation, part opinion. We call it "solving the world's problems." And sometimes we say everything by saying nothing at all.

My position as Dale's favorite companion and sole confidante is an honor; it's a role that I relish more than any other in life. I prioritize it over every relationship: the "One Talent Left Standing" (Chapter 2). Becoming his Intimate requires more than talking or sitting together, however. There is much more involved: it is a process that we will look at in the next few chapters. You will want to learn it and work it for the rest of your life because the secret to an easy-open jar (she whispers) is to keep the warm water running.

20
The Laws of Attraction

Still where you have failed your faults have been to me those of one
BELOVED. —*Harriet Beecher Stowe, American writer*

As I have mentioned, Dale and I met doing theater. The troupe of players we performed with that summer traversed West Yellowstone in a big, old van, and the suave, skinny kid from Houston was always at the wheel. How he earned this designation above all the other boys, I never knew. I assumed it was the same way he got cast as the leading man in both musicals...just something about Dale.

Because the van was made for fifteen passengers and there were sixteen of us, I ended up on the engine case, that protrusion between the two front seats. They called it "Mona's Spot." With my back to the windshield, I could see everyone in the van, but especially the driver. From Mona's Spot, I could gaze on his perfectly clear skin, perpetually pink cheeks, sliver-blue eyes, and slick straight hair around the edges of the fedora hat he'd taken to wearing with an old denim jacket.

From Mona's Spot I got my first lesson in becoming his Intimate. He caught me looking at him, and though he tried not to show his pleasure, the corners of his mouth curled up in spite of himself.

Everyone knows the saying, "Beauty is in the eyes of the beholder." In no other aspect of life is this proverb truer or more vital than in the day-to-day, year-to-year, nose-to-nose, and head-to-head dynamic between a husband and wife. As keeper of the relationship you hold the key to the castle: a key I call *beholding*. A Dream Maker has the power to make her Nice Guy's heart her own forever—by choosing to behold his beauty more often than his faults or weaknesses. Remember, he literally cannot resist responding to the faithful, loving attention of his wife; her admiration is almost impossible not to surrender to; his heart takes profound pleasure in it and wants to repay her kindness in kind. For him to feel otherwise would be as unlikely as a ravenous man rejecting the meat he craves! When a Dream Maker understands and accommodates her husband's deep biological, emotional, and spiritual need for acknowledgement and affirmation, his male fears are assuaged and he will bond like glue to her; just as we all (children and adults) bond with the things and people that soothe us. If a man bonds with his wife in this optimal way, because she uplifts and comforts him, then he has the best chance of flourishing, becoming his best, most courageous, most loving self.

A young husband recently summarized this phenomenon for me in one sentence: "My wife shows unconditional love and concern for me in every way, and it makes me want to reciprocate."

I learned the truth of that statement not long after Dale and I had reconciled. Hoping to avoid past pitfalls and excel as a wife and partner, I started earnestly studying relationship books and observing successful marriages. The two of us spent a lot of time with couples much older than we were because I wanted to watch and listen. Putting into practice everything I saw working in these admirable marriages, and putting to the test every theory I read, my cache of wifely skills began to increase until the effect was undeniable. I was astonished. Dale, the rather spoiled, insecure, self-absorbed Nice Guy I had married began to transform into a wonderful man, a generous and engaged father, and an empathetic, attentive husband.

If that sounds something like Beauty and the Beast, you are not far off, except no curses or magic spells were involved. All I had done, without completely comprehending the consequences, was to give him love, kindness, and First Respect, which had created a kind of magnetic field around him. This perimeter of positive energy consisted of certain attitudes—not necessarily actions, but a mindset based on First Respect—that pulled him to me. The power I felt was truly remarkable. Just as the behavior of my Crazy Ladies instinctively repelled him, I sensed that my new attitudes, which I call *the A's*, attracted him like a magnet.

I have read that when a person begins to feel safe with his partner, he will move from less defensive to at least curious. Where the A's are concerned, that's an understatement. Whenever I run the list of A's past male friends and family, they look at me as though I'm describing nirvana. Their eyes widen as though they dare not believe that it's possible, and then they all say something like, "There isn't a man in the world who wouldn't respond to that kind of wife."

It's true. I'm telling you, the A's are that reliable. Their effect is so predictable (at least with Nice Guys) that we're going to call them the *Laws of Attraction*. Laws describe a relationship of cause and effect, and in upcoming chapters I will show you the outcome of steadily applying the A's over a period of years. For now, however, let's just identify these powerful attitudes (the A's) so you know what we're talking about. And don't fret, overworked and over-worried sisters: this is not another to-do list. It's not about doing *for* him, it's about responding *to* him, or in my daughter's words, "It's all in how you treat him." What that means is, you can say the A's, show the A's, or write the A's in any combination, any way you want—any way that works. (Even *thinking* them will translate into treating him more lovingly.) Every castle lock has its own combination, and your castle's combination is unique; it may even change from time to time, depending on what's going on inside.

One more note: as a Creator, you need to think of the A's not only as the keys to your castle, but as the paintbrushes of your evolving relationship. Your masterpiece won't take long to take shape if you start now and apply the A's consistently and uniformly. (Note: They don't work as well when you pick and choose. The Laws of Attraction develop maximum trust and bonding when applied together.)

So are you ready to think reflectively? I am going to illustrate each Law of Attraction with a message that describes the attitude in that Law. Take your time and consider each one carefully. Think about how you could express the Laws of Attraction in your own personal style in the context of your unique relationship.

The First Law of Attraction: Acceptance

The Dream Maker's message in Acceptance: *"You are different from me and that is all right."*

This First Law is the basis for all the others. It acknowledges the peculiarities of his personality, his opinions, his body, and his dreams. Most of all, it communicates acceptance of his maleness. When a man feels an openness in his wife, the nonjudgmental attitude of a true friend (Chapter 19), he feels free to be himself, which, strangely, inspires him to want to improve himself—no nagging needed.

The Second Law of Attraction: Approval

The Dream Maker's message in Approval: *"You fulfill your responsibilities well, and I trust you to do your best for us."*

If Acceptance is the beginning of any healthy relationship, then Approval goes one giant step beyond that. It doesn't mean you have to agree with him all the time, but it does mean that you assume his heart is in the right place. As we learned in our discussion of male fears (Chapter 8), men are petrified of failure: his drive to succeed spills into every aspect of his life. When he is assured that his wife believes in him—affirmation he can get only from her—it stokes his manly confidence and feeds his desire to be worthy of her.

The Third Law of Attraction: Appreciation

The Dream Maker's message in Appreciation: *"You are so helpful to me."*

While Approval conveys trust, Appreciation communicates recognition of a man's contributions to the family. He craves, for instance, appreciation for his labor to provide for the family, no matter the actual hours or the dollar figure involved. This cannot be overstated (and we will discuss it in more detail in Chapter 21). It's not just the paycheck that it would be kind and wise to thank him for, however. When you decide to verbally express simple gratitude for his attempts to help around the house—even if you have to ask for the help specifically (Chapter 12), or though you consider it his responsibility anyway, or it's not quite up to your expectations, or you feel under-appreciated yourself—you will be celebrating what you want more of. Appreciation makes your Nice Guy want to please you again and again. A husband married eight years wrote me: "Nothing says 'I love you' to me more than to be appreciated. She acknowledges and often tells me how much she appreciates all that I do to support our family and that means a great deal to me. When she throws her arms around my neck, gives me an extra smooch, and tells me I'm her hero for emptying the garbage or cleaning the toilets, that makes it all worth it. It is both validating and gratifying to hear her sincere appreciation. Nothing makes me more desirous of pleasing her."

The Fourth Law of Attraction: Admiration

The Dream Maker's message in Admiration: *"You amaze and thrill me."*

Many women fail to maximize attraction by confusing the Third Law, Appreciation (which women need badly), with the Fourth Law, Admiration (which men need even more). Thanking your husband for changing a diaper is important, but it is not the same as esteeming his ability to rebuild a car engine, solve a complex problem, or pump a lot of weight. Admiration is at the center of this list of laws for a reason: it is the strongest magnet of all. Though your man longs for appreciation, it does not deeply stir his soul like admiration of his masculinity or personal strengths and talents does. He will never verbalize this need or thank you in words for it, but when he believes that you not only accept and approve of his accomplishments but take pleasure in them, it gives him the highest high a man can feel in relation to his wife. He instantly bonds with her.

The Fifth Law of Attraction: Availability

The Dream Maker's message in Availability: *"I have time and energy for you."*

It should be obvious that none of the preceding A's can have much impact if your husband feels discounted or neglected by you (Chapter 8). He needs to feel that he is your priority in life, and that kind of dedication is manifested primarily by your physical presence and how you allocate your time. Availability is one of the most important aspects of Dr. Gottman's *turning toward* theory (Chapter 16) as well as of shoulder-to-shoulder communication (Chapter 19). Remember the husband of six years who appreciates how his wife is happy to take walks with him, go out to eat together, or just sit companionably? Surprisingly, the Law of Availability will actually give you more energy for other relationships and pursuits (Chapter 2) because of the abundance of love and security in your marriage.

The Sixth Law of Attraction: Affection

The Dream Maker's message in Affection: *"I enjoy your company."*

As we learned in Chapter 14, men badly need nonsexual affirmation from their wives. When you reach out to hold his hand, link an arm through his, or offer to give him a back-rub, your Nice

Guy is reassured that he is dear to you. Chuckle at his jokes, show interest his stories, or listen without interrupting, and you send the message that you enjoy his company. Affection is the simplest of the A's, the sweet little dance of give-and-take pleasantries between any husband and wife on their way to becoming grand. It comes more naturally to some people than to others, but like all the A's, it is a choice and it can be learned at any stage in marriage. It just takes practice, and you have the rest of your life to make a habit of it: affection never goes out of style, no matter how long you have been together. Just watch a grand, white-haired couple: you will see that they still share the knowing look, the tiny touch, the secret smile.

The Seventh Law of Attraction: Arousal

The Dream Maker's message in Arousal: *"I try to be beautiful for you and I love being physically intimate with you."*

Though derogatory clichés suggest that this is the number one law in a man's life (Chapter 5), it's not true. Most Nice Guys do not prefer sex for sex's sake. They crave the affirmation that precedes the physical and which is built into real lovemaking. When a woman applies the A's, sexual misunderstandings and frustrations can be greatly minimized (unless there are psychological or physiological issues that require professional intervention). As husband and wife are drawn toward each other in the positive atmosphere created by the A's, they find themselves increasingly on the same page about their physical intimacy. If not, working it out together honestly and pleasantly becomes a mutual desire and priority, like everything else in life. Shared joy in physical union begins when the Dream Maker comprehends that her man dreads rejection, disapproval, and failure in any way, but especially when it comes to sex. Because she is aware of this sensitivity, she tries to receive him (even encourage him) with open arms and an open heart as often as she can. If she feels temporarily unavailable, she at least is sweetly honest with him, and assures him of her love and attraction to him. In treating him this way, she is breaking down his manly reserve through physical intimacy, so that they can both experience the exhilaration of emotional intimacy.

The Eighth Law of Attraction: Accommodate Accomplishment

The Dream Maker's message in Accommodate Accomplishment: *"You can do it, and I want you to do it."*

Since we know that the male quest is at the heart of his why for both living and loving (Chapter 4), the woman who graciously, even enthusiastically, makes allowances so that her Nice Guy can achieve and progress in the world, is actually securing the most honored place in his heart (and at his side). Ironically, when she gives him permission to fly, she mitigates the male need for autonomy. A man doesn't mind feeling dependent on a powerful woman when he thinks of her as the wind beneath his wings. Look how this husband of ten years describes the impact of his wife's support: "I'm afraid I give the term nerd a whole new meaning with my zealous, even gluttonous interest in technology and particularly in computer programming. I have an unquenchable thirst for knowledge that can consume substantial amounts of time and energy, yet my wife is more than accommodating. She encourages me to pursue my interests, and her encouragement is sincere, even enthusiastic. She even asks me about what I am learning, and her sincere interest in my accomplishments deeply endears her to me. I find myself eager to please her and support her in her interests." When a wife accommodates accomplishment, then wherever her Nice Guy is, or whatever he is doing, she can be sure that he is counting the hours until he can be with her again and that he is thinking about how he will help her achieve her dreams.

The Ninth Law of Attraction: Allegiance

The Dream Maker's message in Allegiance: *"You have all my" heart."*

This law might sound the alarm for women who are protective of their individuality, but allegiance is not submission. In the context of Wife for Life it is defined as loyalty—to the man who married you and to your commitment to join forces. People are attracted to people they feel safe with: the intimates we can trust our secrets to, the friends who would never purposely hurt us or tarnish our reputation. If a Nice Guy can count on his wife to praise, even defend, him to others (including their children), and to keep their private matters confidential, he is strongly motivated to do all he can to respect her rights and her dignity. A husband of nine years sent me this tribute to his wife: "It's easy to be faithful to someone when you're with them. But one of the things that I'm most grateful for about my wife is that she's faithful to me when I'm not around. I never have to worry about what she's going to say about me behind my back. She doesn't complain about me to her parents or gossip and get into husband-bashing sessions with her girlfriends. She not only compliments me, but she does it behind my back. Nothing builds trust like hearing the nice things your wife just told somebody else about you." The Hebrew proverb says it all: "Don't kiss and tell; honor in love is silence." When you honor your marriage this way, something magic happens inside your relationship as well as inside your heart: your husband trusts you more, and deep inside, you perceive your*self* as trust*worthy*.

The Tenth Law of Attraction: Authenticity

The Dream Maker's message in Authenticity: *"I mean it."*

Though it's true that none of the Laws of Attraction will have a lasting impact without this final A, don't worry. Authenticity takes practice—just as all the other A's do. If your first attempts to apply the A's feel silly or unnatural, keep trying. Focus less on impressing your *husband* and more on letting his devotion, masculinity, and good intentions impress *you*. With consistent, concerted effort, the A-way of relating to your husband will become beautifully ingrained. Your efforts will become increasingly genuine as you see him respond positively, and he will naturally give you more of what *you* need: Romance, Security, Trueness, Understanding, Validation, and We-ness. If it helps you to commit to living the A's, think of R, S, T, U, V, W (the end of the alphabet— you can figure out what X, Y, and Z stand for), as starting with A, A, A, A, A, A, A, A, A, A: Acceptance, Approval, Appreciation, Admiration, Availability, Affection, Arousal, Accommodate Accomplishment, Allegiance, and Authenticity.

I hope it is clear now why the A's are such a magnet for your man: they soothe his fears, meet his needs, and feed his passions. What husband can resist that kind of attraction? According to the experts (all the guys I know), no man can, as demonstrated by the tributes husbands paid their wives in this chapter. Did you notice how the men I quoted have all been married ten years or less? Imagine how devoted they will feel after two, three, or four decades of living with the A's. My own loving husband is a case in point.

How thankful I am to the young girl who had vision enough to claim the seat closest to the young man named Dale. I may have forfeited the actual engine case long ago, but I have never relinquished Mona's Spot. I am still *beholding* the beautiful boy from Houston with amazement, up close and personal. On the rare evenings he falls asleep before I do, I like to trace his cheeks, his nose, and his lips with my finger. Charmed by the way his face is pressed into the pillow, I can't help kissing him on the cheek. To me, he will always be the most fabulous man on the planet.

You can feel that way too. As the A's do their wonderful work, your Nice Guy will mellow and ripen, becoming increasingly delicious, more and more appetizing. Your cup of love can run over and refill itself year after year as long as you believe in him and thereby become, in the most beautiful sense of the word, his Intimate.

21
Masculine Zest

Love seems the swiftest, but it is the slowest of all growths. No man or woman really knows what perfect love is until they have been married a quarter of a century. —*Mark Twain, American writer*

Now that you have all those A's on your castle key ring, I expect you are chomping at the bit to try them out. By all means, let 'er rip. If you apply the A's and all the other Dream Maker principles consistently, you can look forward to more emotional and physical intimacy. You will feel more loved than ever before.

You can also look forward to watching your husband become not only the man of *your* dreams, but the man of *his* dreams. (Slattery, p. 9) A wife's love flows like gentle rain into a man's roots; her positive affirmation penetrates deep, helping him feel more secure in who he is, which in turn inspires him to become his best self—for you, for the children, for your family, for your community. It is one of a Wife for Life's greatest rewards to see how he loves others better because of you.

I was thinking about these things when Dale and I visited the redwood forest of Northern California recently, home of the world's tallest, grandest trees. I was awestruck. On the Father's Day soon after, I wrote my husband a concrete poem: a type of poetry that paints a picture with words—literally. The arrangement of each line on the page turned the poem, visually, into a grove of trees. I called it "Let Me Look Up at You." It was the only way I could think to express how much he had become like those redwood trees to me. When he read the last stanza, he was particularly touched: "Your gentle power spreads an aura of love, sincerity, and reassurance that life can grow men solid enough, giant enough, to deserve the title tall enough: Husband and Father."

As a castle, your husband surrounds and protects the two of you; but as a mature tree, he will bless and protect others as well. Developing the desire, ability, and courage to serve selflessly takes time and effort; it may take years for his confidence to increase sufficiently to support a mighty trunk and heavy branches. But if you are patient with him, his trunk—essentially his character—will gradually expand in circumference, ring upon ring, experience upon experience, success upon success; and his branches, which symbolize his desire and ability to bless others, will lengthen and thicken through work and sacrifice.

If you want to facilitate that kind of growth in your husband, allowing him to stretch as tall as a redwood or as broad as an oak, then you must understand that he needs the special energy I call *masculine zest*, which comes from a combination of...

- work,
- play,
- adventure,
- and a quest.

Though the masculine quest appears at the bottom of this list, it is the pinnacle of all Wife-for-Life principles, and we will spend most of the remaining book on it. But first, a prerequisite lesson on the other ingredients in masculine zest: work, play, and adventure. These are the secret ingredients in your Miracle-Gro™ for husbands. When combined in just the right proportion they create the perfect soil for growing the tallest, healthiest tree. Unfortunately, many wives don't understand that. When a woman improvises her own formula (born out of *her* needs, not those of her husband), she not only stunts his growth but may actually contribute to his unhappiness. Like the cedar in our backyard that is rotting from the inside out, a man may silently wither away if he lives an unbalanced lifestyle. When a woman underestimates her man's need for work, play, and adventure, she is killing him softly —right along with her own dreams of becoming his Intimate, let alone his inspiration.

If you don't want your relationship to shrivel up, it is vital to understand how play and adventure give your man relief and joy in a world that is otherwise his foe, a world that forces him to fight or founder. Life, to him, is work; in fact, it is sometimes nothing but work. You may feel the daily grind separates the two of you too often and for too long, but to him, work is Life with a capital *L*. Your man struggles relentlessly (for reasons so imbedded in his nature he's hardly aware of them) for influence and distinction among his fellows. And he is constantly compelled to earn not only respect but money. In his mind, his wages correspond directly to his worth in the world and his value to the family—even in today's egalitarian households. Nice Guys take very much to heart both views of work—the philosophical (I need respect) and the practical (I need to provide). They feel keenly the responsibility to earn money, even more acutely than most women do. How can I say that? Because, as we've discussed: men depend wholly on performance and external recognition for a sense of worth. You, dear woman, do not. Don't get me wrong: you want to work and you need respect and money as much as the next guy, but deep down you don't believe that your merit as a person, your right to respect, your value to your loved ones, and your significance to the world *depends* on it. Your esteem is much more inherent.

Gender experts will back me up on this, including funny guy Tim Allen. I once heard the *Home Improvement* star joke that men have far fewer choices than women do. A man has to work, he said, or go to jail. I laughed, until I realized the truth wasn't so funny. Even though crime and vagrancy are repulsive alternatives to a legitimate job, a man works not just to avoid life behind bars or to put food on the table, but because if he doesn't work *he will die*. A husband who feels useless, unproductive, or undervalued will eventually destroy himself with doubt and despondency (sometimes literally). The psychological trauma my own grandfather experienced during the widespread unemployment of the Great Depression twisted his mind and scarred him for life. Many men today are in the same predicament. In too many countries, the male drive to work and earn money cannot be satisfied. Male joblessness on a global scale is contributing big-time to unrest and violence, a phenomenon I saw with my own eyes while traversing Europe and the Middle East. And I will never forget the sight of my own man sobbing at his desk, a deluge of grief and shame bursting like a dam all over a paper pile of collection threats.

Myles Munroe, president of the International Leader Training Institute, explains this innate connection between men and employment in his book, *The Power and Purpose of Men*:

> "When a man loses his job, it's as if his life has fallen apart. Some men actually end up losing their minds after they lose their jobs. Why do they have such an extreme reaction? It's because it's not just a job to them. It's their means of providing. *One of their purposes for being has been taken away from them*" (page 154, italics mine).

So, if your Nice Guy swings a shovel over his shoulder and sings, "Hi-ho, hi-ho," all the way to the office, he's lucky. He's even luckier if his wife kisses him on the forehead for it (even as she marches out the door with her own shovel). And he's King of the World if she generously, graciously, and whole-heartedly understands that as much as he has to work, he also has to play. Your man needs a breather—a regular and frequent time-out from the intense fears, needs, and responsibilities of manhood. He also needs an adventurous break from routine on occasion—daring exploits that challenge and confirm his masculinity.

These regular reprieves from routine and the occasional hiatus from habit is something your man craves just as much as he needs work. Though his escape might not take a form you think of as relaxing (it may seem over-stimulating or even dangerous to you), he knows instinctively that it will save his life.

Here are the facts: working, thinking, and problem solving continuously without replenishing his hormones and energy will kill a man just as certainly as if he could not work at all. Your man is not a Pioneer Women, milking the cows at sunrise and going with gusto all over the farm until midnight. His brain cannot and will not run nonstop like a computer. No, your Nice Guy has to *rest* and *test* his masculinity in between building a barn and bringing in the hay. His biology and his physiology require it.

Shortly after learning about this male-specific trait from the scientific literature that I was analyzing for this book, Dale and I made a trip from the U.S. Mountain West to the Pacific Coast, driving through the Sierra Nevada mountain range on our way to California's Redwood Forest. At historic sites along the way, we learned about pioneer families who, while crossing the mountain range on foot and wagon, lost members of their expeditions one by one. Because I was studying the subject of male exhaustion, I couldn't help but compare the men I know today to those pioneers; men who rarely, if ever, get a real break from the stress and strain of life, their own mountain march at work and at home: husbands and fathers who push or pull a heavy wagon of responsibilities without reprise or affirmation until they are in danger of dropping out of life emotionally and physically.

Dear lady, won't you think twice before you and your girlfriends scold your husbands for boyish behavior? Hold your tongue before you rattle off all the reasons he shouldn't go play. Remember those ill-fated pioneers as you weigh down his wagon with more obligations, and don't ever tell him he's too young, too old, too inexperienced, or too ridiculous for adventure. He may be in pain, he may seem possessed or even puerile—but your Nice Guy needs you to encourage his play (if he's afraid to take a break), facilitate it (if he can't figure out how), or give him the go-ahead (if he's got a plan). Whether he's shooting hoops, climbing rocks, reeling in fish, racing engines, zapping zombies, banging drums, sawing wood, or reading fiction, his activities are *not* as slight, silly, stupid, or scary as they may seem to you.

A Real Adventure

My sister-in-law, Susan, a real Dream Maker, understands this principle and accommodates her husband's need to offset his hard work with hard play and adventure. Several months ago, Susan called to report that she hadn't heard from her camping husband and their teenage son in five days. Though cell coverage may have been an issue in the mountains of America's Central Oregon, I personally found it worrisome that Oscar hadn't made some kind of attempt (smoke signal, carrier pigeon, something) to communicate with his wife. Could elk hunting be that absorbing?

"When will you be home?" Susan had asked before he left.

"Oh, when we're done."

Oscar and Cooper had obsessively plotted this father-son adventure for weeks, investing a lot of time, money, and dreams. Susan had supported the enterprise all along—even though it was the last thing in the world she would do herself. Yet, as she and I hung in suspense that night, debating whether to call out the canines, I wondered if her heart would override her intellect. I wondered if mine would.

Then, just as I found the Park Service phone number, she gasped, "You're not going to believe it! The car's pulling into the driveway!"

She hung up before I could give her my last piece of advice: "Don't yell at him!" Turns out, she didn't need it.

At dinner the next night, Oscar regaled Dale and me with his exploits, while Susan beamed. Susan beamed and I marveled. How many wives would let their husbands disappear into the wilderness like that, respecting his masculine need for adventure, sympathizing with his motives, trusting his abilities to stay safe, believing in his promises to return home; not undermining the whole thing because she was out of her comfort zone while he was ensconced in his?

I'm thinking not many.

I leaned over and whispered in her ear, "How did you do it?"

She looked at Oscar, who was busy telling Dale about near-zero temperatures and getting lost in the snow-covered forest.

"He grew up on a remote ranch," she explained, "with more freedom than anyone would give a kid today. In his mind, staying in constant contact is unnecessary. It's taken some getting used to, and it still frustrates me once in a while, but that's just the way he is!"

Wow, I thought, *with that kind of understanding friend at home, how could a Nice Guy return with anything less than a big smile, a big kiss, and a big, smelly elk?*

"How many did you bag?" Dale asked the hunter.

"Two." Oscar answered with a straight face. "Elk burgers. They make great ones in the little café at the foot of the mountain."

I looked at Susan. She was still beaming.

Whatever he considers play and however the adventure turns out, it's important to control your fear of losing him and employ instead First Respect, treating his diversions and his exploits not as a mere recreation or pastime, but as a biological drive, essential to his manhood. If you can do that, your support will come back to you in conversation and kisses. Just as your feminine delights refresh you so you can be a more understanding wife, play and adventure physiologically rejuvenate your man so he can be a more attentive husband. Nice Guy becomes Really Romantic Guy when you approve of, admire, and accommodate his masculine zest. Not to get too corny or too personal here, but whether Dale's strumming a guitar, strutting on stage, or conducting a choir, tuning the truck, putting for par, or sliding to second, his happiness makes him hot. His zest gives me zing. Back in my arms, as he peels off the grease, sweat, or bravado, he always says, "Thank you," and I say, "My pleasure."

The first step toward becoming his inspiration is to help your Nice Guy balance the male imperative to work with the drive for play and adventure. You can draw him even closer by *joining* his Great Escape: there's no doubt he'd rather have you for a playmate than anyone else in the world, and grand marriages always have common pursuits and interests. If that's not possible, or you just can't bring yourself to go elk hunting (or whatever), at least you can say, "Have fun, honey!" instead of "Don't kill yourself!"

Watch him if you can. Cheer him from the stands. Be his biggest fan. Try to understand. Let him be a man. Because trees that are grand have a helping hand that wear a wedding band. Make sunshine in the land if you want him to expand and grow.

Up.

22
His Inspiration From The Start

I think my understanding about how to support men as they grow *up* actually began with *my* growing up in the company of four little brothers (no sisters). I also raised two sons of my own (both of whom have given me grandsons exclusively to date), and I have worked closely as a teacher to and mentor to male children and teens my whole adult life. Some of my best friends—quite seriously—have been boys. Practical experience like that has to count for something, because it certainly doesn't take a scientist (although plenty of researchers have come to the same conclusions I have) to see some rather obvious differences in the behavior of boys and girls: common knowledge that can actually help us become more effective wives if we know how to interpret it. For instance, Michael Gurian, in *What Could He Be Thinking*, cites a number of indications of the biological basis for the male quest (p. 64-65):

- toddler boys start exploring outward, away from safety and toward external performance earlier than little girls do;
- starting very early in life, boys generally take more risks and experience less physical fear than girls;
- when deprived of a toy, six-month old boys respond

- by pushing, pulling, and grabbing, while baby girls are more likely to cry;
- from the time a tiny boy stands on his own two feet, he is often brandishing a stick, a broom handle, or some other weapon-like implement.

As Gurian writes: "The hero is biologically wired into men's minds. Testosterone, vasopressin, greater spinal fluid in the brain, less serotonin, less oxytocin, and the way the male-brain system projects life onto an abstract and spatial universe, lead men to see the world in terms of action, heroes, warriors, even lovers who must negotiate landscapes of challenge" (p. 62). So, though boys may growl and shout and wrestle and punch and jump and climb and throw and test themselves against themselves and others in ways that are guaranteed to make Mom's eyes roll or her heart stop, parents can take comfort in knowing that Mother Nature is preparing their little man for a big quest.

And so go those treacherous boyish days, until, by the time he reaches adolescence, a young man has zeroed in on a life-challenge, or rather, the need for one. The craving for an external journey as proof of his independence and distinction grows so acute, in fact, that unless he's given a structured way of gaining competence and confidence, of showing his mettle, of substantiating his emerging manhood in a positive way, a teenage boy is in real danger of succumbing to destructive hierarchies, such as gangs, or aligning himself with a misguided cause (such as terrorism in some cultures). It's a scary time. Young male fears and immature male drives can be a perfect storm—or a perfect opportunity. How it turns out depends a lot on the men—and the women—in his life. Lucky boys have at least one responsible, caring male to look up to, as well as a mother, grandmother, or sister who treats his sometimes irritating or juvenile ways with forbearance and respect. If he is *that* lucky—with a tree of a father or role model, and a Dream Maker of a mother or other female—

he is optimally poised for a successful adult quest: a quest that will bless himself, his wife, his children, and even the world.

If a man does not come from such a supportive, nurturing, balanced background, however, his wife becomes not only the most important but perhaps the *first* source of support and inspiration he has ever really had. Becoming a Dream Maker for such a man is crucial. Roll up your sleeves and flex your muscles. The Creator, the Talent, the Dream Maker is on the job. Somewhere out there is a quest for your man—waiting to be sought and fought for. It is a journey that will be *his* salvation and *your* secret for drawing him in as you draw him up; a voyage of discovery that will allow him to triumph over his fears, and in the process, own his soul. It is out there—or rather, *in* there, deep in his heart—and for him to find it, continue it, or expand it, you must be the light at the beginning and the end of the tunnel. As Joseph Campbell puts it in his archetypal masterpiece, *The Hero With a Thousand Faces*:

> "Woman, in the picture language of mythology, represents the totality of what can be known. The hero is the one who comes to know...She lures, she guides, she bids him burst his fetters. And if he can match her import, the two, the knower and the known, will be released from every limitation. Woman is the guide to the sublime acme of sensuous adventure" (p. 106).

At the Start

In the course of this book, I have shared personal letters or poems that I wrote to Dale through the years. Let me assure you, there were never an equal number of words composed at his pen (or keyboard). The box of correspondence from him is not even a box —it's an envelope. That plain manila love bank, though hardly bulging at the creases, holds the most thoughtful of his birthday,

Mother's Day, and anniversary cards through the years, as well as a few sticky notes (which I find inside cupboards or on bathroom mirrors); lots of business cards that were delivered with flowers; and several other rather private emails from far-away places. The most precious of the envelope's contents however, is the missive he wrote in his own hand. These three short sentences in all capitals deserve the exalted title of *letter* because they have enough heart and soul to qualify as reams and reams of romance. Like an archived treasure, this single, folded piece of stationary has been prized, protected, and kept private for over two decades.

My castle wrote, "OH MY LOVE! YOU GIVE ME GREAT STRENGTH! I CAN'T EXIST WITHOUT YOU!"

It was 1986. Do you know what happened that year?

We were betrayed. Trusted associates publicly trounced us in a hostile, underhanded takeover of our non-profit corporation. We were broke and homeless. I was pregnant, on the verge of delivering our third baby, living in a borrowed bedroom, caring for our four-year-old son and six-year-old daughter (with severe disabilities) all by myself because Dale had left for another state to look for work. A Dickensian winter of despair if ever there was one, I should have been depressed. And yet...*he said he could not exist without me*, which was the *best* feeling in the whole wide world!

Katherine Hepburn, as Christine Drayton in the Stanley Kramer film, *Guess Who's Coming to Dinner* (Columbia Pictures, 1967), makes a speech to her successful businessman husband of several decades that applies beautifully here. "You know," she confesses, as she and Spencer Tracey contemplate the just-announced engagement of their daughter, "for us it's all been great, but do you know what was the best time of all? It was the beginning, when everything was a struggle, and you were working too hard and sometimes frightened...there were times when I felt that I really knew that I was a help to you. That was the very best time of all for me."

A mature Dream Maker will tell you that the pinnacle of the quest is very thrilling, and the end of the quest is very rewarding, but it is at the *start*, while the quest is being defined and refined by the two of you—both the grand objective and the million necessary nuances—that you feel the most needed and therefore the most gloriously feminine and powerful. You can't see that when you are in the thick of it, only when you are on the other side of it, but I'm telling you now that if you seize a bright beginning for what it is, the chance to exalt your marriage by inspiring your husband at the starting gate, then when you cross the finish line you will remember the worst of times as the best of times.

A young wife validated this for me just a few days ago. She knew nothing about *Wife for Life*: her family is new to our neighborhood, and we were having our first friendly conversation. I learned that her husband recently completed eleven years of schooling, including lots of grueling medical school, and that he had accepted a position with a local clinic as an OB-GYN. As I looked into her glistening eyes (they were big and brown and gorgeous), I admired the serenity and natural beauty there. She was obviously a very happy woman and an accomplished Dream Maker. And yet, she said to me wistfully, "the best days were the days we were both in school, having our babies, working part-time jobs, moving in and out of seven different states. We were so poor; we had nothing. It was wonderful."

A well-worn debate about the optimal age at which to marry has been circulating for years. Though everyone agrees adolescence is risky, an article in *USA Today* reports that "those who marry in the early to mid-twenties are slightly happier and less likely to break up than those who marry in the later twenties, and that they are significantly more satisfied with their relationships than those who marry at thirty or older" (November 9, 2008). Young women obviously don't care about this research. They are marrying later than their mothers or grandmothers overall, which may very well be best for the majority of couples.

On a personal note, however, I am glad that for Dale and me, "growing up together," as we call it, turned out as well as it did, against the odds. At that stage of life, marriage was not a risk that interfered with our independence, but a totality of spirit and purpose that spawned a quest that was *ours*, not just his or mine.

Whenever you marry, and whatever stage you may be in now, an attitude of "let me add my strength to yours" will do wonders for your relationship. Women today do not wave handkerchiefs from the bedroom balcony as their knights ride out in dawn's light. They don't have to wait to be rescued from an unruly band of gypsies or watch from the sidelines as he discovers gold and slays dragons. No. Today's Wife for Life is a different breed from the maidens of the past. With her education and worldly sense, she is an indispensable asset to the two-some.

And so the conversation goes between the leading actors in the 2011 BBC Films', *Salmon Fishing in the Yemen*:

Harriet: Do you need an assistant, Dr. Jones?

Alfred: An assistant?

Harriet: A partner.

Alfred: *More than anything.*

Remember the Why

I knelt on the rock-hard floor of the abbey. It felt uncomfortable and a little awkward but it was the only way to hide behind the pew and thus avoid the curiosity of pilgrims and the disapproval of parishioners. I stared up at a large stone memorial while my fingers (which were still getting used to the tiny keyboard on my phone) shook with excitement as I transcribed:

"Sacred to the Memory of LUCY CRICLOW, daughter of JOHN COBHAM Esqr & Wife of HENRY CRICLOW Esqr who died in the City of Bath in the Kingdom of England on the 7th and was buried in the Abbey Church of that City on the 14th Jan-ry 1801, Aged 65 Years.... Most carefully educated and bred up in the doctrines of the Church of England, Her faith therein firmly fixed, a true disciple of JESUS CHRIST. Possessing and practicing all that belongs to that character, she proved one of the best of Wives, and by her matchless conduct as a Mother in law, called forth & deserved at the same time the warmest tenderness and attachment from her loving Husband & his grateful Children, and universal admiration from all who had any means of estimating her merit. Most sincerely and affectionately attached to her Relations she was by all of them revered. In her friendships, steady and sincere, to her domestics, indulgent, kind, humane. Courteous, benevolent, charitable towards all ranks of people, her various virtues excited general approbation while living, and cause her the more to be regretted, by all who knew her, now she is no more. This monument is intended to record the well tried worth of a Woman, who for upwards of 26 years living in the conjugal state, approved herself in sickness, and in health, a most unremittingly loving, tender, and condescending Wife, and to express due acknowledgements of her most grateful and afflicted husband, H.C. Henry Crichlo"

I misspelled that last name because a priest strolled by and gave me a stern look. I smiled weakly, shut down my phone, and scurried out the door. Standing outside in Bath's town square, with rain rolling off my umbrella, I read Henry's tribute to Lucy again and again. It affected me deeply, and though I didn't know it at the time, Lucy's memorial had become another prompt (like the one I felt at the Wailing Wall in Jerusalem) that I was supposed to do something important for women.

Mrs. Lucy Cobham Criclow had inspired me.

Thus began the pursuit of my new dream: to find women from

the past who could teach me about grand marriage. With dogged delight, I digested biography after biography, probing and delving and scrutinizing, immersing myself in the hearts and marriages of women who were cherished by their husbands because they were an inspiration.

- Consider Anne Morrow Lindbergh, who acted as copilot, navigator, and radio operator for her legendary aviator husband, Charles, as they pioneered air travel around the globe in the early 1930s.
- Imagine life as Abigail Adams, supporting founding father John Adams during the tumultuous birthing of the United States of America.
- Put yourself in the leather lace-ups of Lillian Moller Gilbreth, mother of *Cheaper by the Dozen* fame, who in the early 1900s collaborated with her husband to leave their mark on the fields of engineering and management.
- Or for just a moment, become Emily Roebling, who was her chief-engineer-husband's indispensable partner during the fourteen-year building of the Brooklyn Bridge.

The list goes on and on. I personally found it very uplifting to know that many, many women have succeeded at becoming an inspiration to their husband. They don't all have a biography at the library, of course, but there are enough who do. We can draw from their exemplary lives the instruction we need to become exemplary wives. They are my mentors, the way I want to be your mentor, and in the rest of this book, I will share with you their secrets. Just remember, each of these women had a husband who loved her fiercely because she understood that her man's *why* for living (his quest) was the same as his *why* for loving (his wife). As we said in Chapter 4, his impossible dream is only possible, only noble, only beautiful and worthwhile if it is for someone else. And that someone must be you.

Whether a man runs for public office like Ronald Reagan, writes the great American novel like Mark Twain, or enacts social reform like William Wilberforce, he believes with all his heart that he does what he does not only because of his wife, but *for* her. As Johann Christoph Friedrich von Schiller, German poet, dramatist, historian, and translator, wrote in a letter to his wife, Charlotte von Lengefeld, in 1789: "My whole existence, everything that lives within me, everything, my most precious, I devote to you, and if I try to ennoble myself, that is done, in order to become ever worthier of you, to make you happier" (*Love Letters*, p. 46). In other words, Schiller is offering his Wife for Life a reason, through his quest, to admire him, to desire him, and to hold fast to him, which he believes will make her happy. A husband's magnificent obsession is born out of his love and desire for his wife.

"Wait a minute," I hear you saying. "Waaaaait a minute! My husband? Change the world for me? My husband is sitting on the couch right now in a T-shirt, watching *Sports Center* and eating Cheetos!"

Well, that doesn't mean he doesn't want and need a quest. Take advantage of these few quiet minutes (while he's absorbed in whatever) to read and contemplate the wifely secrets in the next chapter: how to help him *find* a quest.

23
Dream Seeker: Finding and Refining The Quest

There should be something timeless about a woman—something eternal.
You can see it all in the great portraits of the past...like you could meet
those women anywhere and be inspired by them.
—From the 1948 Selznick motion picture Portrait of Jennie

Dale's parents, Ken and LeOra Zabriskie, treated me like an angel until their dying day for one reason and one reason only: they believed I was heaven-sent. For a long time his mother and father had fretted over their lost boy. Dale seemed so adrift, completely disoriented. True love, his parents reasoned, in the form of a good woman, stood the best chance of straightening out Dale's meandering trajectory. So they prayed for one (a good woman that is), and in short order, out of nowhere, came Ramona. Their parental plans and prayers worked: with little more than love in his pocket, the Family Baby became the Family Man as he realized that he had to fill those pockets with a lot more than love; that he had to *go* somewhere; that he had to *do* something; that he had to *be* somebody.

He just didn't know what.

As much as the lack of specifics worried me, Ken and LeOra didn't worry about what Dale would do in the end. They believed he would figure it out eventually—now that there were two of us. I just wish a mature somebody had warned us that it could take fifteen years of starts and stops and winding and rewinding before we would land on the right quest. The entire process might have gone faster and smoother, too, if we had known from the beginning *why* a quest is important. And if someone had just helped us understand how to *define* a quest from the start, finding and refining one would have been so much simpler.

Let's talk about all of that. How does a woman become indispensable to her husband, his Intimate in his life's work, loved for her understanding and support, cherished for her contribution to the quest?

Since you already understand *why* he needs a quest, the next question to answer is what his quest should be. In other words, *what* kind of dream qualifies as a quest?

Defining a Quest

A quest helps your man take his place in the world because it distinguishes him from everyone else. A man's quest must embody his voice, his value, his exclusive mark on history and humanity. This might be achieved on a very small scale or a very grand one, it doesn't matter. All that matters is that he believes he matters. The quest will ideally become his legacy, a symbol of what he believes in, of what he feels most passionate about. It will represent his essence, the one thing in life that he owns completely.

A quest is Sizeable. As James Allen, the British philosopher, wrote in *As a Man Thinketh*, "Dream lofty dreams, and as you dream, so shall you become." What this boils down to is *dream big to grow big*. A quest has to be a challenge mighty enough to command your man's full concentration, something that will rouse his highest faculties and muster his greatest energy. A quest cannot be a trivial pursuit, or a man will not find fulfillment in it. Simple, easy, or half-hearted won't do. To feel invested and driven, his quest has to be much bigger than he is at the start. Remember: you are growing a redwood tree, not a crabapple or a crape myrtle.

A quest is Showable. To bring out the best and biggest in your husband, his quest must ultimately allow him to express his strengths and passions, to become *creative*. Smothering innovation stunts the spirit. Freedom to create inspires and empowers. As the physician and inventor Edward de Bono pointed out, "Creativity is a great motivator because it makes people interested in what they are doing." If your man is going to devote enormous effort to a challenge over many years, the opportunity to be resourceful, visionary, or inventive must be inherent in the quest.

A quest is Stretchable. By its very definition a quest is a long, long road. You can't possibly know exactly where it will lead you; the important thing is to choose a direction and trust that you will gain the talents, abilities, and insights needed as you go. Woodrow Wilson, for instance, never considered politics until observers convinced him that his career as an outstanding thinker and leader in the academic world had prepared him for a governorship and then the Presidency of the United States. The right quest will stretch and expand as your husband does. Like a video game, a proper quest is linear in essence, but it evolves level by level.

A quest is Shareable. To experience ultimate fulfillment, your husband must believe that his exertions are helping or motivating others in some way. It is a given in his mind that his work will benefit you (and the children); this parameter goes beyond that. Your Nice Guy needs to feel that his efforts are of service to a greater community. Whether he acts as a leader or team player, a teacher or mentor, an innovator or producer, a public servant or private businessman, it brings him great satisfaction to feel uniquely useful to the world by providing opportunities or products for *others* as he pursues his quest.

How Do I Help Him Find Such a Quest?

Most women do not fall in love with a ready-made hero, as Anne Morrow did. At twenty-one, her head was in the clouds (literally) with twenty-six-year-old Charles Lindbergh—already world-famous for making the first solo nonstop flight across the Atlantic Ocean. Even so, Lindbergh's life quest had only just begun, and without a strong wife at his side, he believed his ultimate mission remained foggy and unattainable.

Pierre Curie, an admired academic and a celebrated physicist, pleaded with fellow scientist, Marie Sklodowska, to marry him and pool their remarkable ambitions. As their daughter, Eve, wrote in her biography, *Marie Curie*, "For Pierre, science was the only aim. Thus his was a strange and almost incredible adventure, for it missed the essential aspiration of his mind into the movement of his heart. He felt himself drawn toward Marie by an impulse of love and at the same time by the highest necessity" (p. 137).

A more contemporary example is Ronald Reagan, who made several Hollywood films as a leading man in the 1930s and 1940s, but still felt unfulfilled and troubled by a divorce and a declining career. He later admitted freely and repeatedly, as reported in Nancy Reagan's memoirs, *My Turn*, "...if Nancy Davis hadn't come along when she did, I would have lost my soul" (p. 126).

The point is, regardless of their previous attainments in life— whether negligible or considerable—most men feel their quest is undefined or incomplete without the whole-hearted support and involvement of a loving wife. He is counting on you, consciously or unconsciously, obviously or intuitively, to be his "guide to the sublime acme of sensuous adventure," as Joseph Campbell put it. Like Anne Morrow Lindbergh, you must resolve to give your husband "a sense of freedom and power and fulfillment"— consistently treating him with First Respect, offering shoulder-to-shoulder companionship, filling him up with the A's, and accommodating his need for masculine zest. As his love and trust deepens, your reassuring presence will naturally lead him to reveal more and more of his buried or undiscovered dreams.

Refining the Dream

Slowly, gradually, and maybe over years and years (because you will never rush him), the two of you will piece together what he's really made of and what he's really meant to do in this world. Here are some ways to help him on the road to discovery.

Encourage his individuality. The courage to be himself—to form and share his unique opinions and approach to life—rests largely, if not exclusively, on you. How you respond to his ideas and impressions has the power to inhibit or to liberate him. You don't necessarily have to agree with everything he says, but you have to give him the First Respect he deserves as a man and as an individual. Let him be passionate, dramatic, and ambitious as he brainstorms his quest. Try not to worry at this point about the practicalities, or get overwhelmed by the scope of his ruminations. You're a Dream Maker, not a Dream Breaker. The world will cut him down to size if given half a chance—you don't have to. Keep the air clean and clear of skepticism so that he is free to try out his opinions or experiment with his thoughts out loud.

Spur his creativity. This is absolutely critical not only to finding a quest but to fulfilling it. The global economy rewards and relies on creative people. Companies are outsourcing the mundane pieces of their business, anything that is routine or automatic, and hiring instead thinker-innovators who add creative instinct and solutions, strategic insight, even artistic flair. Every aspect of life is better when approached creatively, and those who want to leave their mark have to unleash and develop this capacity. You can help your man do this by

226

instigating a running dialogue between the two of you about the world around you. Observe people, organizations, nature, products, the arts, media, religion, politics—everything! Ask him what he likes or doesn't like about the way something is designed or functions. Ask him what could be improved about it: what would he do to make it better? Travel. Read together. Watch the news together. Attend the arts. And then analyze and talk about it. (Dale and I have been doing this for thirty-five years.) Remember, you are creating a quest that expresses his unique essence.

Spend time with positive, creative people. It takes an effort to be social—and I'm talking in-person, not on-line, social. It takes even more effort to purposefully arrange how and with whom you spend your precious leisure time. But if you want a husband who is jazzed about life—who learns to see and seize opportunities and overcome obstacles—then you would do well to expose him (and yourself) to enthusiastic, creative people. Such people talk about ideas, live optimistically, respect your marriage, and leave you feeling invigorated and closer to one another. They will spark your imagination and fire up your enthusiasm. Friendly, confident, exuberant attitudes are contagious. You want that influence in your life. If you don't know people like that already, get involved in local congregations, nonprofit or neighborhood organizations, and children's teams or activities. Great people are always engaged in helping others. Meanwhile, it's just as important to avoid the downers, the stuck-in-the-muds, the caustic or toxic people. Remember, you need happy, courageous influences in your heart and home—those who will give you truly helpful support and feedback as you orchestrate your big, bold dream.

Look at a variety of sources. Ideally a man's job and his quest would be synonymous, but it ain't necessarily so. Plenty of men discover their ultimate satisfaction in a challenge outside their employment. As a Dream Seeker, you must remain open to all kinds of possibilities, so don't rule this one out. Growing a tree (rather than a Swiss bank account) might mean investing in an occupation other than his nine-to-five. It might also mean that his future mainline is a sideline at the start. With creativity, the two of you could turn it into a career. Of course, there's always the chance that a man's fantasies will remain just that. He might not get the specific shot he's looking for. He might be reticent to settle on a job (though he needs to for the family's sake) because it's not the ideal. In circumstances like these, a wife can inspire her husband in a different way. Analyze together the essence of his original dream. Ask him what it is about his dream occupation that really appeals to him. Keep digging until you can take his answers—the values inherent in his dream occupation—and apply them to his present work, or to a completely different, but similarly challenging, endeavor. For instance, chances are he hasn't thought through what *really* thrills him about the idea of pitching for the major leagues. When the two of you analyze it, he may discover that what he loves most about the idea is the pitcher's control over the game. Well, there are obviously lots of opportunities in this world for exerting control over the game that could be just as rewarding, but that don't require a ball and a glove. In reality, dead-end jobs don't have to stay that way: nearly every position offers an opportunity to learn something (if you have the right attitude), which can lead to something else, something better, something closer to the dream. A quest is a step by step journey, not a destination. Growth is in the challenge, not the prize.

My Dale is an example of this. When we met he wanted to be an actor. That idea morphed over time into a desire to become a radio broadcaster, which eventually mutated into a fascination with the technical side of the business, which evolved into an exploration of technology in general, which led him to the broader aspect of the business side of technology including manufacturing, research and development, sales and marketing, and so forth. Eventually, he found himself a niche with a global software company, a job that perfectly melded his technical experience with his presentation skills. Now a busy keynoter in the field of network security and information protection, his ride-of-a-lifetime has fulfilled all the criteria of a quest:

- Sizeable,
- Showable,
- Stretchable,
- and Shareable.

My in-laws would have loved this moment. I pray the angels will let them have a peek from the top of their cloud at their son, who is at the top of his game. As his Dream Seeker, it's all I ask.

24
Dream Believer

There are times when you have to give 90 percent,
or when both of you have to give 90 percent.
—*Nancy Reagan, wife of U.S. President Ronald Reagan*

Cassie the doggie and I usually bounced along at a nice clip, thinking of little more than pace, heart rate, and scampering squirrels. But this day was different: our clip slowed down to a jog, to a brisk walk, to a saunter. I just couldn't focus on running while I focused on worrying. We had received a job offer the day before: a good job, a great job, maybe even Dale's dream job: the kind of work with the kind of potential inside the kind of company that we had prepared for over a very long time. So why was I dragging my feet?

John Adams, one of the fathers of the United States of America, called Abigail Adams "my partner in all the Joys and sorrows, Prosperity and Adversity of my Life" and pled with her "to take Part with me in the struggle" (*Adams Family Papers*, 1 July 1774, Massachusetts Historical Society). Men rarely write like that anymore, but how many women even today, in the twenty-first century, could resist such a grand proposal? All Dale had to do was use the words beautiful life and I said yes. I communicated in my own way the same sentiment John Adams' young woman from Weymouth expressed in these words, "I long impatiently to have you upon the Stage of action" (*Adams Family Papers*, 19 August 1774, MHS). It all sounds very noble, but if you look at the date on

Abigail's letter to John—and the date I said yes to Dale—you will realize it was the spring of marriage for both of us. The proverbial rubber had yet to hit the road.

The distance between New York, Philadelphia, and the Adams home in Massachusetts was much greater in the eighteenth century than it is today—at least in terms of time and trouble. Once John stepped onto that "stage of action" it took him several days to get home because of the difficulties involved in travel, and it was always complex to extricate himself from the First Continental Congress. He and Abigail necessarily lived apart for six months or more at a time, and during his diplomatic mission to France, they were separated for years. We don't have to imagine their sacrifices to sympathize; her letters tell all.

> "The unbounded confidence I have in your attachment to me, and the dear pledges of our affection, has soothed the solitary hour, and rendered your absence more supportable for had I loved you with the same affection it must have been misery to have doubted. Yet a cruel world too often injures my feelings, by wondering how a person possesst of domestick [sic] attachments can sacrifice them by absenting himself for years" (*Adams Family Papers*, MHS, 23 December 1782).

I completely relate to Abigail. When Dale received that life-changing job offer, he was handed the world—he literally began traversing the globe. I, on the other hand, was handed a list of bills to pay, a house in the middle of a remodel, and four energetic kids, including our daughter with severe disabilities. It frightened me to think of long days, let alone long weeks, without him, and I wondered how I would ever meet the challenge.

But then again, how could I ever *not*?

By this time in our marriage, I had come to accept the fact that I'd wed a man who liked to work. I might have caught on sooner if he had warned me the way legendary engineer, Frank Gilbreth, warned his future bride. As recorded in Edna Yost's *Frank and Lillian Gilbreth*, Frank told Lillian flat out that "he lived to work, that he rested only long enough to get back to it, and that he shared to the full the New England ideal of the importance of work and of making the most of himself" (p. 13). Dale had never said as much, but I got it. What I couldn't comprehend was that his self-worth had to be fulfilled and validated *through* that work *before* I could claim his full attention. It was difficult, if not impossible, for him to give to me until he felt certain he had something to give. With the typical male tendency to concentrate on one thing, one project, or one relationship at a time, he found it excruciating to release himself from a task—mentally and sometimes physically—until he had succeeded at it. He needed to feel proud, satisfied, finished—not just for himself, but for me.

I couldn't see that at the time. Still trying to shove my way to the front of the line, I too often missed a truth that would have made life so much more pleasant: *in his mind, I was already at the front of the line*. To the Boy Wonder, his work was not Ramona's competition. His passion was not a limited commodity. His dreams did not threaten mine. They *were* mine. He truly believed that. He *had* to believe it in order to thrive and progress. When I learned to Accommodate Accomplishment (the Seventh Law of Attraction), and not only avoided giving him a hard time about working so hard, but actually helped him meet his commitments, he came back to me sooner and in full force, having (in his mind) never left me. Like waiting out the seasons or the sunrise, allowing my man to *do* his quest so he can then *do* for me is actually the most natural thing in the world.

Mother Nature does everything for a reason. The male quest is meant to not only strengthen the relationship between a man and a woman but to protect it, to serve as a check or balance in your family's ecosystem. What do I mean by that? Just this: though it may seem all wrong to a wife that her husband sacrifices some of their togetherness and home life in order to gain status in the world, the fact of the matter is, you don't *want* him focusing on you 24/7. He is biologically impelled to test his masculine prowess, to assert himself in situations that prove his exceptionality and worth—so just what do you think would happen if he had nothing to engage in but you and the family? Having Mr. Help-More or Mr. All-Romance at your constant beck and call may sound idyllic, but it's almost certain you would take your wish back once the power struggle began. As Michael Gurian warns in *What Could He Be Thinking*, women who expect their men to "curtail these callings, bringing their focus of power away from external pursuits and directly to providing for women's emotional and romantic needs" ought to also consider "the biological necessity of males to involve themselves in dominance activities and the human tendency (both male and female) to struggle over emotional power" (pp. 51-52).

The bottom line, which remains invisible to a lot of women, is that you want him *out there*: challenging himself, challenging the world, challenging something or someone—besides you!

That may sound unfair at first, and you might be thinking, "But what about me? Don't I need to be out there, too?" You may very well, but here's the deal: women, in general, are content to nest for longer stretches then men. Forcing a man to think like that will lead to misunderstanding at best and alienation at worst. As Pierre Curie astutely observed:

> "Woman loves life for the living of it far more than we do...Thus, when we, driven by some mystic love, wish to enter upon some anti-natural path, when we give all our thoughts to some work which estranges us from the humanity nearest us, we have to struggle against women. The mother wants the love of her child above all things, even if it should make an imbecile of him. The mistress also wishes to possess her lover, and would find it quite

natural to sacrifice the rarest genius in the world for an hour of love." (*Marie Curie*, p. 120).

It has always been hard for women to accept this aspect of masculinity, but the world out there is constantly, subliminally calling him. Ancient nomadic instincts, when combined with masculine independence, stir up a nearly irresistible urge to prove himself beyond home and family. Captain Alfred Bland tried to explain this in a letter to his wife from the battlefield in 1916:

"My only and eternal blessedness, I wonder whether you resent my cheerfulness ever! Do you, dear? Because you might, you know. I ought, by the rules of love, to spend my days and nights in an eternity of sighs and sorrow for our enforced parting. And by all the rules of war, I ought to be enduring cold and hardship, hunger and fatigue, bitterness of soul and dismay of heart....Would it rejoice you if I confessed to being utterly miserable every now and then?...Would you be glad or sorry? Oh, I know how sympathetic and sad you would feel, and I know you would not be glad at all. Would you? And if you were glad, you would be all wrong; because, even if those things were true, it wouldn't bring us together again, it wouldn't make me love you more, it wouldn't sweeten those embraces we are deprived of for the moment, it wouldn't strengthen our divine oneness one scrap. Would it?" (*Love Letters*, p. 138).

It really is true what they say: You can't keep a good man down, or in this case, home all the time.

So what's a girl to do when her man leaves in pursuit of his quest? Sulk in silence? No! No! No! If that were true, I'd go *Crazy Lady* and club us both senseless! You naturally crave, and deserve, your own form of expression, your own employment, your own sense of fulfillment. Your wants and needs must also see the light of day and have the spotlight at night (see "Teaching a Knight to Knit," Chapter 11). He is your castle after all, and you absolutely need him to understand and accommodate you as well. He wants to do that when you are his Intimate; and in fact his happiness is based on it. But at the same time, he doesn't want to feel guilty about pursuing his quest. How you balance all that is something we'll continue to discuss, and I will share examples of husbands and wives who have joined forces to achieve both his dreams and hers. Believe me, it is totally, wonderfully possible; but it is also a fine line. I know; I've walked it for years, beginning that day on the running trail.

The rising sun became as bright and hot as the lamp of an interrogator while I asked myself a lot of hard questions that morning—not questions about the quest, but about me. Am I willing, I wondered…

- to go through the process?
- to stick out the tough times?
- to actually contribute to the cause?
- to share my man?
- to let him shine?
- to defend the dream?

After several miles of prayerful, meditative Q&A, I made my final decision. Cassie looked up.

"It's okay, girl," I whispered. "He will do his best for us. I trust him. I have to."

Committing out loud sealed the deal. I would not prevent my man from reaching his potential; I would see that he achieved it. Love left me little choice. As a much older Abigail Adams wrote (after decades of marriage), "Who shall give me back Time? Who shall compensate to me those years I cannot recall? How dearly have I paid for a titled Husband; should I wish you less wise, that I might enjoy more happiness? I cannot find that in my heart" (*Adams Family Papers*, 25 October 1782, MHS). Like Abigail, I couldn't bear to limit what he, and consequently *we*, would become.

I ran all the way home to tell him.

"Honey!" I burst through the front door, panting. "You can do it! I want you to do it."

It took a minute for him to track what I was saying. Then, with something between a laugh and a cry, he picked me up and kissed me hard. It was only a kiss, but it felt like much more.

It felt like the birth of a nation.

25
What Dream Makers Are Made of

You don't marry one person; you marry three: the person you think they are, the person they are, and the person they are going to become as a result of being married to you.—*Richard Needham, British politician*

So now it's your turn. Take a break, take a walk, and take this book. It's time to consider: whose dream is it, anyway...*yours, mine, or ours*?

Becoming a Dream Maker involves a number of prerequisites, which we have spent a whole book discussing. We learned how to identify and avoid behaviors and attitudes that push him away, as well as how to cultivate habits and outlooks that draw him toward you. All of that is necessary to becoming his companion and Intimate, but if you want to go places that only a few even dream of, you have to go one step further. You have to become his inspiration; that is, a fully-vested Dream Maker.

So far, we have discussed the first step in that process: becoming a Dream *Seeker*, the partner who helps him find his quest. Once the two of you have that settled—and maybe even before then—you will need to go through some serious self-analysis: the same introspection Abigail Smith Adams, Nancy Davis Reagan, Lillian Moller Gilbreth, Anne Morrow Lindbergh, Ellen Louise Wilson, Emily Warren Roebling, and many other powerful wives have undertaken. I'll guide you through it, step by step. I highly recommend journaling your answers as you go, even augmenting them as your thoughts change and develop. I'll warn you though, that doing this right will take more than a couple of hours; it could take days or even weeks. Deciding when you are ready to become a Dream *Believer*—the pre-requisite to becoming a Dream Keeper and ultimately, a Dream Weaver—is a very personal process. It will be different for every woman, individual to every Wife for Life.

Ready to start?

Your Dream Believer Q&A

Am I willing to go through the process with him? Since pursuing a quest is not only about action, it's about ideas—and good ideas are as much evolutionary as they are revolutionary —your husband's quest will take a lot of processing. That means you can anticipate going backward as often as you go forward, subtracting as much as adding, breaking down as much as building up, decreasing as much as increasing. Together, you will mold his dream like a piece of clay, shaping and reshaping as you discover something new (an opportunity, a perspective, a talent) or cast off something old (a plan, a relationship, a failure). Dream-Believer flexibility takes commitment. Dream-Believer elasticity takes discipline. Though it may appear ironic—like a supple dancer (flexibility, elasticity) beside a rigid soldier (commitment, discipline)—you must see yourself as both. Reality will demand it as you journey through the *process.*

Am I willing to go through the tough times with him? Life isn't all fun and games, as they say, and pursuing a quest, while rewarding, is also rigorous. As Anne Morrow Lindbergh reminisced: "I was plunged into life— active life—loving and living and having children and those terrific trips and the suffering too" (*Anne Morrow Lindbergh*, p. 205). You must remember in the midst of such trials, however, that men, in general, want to solve problems and confront challenges. Your man may appear consternated when blocked or foiled, but pushing through complicated times is what he's all about. The real problem is how hard those times are on you— especially if you feel responsible for smoothing the way or alleviating the pain. You are *not* wholly responsible for doing either. The quandaries of a quest are part of the grand glory in it. Fixing a mess that's he's stumbled into (by his own actions or those of others) is not what he most needs from you; it may even push him away. What he craves from his partner is calm confidence and sympathy, even a light touch of optimism. If he wants to talk it through and get your input or expertise, you will roll up your sleeves and get to the dirty jobs, but first you must be willing to let him do what he can and must, even if that means his working it out silently and independently while you stand by ready to back, boost, or belay as needed.

Am I willing to contribute to the cause? Taking an idea and turning it into a reality is what *Wife for Life* is all about. I hope I've made it clear by now that the process of going from a concept to something you can see, hear, feel, or touch takes work. That's why, frankly, so many people fail to achieve their dreams: they aren't willing to put in the blood, sweat, and tears. It may be even more daunting to have to learn something new, to stretch yourself personally. Every one of the amazing wives I studied not only supported her husband's dream but she got her own hands muddy by lending a hand. These wives were also willing to learn new things. Anne Morrow Lindbergh, for instance, became Charles Lindbergh's relief pilot, radio operator, copilot, and navigator during their expeditions around the world in the 1930s, receiving prestigious awards and worldwide acclaim for her skill—and she had never flown before meeting her husband. Lillian Moller Gilbreth became an astute research partner to her husband, earning a Ph.D. and accolades in a field completely foreign to her until she met Frank Gilbreth. And reserved Nancy Reagan found herself out on the campaign trail all by her lonesome during Ronald Reagan's political bids—despite her dread of public speaking. Like Bess Read, of whom it was said, "When Bess Burdine married Lieutenant Commander Putty Read, the U.S. Navy got two for the price of one," all these women had so much faith in their husband, they were willing to add personal value to his quest.

Am I willing to share my man? This question proved the hardest for me to reconcile. I expect it will be for a lot of women. But if a real quest is Shareable—in that it's about benefiting others—then your *husband* will necessarily be as shareable as his *dream*. In other words, other people (maybe a lot of other people) will need him. They will expect his time and energy. Additionally, since a quest is sizeable and showable —in that you want him to excel at some creative endeavor— you will have to encourage him to improve himself. That may mean regular time away from you while he attends class, works out in the gym, meets with a mentor, goes on an adventure, or serves in the church or community. I love the example of Woodrow Wilson's wife, Ellen, in this regard. She was proud of her husband when he was unanimously elected President of Princeton University, but she also wept over the bigger world he was stepping into and the social activity it would necessarily require. Until then, they and their two daughters had enjoyed such a pleasant, private family life. The new service predictably drained her, but when it almost killed Woodrow, she persuaded him to take an ocean voyage to England and from there, a bicycle tour of Scotland. The fact that they could not afford for both of them to go did not keep her from sharing her husband—even with himself.

Am I willing to enjoy his success and let him shine? This may be sticky if you have any sense of competition with your husband. The woman who can turn off those instincts so as to graciously let her man feel the full impact of his success (which, remember, is integral to his sense of worth) is a woman truly in love. Though she may have worked just as hard, or maybe even harder, to achieve, she will appreciate the fact that her husband has a great, perhaps a greater, need for recognition from the world than she does. There is no place, really, in a wife's loving relationship with her husband for competitive pride. I find the accounts of Elizabeth Bowes-Lyon, wife of Albert, Duke of York (reluctant inheritor of the British throne as George VI in 1936), very beautiful for that reason. Elizabeth was a supporter, facilitator, and confidante to her husband, who had a speech impediment that threatened to make him an object of ridicule in the public eye. She grew accustomed to stepping forward in many situations to do the talking for him and thus saved her husband the embarrassment of speaking. However, they worked hard to overcome his handicap, and as he became more and more adroit at speaking in public, she knew when to step back. After one of his speeches to Parliament a newspaper reported, "One does not need to be clairvoyant to understand what was passing through the Queen's mind. When the King had finished she could not keep from her eyes the pride of a woman in her husband" (*The King's Speech*, p. 134). Elizabeth so appreciated her husband's need to shine that she not only allowed it, she did everything she could to make it happen.

Am I willing to defend the dream? In the 1947 Western, *Sea of Grass*, starring Katherine Hepburn and Spencer Tracy, a young wife from the city cannot accept her husband's dream of protecting the pristine American prairie for cattle grazing. She believes the land should be open to settlers. Her very basic difference of opinion, or as he saw it, lack of loyalty to his quest, eventually erodes the marriage until the couple becomes alienated for years. In the end, after much tragedy, they are reconciled, but it's too late to save the prairie. Her rancher-husband's prophecies about how greedy use of the land would devastate it prove true. The same scenario could play out in your house—not the ruin of the prairie, obviously, but the ruin of your marriage. It is critical that you think long and hard on the question of loyalty at the start of the quest because if you have any philosophical issues with his dream, the split in your belief systems could rip you apart.

Emily Warren Roebling must have gone through that kind of deep reflection when her husband became chief engineer of New York's City's most ambitious public-works project in the mid-nineteenth century: building the Brooklyn Bridge. For the next fourteen years he would be obliged to court public opinion constantly while fighting the politicians incessantly—in addition to supervising construction. It was absolutely critical that his wife and partner stand on *his side* of the bridge, so to speak. And she did. In fact, the project tested her loyalty far more than either of them had anticipated. Five years into the mammoth enterprise, when most of the bridge was still a blueprint, Washington Roebling became permanently disabled in the execution of his dangerous duties. Refusing to give in, Emily assumed several important roles: constant companion, nurse, private secretary, emissary, and unofficial aide-de-camp; so great was her involvement that many people insinuated she had taken over as chief engineer. Her extraordinary strength and resolve made it possible for Washington to direct the work from his sick room while watching the construction from a window. I like to imagine the two of them sitting at that window, discussing the dream as it takes form right in front of their eyes, day by day, year by year, despite pain, tedium, and exhaustion, overcoming all obstacles, defying every political scheme— together.

Now I ask you: whose dream was it, that bridge? Did it belong to Washington, to Emily, or to the *Roeblings?* Emily was the first to actually ride across the finished product, by the way, and took a starring role in the greatest fanfare and celebration of the century. Do you suppose, amidst bells, whistles, trumpets, rockets, and cheers, that Emily cared one whit which of them originated the dream?

So there you go: six life-staking questions. I know they're not easy to answer. They are not supposed to be. Your responses will lead you to places you can hardly conceive of right now, and they require acting on your gut. I, for one, believe you will find the faith you need after honest introspection, as well as the creativity and the courage you need to demonstrate that faith. Your heart will eventually tell you what powerful wives already know: to cherish the man but not his quest is virtually impossible. Confidence in the one is faith in the other.

26
Dream Keeper

When you look at the ones that went on forever, it's not because they were based on love, sex, romance, passion. It's because the woman was made of granite.
—*Cindy Adams, syndicated columnist*

Washington Roebling honored his wife, Emily, with these words: "At first I thought I would succumb, but I had a strong tower to lean upon, my wife, a woman of infinite tact and wisest counsel" (*The Great Bridge*, p. 452). How wonderful for a bridge builder to talk about his wife as a "strong tower," because the towers on either side of a bridge are exactly what supports the superstructure. When completed, the towers of the Brooklyn Bridge stood 278 feet above the East River and rested upon 3,000-ton caissons—a foundation that has lasted about 130 years to date.

Lionel Logue, personal coach and speech therapist to King George VI, used the same tower metaphor in a letter to Elizabeth, the queen, when she became a widow:

> "Since 1926 he honoured me, by allowing me to help him with his speech, & no man ever worked as hard as he did, & achieved such a grand result. During all those years you were a tower of strength to him & he has often told me how much he owed to you, and the excellent result could never have been achieved if it had not been for your help" (*The King's Speech*, p. 225).

The point is clear: bridges and kingdoms would fall without women standing strong. Men are *not* naturally confident—despite the bravado—and when their abilities are in question (especially in their own minds) they hunger for a woman's reassurance. No matter what stage of the quest is before him, your husband will stop, turn, and look back at you before stepping into the unknown. He needs the kind of courage only a life partner can give— especially when his quest is in jeopardy. He will lean upon you, his inspiration, not only to soothe and buoy him, but to direct and even mold him. If you can do this with Emily Roebling's "infinite tact," you will go from being his Dream Seeker and Dream Believer, to becoming his one and only Dream *Keeper*.

To earn and hold the precious position of Dream Keeper, you need to arm yourself with the proper responses for those days he needs you most: when he's afraid that he doesn't matter or that he can't do it. As a former student of mine wrote to his wife in the dedication of his Ph.D. thesis: "To my wife, Kira, thanks for your love, understanding, and support through these years, and for keeping me going the many times I was close to giving up." A Dream Keeper uses her power to dispel doubt. Singlehandedly, she can often reignite his fire just by adding a little fresh kindling. As the flame spurts to life and gains momentum, she can judiciously add more fuel until she's got her man roaring again.

I've tried to help you remember the reignition process, by giving every *stick of kindling* a phrase that begins with the letter "R."

Reassure him of your devotion. The easiest thing in the world for a truly nurturing woman to do is reassure. She doesn't do this by insisting a man think like she does, but by lovingly asking questions and listening sympathetically and empathetically to his answers. She speaks to him physically as well, with whole-hearted intimacy. In this gentle way, she assures him that he matters a lot—at least to her. For example, when King George struggled in public with his stutter, Elizabeth communicated her reassurance by reaching out and squeezing his fingers; the flustered king, ready to give up, would regain control and go on. His wife's opinion mattered far more than anyone else's. Just as a tiny twig gives a dwindling fire new hope, it takes very little to reassure your man that he matters to you.

Review the positives. While your husband may be vulnerable to the criticism of others, it is the Dream Keeper's job to remind him that a quest is about living *his* truth—no one else's! If all he ever accomplished was to live a life congruent with his beliefs, he would be making a significant contribution to the world. His example of doing his best as he follows his quest has a profound impact—on you, on your children, on family, on friends, and on the many others who become aware of what he is doing—whether or not anyone else's expectations are met. One way to help him overcome frustration or disappointment is to focus on the *journey* instead of the *results* —a healthy way of approaching the quest anytime. Notice and point out what he's learning or how he's growing along the way, as well as the people he influences and inspires. There is a beautiful example of this in the 1939 film, *Good-bye Mr. Chips* (Denham Studios, 1939), in which the lovely Greer Garson consistently steers her husband's attention toward his impact as a schoolmaster on young boys. Because of her ability to see the positive and draw timely attention to it, the meek Mr. Chips becomes the most legendary and influential headmaster the school has ever seen. If you can help your husband look beyond his unfulfilled expectations to his accomplishments, especially as he ages, you have added another log to the fire.

Restructure the vision. While reviewing the positive is basically about looking back in time, or at least at the here and now, restructuring the vision is focused on the future. Though events or circumstances may defer or derail his quest, a discouraging episode or stage of life can also prove advantageous. Life has a way of redirecting us when we need it, and a wife can help her husband see this, though the ultimate destination may be obscure at the time. Ronald Reagan's declining Hollywood career, for instance, as demoralizing as it was, forced him to accept the invitation to become a celebrity ambassador for General Electric (just to pay the bills). The job required appearances and speeches at GE factories across the nation, which exposed him to thousands of American workers. Their collective plight gradually affected his views, not only reversing his political opinions, but inspiring him to become part of the solution. His wife helped him to see in this, a new calling and supported his run for office—first as the governor of California and eventually as President of the United States. Just think: What if Nancy had lost her head under pressure when her husband was in crisis? If a man's passion is declining, he needs a partner who will help him regroup. That may mean restructuring the vision in order to approach the quest from a completely different angle.

Recommit yourselves to the dream. I love the story of Jeffery and Patricia Holland. They married as college students and predictably began life with absolutely no money. One day, walking hand in hand across campus, the couple contemplated their austere life. As undergrads, earning a Ph.D. seemed light years away. Jeffrey turned to his wife and said, "Honey, should we give up? I can get a good job and carve out a good living for us. I can do some things. I'll be okay without a degree. Should we stop trying to tackle what right now seems so difficult to face?" ("Remember Lot's Wife," *http:// speeches.byu.edu*) Pat must have felt just as hungry, scared, and overwhelmed as he did. But instead of agreeing with him, or letting his desperation get to her, she responded in a way that her husband would never forget: "She grabbed me by the lapels and said, 'We are not going back. We are not going home. The future holds *everything* for us.' She stood there in the sunlight that day and gave me a real talk." It must have been some kind of talk, because twenty years later, Jeffery R. Holland became president of the very university he had wanted to quit. (Can you imagine all the kissing and reminiscing that went on that day?) Like a fresh wind, Patricia's foresight and recommitment lifted their ship of dreams out of the doldrums.

Reenergize his masculine zest. Though any or all of the first four suggestions can help reinvigorate your man when he is questioning his worth or his future, there is one last tactic you may need to use for reigniting the fire. Since masculine zest is the energy source for a masculine quest, he may be dangerously low on zest. This is different from feeling tired— something sleep, rest, exercise, nutrition, or medical help will resolve. If you've tried all those remedies with no effect, you may be looking at what I call zest depletion. This is your man in an ongoing funk because he doubts himself or his quest in ways that you can't seem to shake him out of. Day after day he is troubled, even paralyzed, by despondency—which you know is not his usual mode of operation. One way to refill his tank is to send him on an adventure—one of those exploits we discussed in Chapter 21. Encourage him to challenge himself in a setting or at an endeavor totally unrelated to his quest, something very appealing to him, something he normally wouldn't have given himself permission to do, or that he worries you wouldn't approve of because it seems extravagant or stressful. If he can spend several hours (or better yet, several days) concentrating on something that excites him, that challenges him, that reaffirms his masculinity outside of his work or quest, it can kick start his sputtering engine. Restore his zest and you'll reenergize the quest (or the quest for a quest). Remember, he needs his quest to thrive.

I want to emphasize that helping your man take up arms and rejoin the fray is a reoccurring responsibility. He's not a one-time fixer-upper. Because his confidence will fluctuate for the rest of his life, you may repeatedly have to help him battle his fear of failure or of becoming emotionally overwhelmed. Peaks and valleys will test the strength of his convictions. Contests between heart and fate will challenge his masculinity. The world will throw down the gauntlet again and again as if to say, *Come on then, let's see what you're made of.* But it's not always what he's made of—it's often what you're made of.

The great British social emancipator of the late eighteenth and early nineteenth centuries, William Wilberforce, struggled for years to abolish the slave trade. The colossal odds against him and his fellow reformers, compounded by failure after failure, wore him down to a thread. At age thirty-seven, finding himself wishing "not to finish my journey alone" (*Hero for Humanity*, p. 252), he met Barbara Spooner and fell deeply in love. In her he recognized something that would not only complete him, but could renew his fighting spirit, giving him the muscle he needed to finish the race. Because Barbara was indeed made of loving granite, Wilberforce felt empowered again and again to venture into the conflict, leading charge after charge until the Slavery Abolition Act of 1833 was at last ratified, just three days before his death. In the final scene of *Amazing Grace* (Four Boys Films/Walden Media, 2006), the dramatization of Wilberforce's heroic struggle, he humbly accepts the thunderous ovation of Parliament. With the passage of the act, hundreds of thousands of men, women, and children are freed. At that ineffable moment, when all creation is singing his praises, William looks only at Barbara. Their locked gazes, brimming with emotion, say everything.

A quest in crisis, then, is your prime opportunity to:

- Reassure him of your devotion.
- Review the positives.
- Restructure the vision.
- Recommit yourselves to the dream.
- Reenergize his masculine zest.

When you can do all that with "infinite tact," you will not only keep the fire burning, you will become the strongest, most powerful partner in the world...the *Keeper* of his Dreams.

27
Dream Weaver

I know that my life would be stripped of the great part of its worthiness and its
power to achieve if I did not have you to love and to serve, and from whom to
receive that love and sympathy which are the life of my heart. And our love
warrants me in concluding that it is just the same with you,
that it has been my privilege to make your life complete…
—*President Woodrow Wilson, in a letter to his wife*

On April 25, 2011, Dale and I visited Salzburg, Austria. On April 26, I wrote the following in my journal:

As a child, I nearly wore out my brand new Sound of Music vinyl record–I played it so often, over and over through the years. As I grew up, the movie and the real story behind the Sound of Music *became the lyrics of my life, while the melodies became the underscore. So yesterday when my Captain kissed me in the same gazebo that Liesl got her sweet-sixteen kiss, I figured we must have followed the right rainbows, because we'd certainly found our dream. However, Dale's experience during that kiss was different than mine because the dream he'd found was different than mine. In his version of our kiss, we weren't Christopher Plummer and Julie Andrews, but more Wolfgang and Constance Mozart. Although he appreciates musical theater, Mozart, not Maria, brings him to tears. Imagine his feelings as we walked through the Maestro's town and toured the home he grew up in. His hand gripped mine all the tighter as we entered the very church Mozart played regularly in as organist, and his face became virtually luminous during the concert at the top of Salzburg's world-famous Hohenwerfen Fortress. We spent half the day in my dream and the other half in his.*

Dale and I have lived in and visited a lot of places and done a lot of interesting things, always in pursuit of one thing: our dreams, meaning the dreams of both of us. Like two sets of threads woven to form a single fabric, we have turned toward each other for help in fulfilling our individual ambitions while balancing a life full of practicalities. Over-under, over-under, over-under: sometimes his quest is the priority, and sometimes my dreams take precedence. Give and take for the sake of mutual progress and happiness is one of the highest orders-of-living a couple can attain, but it requires lots of love and patience—years of investment. The surest way to a married life of accomplishment and personal growth—not just for him, but for you—is to offer him First Respect while responding to him with the A's as well as taking up your critical role as Dream Seeker, Dream Believer, and Dream Keeper through the decades. When you consistently respond in a loving way to your Nice Guy, he focuses on making your dreams come true. As George Bailey says to Mary in It's a Wonderful Life (Liberty Films II, 1946), "What is it you want, Mary? You want the moon? If you do, just say the word; I'll throw a lasso around it and pull it down for you." Remember: He lives and longs for your happiness.

Once, in a workshop on finances for writers, something the teacher said riveted my attention. She told us that she handled the money side of her husband's business, a family business really, which I didn't think all that remarkable. However, what did strike me as curiously wonderful was the fact that she had hated math all her life and possessed no accounting skills when she got the job, and yet, here she was—standing in front of dozens of inept bookkeepers as an expert! I had to know this woman. A few weeks later, she confirmed my suspicions in a video-call interview: the math flunky turned business manager is actually a fully vested

Dream Maker.

It all began for Sandra when she married Howard, her Nice Guy. Though he was a very artistic guy, Howard climbed the corporate ladder to fill the cupboards. For eleven years. Meanwhile, Sandra, who had not forgotten her husband's creative side, determined they would be ready when the right idea and opportunity came along. She saved. She paid off debt. She watched and listened and engaged her husband's creative juices like a Dream Seeker. Then, about eight years into their marriage, Howard picked up a pencil and doodled. Something clicked. With every spare minute and on every spare piece of paper, he sketched a comic strip world with fully developed characters and story-lines. An online community started to follow his strip (called *Schlock Mercenary*) and gave him so much confidence that, after four years of doodling for fun, they both knew it was time to jump. He left his seventy-hour workweek in upper-level management and became a full-time artist. The transition was not easy; in fact Sandra says it was downright terrifying. For the next two years they couldn't see past the next three months, but she believed in him, and not only pared down the family budget, but became very good at both financial management and book publishing. Today, their family business supports a household of six. Howard is very happy. And Sandra is a writer, her life's dream. Working together, they did what they had to until both their dreams began to come true.

Sandra is in good company. Of all the powerful wives I studied in biography after biography, the ones that impressed me the most were the Dream *Weavers*: women like Anne Lindbergh, who wrote several critically acclaimed memoirs detailing the couple's aviation feats. Another renowned author, Ayn Rand, published her popular novels in the mid-1900s while supporting her husband's artistic talent. And of course, the brand "Julia Child" (amateur chef turned world phenomenon), was actually a husband and wife *team*.

One of my very favorite historical Dream Weavers is Lillian Gilbreth. Her marriage is described by the biographer in this beautiful passage:

> "...it was a partnership rooted in the most amazing fulfillments of love and marriage as well as in work of an unusual character for a woman. In the first quarter of the twentieth century these two lived and worked together for twenty years as man and wife in a home to which twelve children were born and, simultaneously, as creative partners in an important profession then in its birth throes" (*Frank and Lillian*, p. 3)

Lillian's beloved Frank (who called her his "absolutely perfect half") died suddenly after only two decades of marriage. He had been about to embark on an important tour of Europe, so Lillian sailed instead and gave his speeches and ultimately carried on their work in management and motion study for another quarter of a century. She became not only an engineer, but a management consultant, a professor, a government advisor, and one of America's most celebrated women in the mid-twentieth century.

Scientist Marie Curie also lost her cherished husband and partner, just as their discovery of radium was making them famous across the world (a dream she had originated). Twelve years earlier he had proposed to her with these words: "It would be a fine thing...in which I hardly dare believe, to pass our lives near each other, hypnotized by our dreams: *your* patriotic dream, *our* humanitarian dream, and *our* scientific dream" (*Marie Curie*, p. 130). His death left his Sorbonne teaching post vacant. Though a woman had never spoken at the University of Paris before, Marie Curie, who shared the 1903 Nobel Prize in physics with Pierre and another physicist, became the natural inheritor of the Sorbonne chair. On the day of her first lecture to Pierre's students, the classroom amphitheater overflowed with additional faculty, reporters, and curiosity seekers. Her biographer (also her daughter) describes the occasion arrestingly:

> "Half-past one....The door at the back opened, and Marie Curie walked to the chair in a storm of applause. She inclined her head. It was a dry little movement intended as a salute...[The ovation] ceased suddenly: before this pale woman, who was trying to compose her face, an unknown emotion silenced the crowd that had come for a show.
>
> Marie stared straight ahead of her and said: 'When one considers the progress that has been made in physics in the past ten years, one is surprised at the advance that has taken place in our ideas concerning electricity and matter...'"
>
> Mme Curie had resumed the course at the precise sentence where Pierre Curie had left it" (*Marie Curie*, p. 259).

I cried when I read that.

My favorite tourist spot in central London is Westminster Abbey. Walking through that immortal church is something like shouldering your way through a crowded, solemn assembly of famous people; their names whispered in stone, rising from the floors to ricochet off vaulted ceilings. Dale stood and cried at the foot of Handel's tomb while I sat in a stupor beside memorials to Jane Austen, the Bronte sisters, Charles Dickens, and Shakespeare. Together we gazed up at statues of fallen soldiers and bent over the tombs of scientists and statesmen. Weaving our way through the memories of this host of human beings both inspired us and made us feel small. Where do we fit in? Of what value are we to our fellow man?

I found the answer in the marriages of historically powerful husbands and wives. Though the kings and queens of England, or the Adamses of America, the Lindberghs, the Gilbreths, the Wilsons, the Wilberforces, the Roeblings, the Reagans, the Rands, the Childses, and the Curies may have come from times and places a little foreign to us—and though they may have achieved feats we will never come close to—they are still in essence very much like Dale and me. Every one of the women in these celebrated couples longed for, more than anything else, to cherish and to be cherished by her husband. And every one of these famous men wanted nothing more than to have an inspiring woman at his side and to please her.

I now fancy myself a marriage protégé of great husbands and wives. What I learned from them—above all the lessons of the Dream Seeker, Dream Believer, Dream Keeper, and Dream Weaver —is this: the spirit of a virtuous romance can be felt everywhere and for eons to come: its beauty and solidarity will affect all who come to know it, as well as all who descend from it. The world needs—even craves—mature, splendid marriages because authentic lovers give the rest of us courage to live up to our promises.

Holding Dale's hand as we exited the Abbey, I began to muse all over again how he and I will never be important anybodys in this life, not by Westminster standards. No ornate crypts or elaborate epitaphs for us. And yet, if a woman can adore her husband with all her heart and inspire him in turn to adore her with all of his, if together they can nurture his quest and her dreams through grand and grievous days, is that not one of life's greatest attainments?

28
Beyond Good and Great, There is Grand

Every joy of [my most happy courtship and honeymoon] is mine still,
undimmed, and in addition—ah, how much deeper, more wonderful joy—
that which springs from the deep confidence and infinite peace
which you have taught me to feel in your love.
—*Ellen Axson Wilson, to her husband, Woodrow Wilson*

We have spoken a great deal about *grand marriage*, and I hope by now you can not only picture it, but want it badly. As one hopeful Dream Maker wrote me, "I'm so excited for the chance to have a grand marriage. In my life, I have not witnessed any grand marriages, yet I know in my heart and soul that it does exist. I would love to provide that example to my children and grandchildren, as well as to all of my family, and now I have the information, support, and resources to make it so." Yes, you do. As you begin applying the Dream Maker principles, you will see your relationship improve almost immediately, but you have a long road ahead of you. If you want more than an initial flush of success, then you will need to regularly remind yourself of everything you have learned by tuning into my social sites and support system at *ramonazabriskie.com,* including helpful videos, video courses, and blog posts. You may also consider joining other women for support and in-depth instruction in one of my popular Wife for Life University classes that meet by live conferencing. Regardless, I hope our association is just beginning. I want to see for myself how you and your husband go from good to great, and I hope ultimately to see you experience a grand marriage that is characterized by:

- Exclusivity,
- Steadfastness,
- Deep Regard, and
- Imagination.

Beyond Togetherness There Is Exclusivity

I have done my best up to this point, to fulfill the charge commissioned me that day in my garden (see Preface); the same hint of an errand I felt standing at the Wailing Wall in Jerusalem (Chapter 4) and the whispered prompt I heard kneeling at Lucy Criclow's memorial in Bath, England (Chapter 22). I have conducted my search for answers with all the breadth, earnestness, intelligence, and determination I could muster. Yet even as I pored over books and studies, talked with experts, and searched my own heart and experience, I remained well aware and humbled by the fact that marriage is always to some extent a mystery.

As Walter Bagehot, mid-nineteenth century English economist and journalist, wrote to his wife, Eliza:

> "We seem to have a deep life together apart from all other people on earth, and which we cannot show, explain or impart to them. At least my affection seems to isolate me in the deepest moments from all others, and it makes me speak with my whole heart and soul to you and you only. And perhaps this isolation is one reason why deep love makes one feel—at least in some moments—so religious" (*Love Letters*, p. 23).

Walter and Eliza's subsequently long marriage can, in part, be attributed to the fact that, from the very beginning, they embraced and protected their isolation. They treated their "deep life together apart from all other people on earth" almost like a religion.

Indescribable feelings between a loving husband and wife become sanctified through secrecy—that is, the guarding of intimate conversation, the protection of confidences, the shielding of shared experience. Private one-on-one is made holy when a couple can testify from the depths of their soul that they know and love each other in a way that no one else can possibly comprehend; the whole of their shared story belongs only to them. If you want a grand marriage like that—a secret, walled-in garden that blossoms more and more each year—then you have to cultivate your alliance using these two important strategies:

> **Spend time with other people.** Didn't we just say that a grand marriage is exclusive? Yes, but keeping company with people who respect and support your marriage can actually strengthen your exclusivity. If your friendships include couples with exemplary marriages themselves, all the better; their influence will intensify the bond between you and your husband. We spent a recent Easter with two of our favorite families. Sitting around the dining room table, I saw each husband put an arm around his wife while they leaned toward one another—and it inspired me. Dale and I surround ourselves with friends, who— like the tulips and daffodils that bunch up around our woods each spring—grow and blossom *with* us. These friends do not have the key to our secret garden, which is closely guarded, nor do we have the key to what belongs only to them, but the roses we see cascading over the walls allow us to imagine the abundance inside those marriages. Our romance is richer for theirs.

> **Spend time alone—just the two of you.** A young husband once wrote me: "I feel you need to go out and do things together to keep the fire going in the relationship. I mean, that's how friendships work, so shouldn't marriages work the same?"

Of course, he is clearly, obviously, let's-get-out-of-here right. This one simple rule, practiced consistently, could take almost any marriage from good to great, and maybe all the way to grand.

Besides our *weekly* date night *away from the house* (absolutely imperative for thirty-five years), Dale has regularly insisted that I wave bye-bye to the kiddies, pack the pretties, and become just his—somewhere else— at least once or twice annually. He knows that a change of costume and character rejuvenates us. Finding out that we're not irreplaceable at home liberates us. Exclusivity as best friends and lovers revitalizes us. And memories pile up like wood for winter fires. For a night or two or three, anything is possible.

Shall I tell you how we walked in the rain on the beaches of Honolulu? Or about the time he kissed me in Times Square? No, I don't think I will; each of these moments is too luscious, too surreptitious, and too secret. What I will tell you is that they didn't happen when we had loads of money or time or independence (quite the opposite), and they didn't happen in the garage, the family room, or even our bedroom. They happened, as those particular moments can only happen, when we took the time and set aside the money to go *somewhere else* on a regular basis.

Grand marriage then is set apart by the rareness of it. The wise husband and wife who respect and protect their singular connection ironically exhibit it to the entire world. Everyone can sense their confederacy and are blessed by it, but no one will ever see inside the private guild, the secret society, or the castle on the hill, because of the couple's commitment to *exclusivity.*

Good marriage: togetherness.

Great marriage: intimacy.

Grand Marriage: exclusivity.

Beyond Commitment There Is Steadfastness

The unity created by exclusivity is absolutely essential to the next characteristic in a grand marriage: *steadfastness*. I think I can best illustrate this trait with a true story about the romance that has affected mine more than any other.

When my parents met at a church dance, they say it only took twenty minutes to fall in love. Soon after their marriage, they bought the house my great-grandfather had built and settled in. All the relatives eventually moved to other places, but my parents stayed on. Then the children grew up and away, but they stayed on. Grandchildren and great-grandchildren came and went by the dozens, and still, Mom and Dad stayed on. In fact, a whopping fifty-six years after their first dance, my parents still live and love from the same house on the same street in the same town I grew up in.

Because of this family pattern, I too am bred for the habitual, the regular, the repetitive. My father and mother have modeled permanence in a way that has made adapting to new circumstances (a house, a neighborhood, a country) a bit uneasy for me, but I have found that their example compensates me with something far more important: a natural desire and commitment to constancy.

A close friend observed a couple of years ago, "Dale and Ramona are acting more and more like Ray and Sharon" (my parents). I wasn't sure what she meant until the day I walked through tiny Bray Village on the outskirts of London. Each adorable, aged cottage radiated contentment and sameness, like art by Thomas Kinkade. The paned windows glowed from inside, and I imagined old men and women spending an evening together exactly like hundreds of evenings before this one. The vision suddenly illuminated what my friend meant to say about Dale and me. In comparing us to my parents, she was referring to our oneness: cohesiveness created by steadiness, by which I am deeply flattered.

Grand marriage then is both undergirded and crowned by the absolutely dependable devotion and unswerving character trait I call *steadfastness.*

Good marriage: commitment.

Great marriage: faithfulness.

Grand Marriage: steadfastness.

Beyond Respect There Is Deep Regard

While exclusivity contributes to steadfastness, the next trait of a grand marriage absolutely relies on both. I want to share a personal story now that I have saved just to illustrate this point.

One day, over thirty years ago, I was with a group of young mothers like myself when I realized that I had an opportunity to get some much-needed support. I suddenly blurted out, "I'm afraid my baby will never grow up."

The other young mothers looked shocked. They immediately dismissed my disconcerting premonition with a round of, "Ohhhh, don't worry. You're just a brand-new mom." One woman patted my hand and the other pulled back the quilt around my Ashley's infant face: a countenance as lovely and flawless as Snow White's.

"They're right. You don't need to worry," she whispered. "Your little girl is perfect."

But within a year, my suspicions were confirmed. Doctors told us that because of Ashley's intellectual and physical limitations, she would never walk or talk. Dale and I held each other and cried.

Though some might call it a tragedy, I'm going to call what we have experienced with Ashley—like many other potentially devastating situations—a trial. Living through precarious circumstances has *tried* us again and again; in other words, it has given us a chance to prove ourselves to ourselves. There have been innumerable occasions when I felt beyond exhausted caring for Ashley while I was pregnant with, or raising, three other children in addition to work and responsibilities outside the home. Dale has often returned from his business totally spent, only to face a pile of medical bills and a mountain of household demands—as well as a wife who needed relief from heavy-duty caregiving. We were able to push through all that, in addition to other upheavals, because we finally accepted that if there is one thing you can expect from life, it's the *un*expected. Once we stopped looking for someone to blame, including each other, we could *brace* each other.

I remember one poignant episode that helped us learn this lesson—a night that, while it robbed us of life, taught us about life.

My pregnancy had been going fine, yet here I was, nearly five months into it, shocked at having just experienced an involuntary, spontaneous miscarriage. Dale, the only other human being present, looked at me through a waterfall of grief and anguish. In that exquisitely personal moment, something passed between us. The English language cannot describe it adequately. The best I can come up with is *deep regard.*

Deep regard goes far beyond respect and is different than love. It is a direct product of facing challenges and adversity not only together or at the same time, but as *one*. If a husband and wife agree to sink or swim in tandem, to stand by one another despite fear and pandemonium, the unexpected will cement their relationship instead of breaking it up. It takes courage. It takes guts. It may take everything you have to give: I've been lifting, showering, dressing, toileting, and feeding my daughter, as well as acting as her voice and her advocate for over thirty years while Dale has worked as many jobs as required to pay for her therapy and care—but you cannot give up on one another during the trials of life if you want a grand marriage.

One of the most impressive examples I have seen of this principle in action is in the life of my friend, Heidi Ashworth. She is a romance novelist who says it's "only fitting that the story of my marriage should be full of drama, passion, and epic challenges." During the course of their twenty-seven years together, Heidi's husband has been out of work eight times due to health problems. They struggled for years with infertility and miscarriage, though they eventually had three children. When the oldest began exhibiting bipolar behavior, it seriously affected the family. Heidi and the younger children eventually developed stress-related problems. "Only five percent of couples who have endured what we did are still married," she says. That feat is even more astounding considering how few resources the family had to draw on during the toughest times.

Luckily, one of those resources was Heidi. A self-described romantic idealist who looks for the happy ending in every story, she has resisted the temptation to pity or to blame, and instead loves her husband for his genuine goodness, talents, and commitment to the family. "It is clear to me," she says, "that he has done his absolute best every minute of every day and has continued to love me even during my lowest points." In reviewing their marriage, Heidi can see that their trials have actually enriched their relationship. She calls it "crazy in love" but I detect something more. The Ashworths clearly have deep regard for one another. As legendary American author, Washington Irving, once said, "No man knows what the wife of his bosom is until he has gone with her through the fiery trials of this world."

In a grand marriage, then, your seafaring blood rises to the surface in order to survive the storms. It is possible to actually benefit from life's trials if your marriage is infused with a combination of exclusivity, steadfastness, and *deep regard*.

Good marriage: respect.

Great marriage: admiration.

Grand marriage: deep regard.

Exclusivity. Steadfastness. Deep Regard. That leaves one more attribute to share in our characterization of a grand marriage. I present it to you last, like a scrumptious dessert carried by white gloves on a silver platter. It is no less than *the* secret that makes everything possible and worthwhile. I call it your *best imagination*.

29
Your Best Imagination

Yesterday's fairy tale is today's fact.
—Anne Morrow Lindbergh, writer and aviator

On the most thrilling day of my life, you and I set sail thinking our waves would be ripples and our winds nothing more than breezes. But the storms came, of course, and we held on with a white-knuckle grip. Shouting through the howling mayhem, our faces drenched with the salty spray of tears, ducking the wild yardarms of fate that threatened to toss us overboard, we managed to stay afloat by batting down the hatches. So, here we are, thirty-five years later, heading into the sunset of our lives. Your cheeks are ruddy, my dear, from weathering the toughest stuff nature can throw at a man, and my hands are calloused from scrubbing the deck, but I think we are beautiful. Let's keep sailing.

I could not have written something like that as an anniversary gift, and my husband could not have read it with tears in his eyes if we were not intimates. Only *he* knows what I mean by "howling mayhem" or "wild yardarms of fate." Dale alone would be touched by the thought of "ruddy cheeks" and "calloused hands" and I can't think of anyone else who would smile about "scrubbing the deck." To you, it's a parable. To us it is real life. And it's in a language only the two of us understand.

Maybe that's why I prefer metaphor to narrative. It reveals so much and so little at the same time and leaves a lot open to individual interpretation. I also love the way a parable, like a piece of fine art, can be appreciated at different levels. The more you contemplate it, the more meaning you discover—sometimes even a completely different meaning than the author or artist originally had in mind. When you personally interpret, decipher, or unravel an artistic mystery, it goes deep. You appreciate it. It becomes uniquely yours.

Think for just a moment of your husband (that magnificent, gorgeous hunk of man you've entrusted your life to) as an artistic mystery: a living poem. I am intrigued by the "poetics of intimacy" as introduced to me by Thomas Moore, in *Soul Mates: Honoring the Mysteries of Love and Relationship.*

"In developing a poetic approach to relationship, we might first recognize that a person is a text of sorts, as are his or her stories, theories, ideas, memories, wishes, intentions—anything that a person expresses. Like any rich text, a person has many, many layers of meaning, most of them unknown even to himself" (p. 246).

People—that is, people's *souls*—are obviously multilayered and constantly evolving; we grow deeper and more complex with experience, changing day by day in subtle ways. Our fluid, ever-changing souls exist in a fluid, ever-changing environment, perceived and influenced by other people, relationships, and stories that are themselves fluid and ever changing. Because life and people are so fluid, something as subtle as thought can gently nudge us toward one destiny or another, as we've discussed throughout the book.

Clearly, we underestimate and underuse our power, especially as women, to influence where life will take us—just by employing our thoughts, or what I call our *best imagination*. Look at how this protégé of mine went from Dream Breaker to Dream Maker:

"I just read all about his "why" in your book, *Wife for Life*, and I cried and cried. I *knew* this, but I didn't get it. I was so confused by it all...I struggled so much to understand... I now realize why every time he expressed his desire to achieve, or to give to me, he was dismayed when I said I didn't want or need it...I get it. *I get it!* My whole perspective is changing. My marriage is changing!"

Because this woman's best imagination was unleashed, she could now see her husband's motivation (his soul) from a completely different angle, and their future was subsequently altered. Just a few weeks later, she wrote to me that her husband was about to take a test extremely important to his quest. I told her that, with his Dream Maker behind him, I had no doubt he would fly. The next morning she emailed me these glad tidings:

"Ramona, he didn't fly, HE SOARED!!!!!!! His score puts him in the 99th percentile; the doors to the top business schools in the world just flew open. I am so proud! We laughed and cried and whooped and hollered. His dreams are becoming reality! And I couldn't be more elated! He thanked me—*me*—for supporting him in this dream. He thanked *me* for that score. He brought *me* flowers and he thanked *me*! I am so full of life and and am thrilled today! *I am soaring too!*"

This young Dream Maker, who had a good marriage to begin with, is now well on her way to having a *great* marriage, and, if she keeps her best imagination in tip-top shape, they will one day have a grand marriage.

But what about a marriage speeding toward alienation? Can imagination put on the brakes? I believe it's possible. When disillusionment or alienation threatens, when your personal universe hangs in the balance—the hard work of recovery and reorientation begins by employing your best imagination to reinterpret the past. Memory can be reorganized with a broader, more creative way of thinking. It can spin us on our heels, just like it did for this follower of mine who was on the brink of divorce. In this letter, notice how *imagination* stimulated her empathy and desire to change:

"I have been able to put myself in my husband's shoes now and can see what he has had to put up with all these years...I have dragged him down. And when I have received nurturing and attention from him, I have lacked appreciation, and in a sense thrown it all back in his face with the belief that it's either not meant, or that I am too busy! Oh, how I miss those heartfelt hugs and kisses...I long for them once more...will I ever get them again and will I trust that they are heartfelt, especially with his recent declaration that he no longer loves me and doubts now that he ever did?"

Though at this point, her husband was filtering their history through an overwhelmingly negative lens, I believed it was possible for her to reorganize memory for both of them. I assured the letter-writer that her husband's love for her in the past was real; it was just buried under an avalanche of hurt. "Instead of telling yourself you have to revive the embers of a dying fire," I told her, "think of melting a mountain of snow to get to the green grass underneath." That little twist of perception was exactly what her imagination needed to move forward with more confidence. She wrote me in response:

"I no longer feel I am going insane. I no longer feel the need to get to those doctors to get myself some antidepressants! I feel liberated! I am so empowered! It is time for me to create!"

As Thomas Moore writes, "The difficult truth to learn is that change takes place in the imagination, and knowing this has everything to do with developing a good, intimate relationship to our own soul and the soul of others" (Soul Mates, p. 42). Indeed, as the woman in an endangered marriage employed her best imagination and followed Wife for Life principles, her husband was naturally drawn toward her. The marriage made a 180 degree turnaround. Within a few weeks, she reported a far different state of affairs:

"A miracle has happened today—about an hour ago in fact. I got my kiss—the melting type! My husband told me that he has seen the change in me, acknowledges my efforts, and most of all that he loves me!"

I believe miracles can happen when a woman uses her imagination so that she looks at herself and her husband not only as they *are* (deep and rich and unique), but as they will *become* (mature, strong, glorious). My dear friend, Hazel Perinchief, is a model in this regard. As part of their fiftieth wedding anniversary, she and her husband, Burt, flew to London where we met them for dinner. We heard all about the formal ceremony where they had recently renewed their vows in front of five hundred people.

"Why," I asked, "did you do it?"

Hazel looked at Burt sweetly and giggled like a girl.

"Because," she said shyly, "I'm only just *now* getting to know him!"

To Hazel, life is a beautiful mystery, and Burt is still an intriguing poem of a man, and her best imagination is always in high gear. As a highly successful Dream Maker, she is more *literary* than *literal* minded. Because she has treated love with astonishment for over fifty years, Hazel lives inside a miraculous relationship. She may still struggle on occasion with relational fears and judgments, but I can guarantee she has learned how to redirect her imagination so as to judge hopefully of her man. Hazel chooses to turn toward her husband with peace, patience, grace, and wonder.

In the 2011 wedding ceremony of Prince William and Catherine Middleton, The Right Reverend and Right Honourable Dr. Richard Chartres, Bishop of London, stated: "Marriage should transform, as husband and wife make one another their work of art..." Dr. Chartres' wisdom for the future king and queen of England is solid counsel for any couple. In the slow, gentle process of Dream Making, you will transform not only yourself, but your husband. Remember the Creator lesson from Chapter 1. Your man is your work of art because he *is* a work of art—a multi-layered parable, poem, metaphor, and mystery; how he matures in the end will have as much to do with your imagination as with his.

The Stories We Tell Ourselves

Since so much is riding on employing our best imagination, not our worst, it seems rather obvious that as women we must do everything we can to nurture and protect that delicate, impressionable part of ourselves. If you want to see your Nice Guy in the best possible light and to love him for not only what he is, but for what he will become—right from the start and all the way to the end—you must be oh-so careful to fill your imagination with stories that help you to love and trust him more, not less. This includes all the stories you are told by other people through conversation, books, the internet, television, music, and movies. This point is terribly important. I have watched marriages fall apart because of the stories a woman overindulges in. People and influences outside your marriage will affect your imagination and thereby the way you approach life—which, in turn, will create or destroy your dream of a grand, lifelong marriage. The wrong kind of stories will subliminally or overtly blunt your best imagination by inciting your worst. Thus, if someone or something causes you to feel discontented with your man or with marriage generally, be wary: there are influences that will strangle your love.

On the other hand, the best kind of imaginative stimulants will breathe fresh life-giving air into your marriage because they fill you with...

- Curiosity (as in, "I wonder what's in his heart?")
- Courage (as in, "We can do anything together.")
- Amazement (as in, "Why am I so blessed with this man?")
- Joy (as in, "Our friendship is my greatest happiness!")
- Compassion (as in, "My sweet, good man.")
- Love (as in "How I cherish my husband!")

On my blog, my team and I frequently post recommendations for inspiring entertainments that are conducive to a positive imagination: beautiful pieces of music, art, and literature that will orient your thoughts toward truly loving and respecting your man, toward crafting a grand marriage. You have probably already thought of many of your favorite films, books, and songs that fill the bill, and I hope you will share them with me and other Dream Makers at my blog and social sites. Of course, I have mentioned lots of personal favorites in previous chapters, and I hope you will seek them out because rich stories like the ones I have cited are, as Thomas Moore puts it, the "raw materials of soul-making."

Frequently feasting on great literature, film, music, scripture, or history will slowly, almost imperceptibly, elevate your attitudes and behavior until you no longer have to be aware of your every move and thought in relation to your husband. Evaluating your choices or his becomes less and less omnipresent. Good habits and great thinking will become second nature, and love will flow through your every act like water through a water wheel. Your positive relationships will naturally generate happiness as you truly *become* a Creator, The Talent, a Pioneer Woman, and a Dream

Maker, your husband's Intimate and inspiration.

Do you know how dictionary.com defines imagination? It is, they say, "the faculty of producing ideal creations consistent with reality."

Good marriage: tolerant.

Great marriage: accepting.

Grand Marriage: imaginative.

I Cherish and Feel Cherished Because of the Stories in My Heart

One of the stories that helps me feel cherished has been repeated so often, it's taken on mythical or legendary status in our family. Dale loves to describe the night he fell in love with me, remembering how we went for a walk one evening in West Yellowstone, Montana. The "big sky", he says, was perfectly clear, the stars especially bright. A letter I wrote to my mother at the time completes the scene:

Last night we went for a walk in the black, starry, cool evening. We made our way to a beautiful open field, surrounded by mountains and trees silhouetted in the moonlight. I was just bubbling over. I wanted to touch the sky, grab a star, and dance with the mountains, but since I couldn't, I leapt, shouted, sang pretty songs, skipped, ran, and danced with Dale. Oh, it was wonderful. Dale just makes me melt. You know, Dale—my leading man.

Obviously, this was very early in our acquaintance, or I wouldn't have had to remind my mother that this "Dale" person was playing opposite me in the musical we were there to perform. The "leading man" comment reads more like prophecy today. So the question is: why did he become enamored with me that night, so early in our relationship? We barely knew each other. Actually, I knew nothing about him until that night, and then, between leaps and lyrics, he told me all about himself. And I mean *all* about him: a little bit of good, and frankly, a lot that could have worried me. What amazed him to the point of admiration, to the point of adoration, was that I barely batted an eye or skipped a skip. I kept right on singing and prancing and pointing at the stars. I listened of course. Of course I listened. But for some reason, none of it alarmed me; none of it threatened me; none of his confessional caused me to think I couldn't be his friend. My belief in him was all his imagination needed to start planning for a future that, before meeting me, seemed all too vague. He set out looking for a quest and six months later, I promised to be his partner in Dream Making.

Of course, as the British say, I "lost the plot." We hit that frustrating, near-fatal disillusionment stage—when I became absorbed in my fears and oblivious to his. Thank goodness my friend suggested watching *Heaven Can Wait* that fateful night. The story of two people who promised to remember, to give each other a chance, and to not be afraid, ennobled my very best imagination.

I hope this book has done the same for you.

Wife for Life UNIVERSITY

Customized Instruction. Personal Mentoring. A Community You Will Love and that Will Love You.

Dear Reader,

You have just learned all about the concept of "Grand Marriage". Well, that is *your* marriage. Someday. A love and a partnership that is so strong and so true that it blesses not only you and your husband, but everyone who comes in contact with it; a romance that is remembered for generations.

But you and I both know that the best ideas from the best books tend to be short-lived without some kind of program or commitment or support system to help us really practice and internalize those ideas; to live them day by day and day *to* day until they become a part of us – natural, almost effortless, like breathing.

That is why I founded Wife for Life University.

Wife for Life University is the best possible combination of concentrated instruction and ongoing inspiration, as well as long-term personal advocacy, accountability, and community support.

And you are going to *LOVE* it.

Just like the wives who share their stories with you at **wifeforlifeuniversity.com/stories/**, you are going to find so much of what's been missing in your life and in the less-effective approaches you've taken to improving your marriage. These beautiful women are just a few of the many from our community who *asked* to share their real, transformative experience because— frankly—*they want you to join them!* Wife for Life University is an incredible sisterhood; uplifting, encouraging, affirming, understanding, and sympathetic. You just can't believe the bond that happens inside a Wife for Life University class.

Listen to this email from a recent Wife for Life grad:

> One does not often have the opportunity to so intimately view, hear, or feel the spirits of other women talking about their marriage as I did during Wife for Life University. I found it revealing, humbling, inspiring. The women I heard truly treasure their husbands and marriages."

Or this one:

> "I couldn't wait to get to class. I love having my own band of Dreamers to lean on!"

So Wife for Life University isn't just a book with a study guide, or a lonely e-course, or an impersonal seminar that expects you to indefinitely sustain all the rah-rah you felt for a few days. And Wife for Life University also doesn't send you home with a stack of material leaving *you* to figure out how to actually apply what you've learned to your unique circumstances. Real learning, real lasting change requires much more than that, doesn't it? It requires *enlightenment*, not just information; *friends*, not just fellow students; and, most of all, customized care from loving *mentors*, not just teachers. All of that, and much more, is waiting for you at Wife for Life University.

So go on, take the next step! Learn more today at wifeforlifeuniversity.com. *WE HAVE A PLACE FOR YOU!*

Much love,
Ramona

Acknowledgements

Though sitting holed up in an office writing a book is a lonely process, I was ever aware of my blessings, including all the people who stood beside me, spiritually and sometimes physically, every step of the way. My own husband, Dale, it won't surprise you, was and is my partner in every single aspect of *Wife for Life*. He is my inspiration. Our foremost support system is made up of our children and in-law children, Hannah and Ken, Grant and Bri, and Chris and Heather, who eagerly contributed every imaginable and necessary expertise and talent, not the least of which is knowing how to love their mom and dad through thick and thin. I especially appreciate the forbearance of our precious daughter, Ashley, and the joy of our grandchildren, Taylor, Bracken, and Elle. And while we are on family, I must also express thanks to all my siblings and to Dale's siblings, who have always been my staunch supporters and biggest fans; brothers Steve and Larry particularly extended themselves in this project.

Of course, a number of old friends gave me ideas for years, and new friends gave me feedback in the final weeks, including the beta readers. I cannot for space and time, mention all of my influential friends, save two who must be singled out: Sue Simper, who spawned the idea for the book in the first place, and Debbie Woods, who has been my muse for over thirty-five years. Sue and Debbie's personalized inspiration would never have taken root, however, if twelve young women named BriAnne, Hannah, Sarah, Sara Lyn, Brooke, Emily G., Emily B., Deborah, Lacy, Katie, Kata and Heidi—who I affectionately call my Dream Team—had not believed in me and freely spent their precious time setting up and maintaining a platform from which *Wife for Life* could launch and thrive.

Among those who also deserve the title of Dream Maker, is my editor, Mary Mohler, who—while she was always very honest with me—treated the manuscript with deference, as though it were some kind of honor. Our relationship as writer and editor was one I had wished for all my life. Her decades of professional experience in the publishing industry helped me craft a book that would resonate with as many women as possible.

During that same period, I was surprised to discover that the most intimidating aspect of my research and writing was not interpreting academic studies or making sense of professional marriage advice; it was asking for, and then truthfully representing, other people's real experiences along with my own. I am grateful to all those whose stories are anonymously quoted herein, but indebted most of all to the forthright men and women who agreed to be named. My own parents are among those so cited, five people who lay down and sustained the foundation of my own marital happiness: my mother, Sharon; my father, Ray; my mother-in-law, LeOra; my father-in-law, Kenneth; and Janet, the amazing woman who married my father-in-law after Mother passed away. I regularly look to Janet for the mentoring I still need myself.

Lastly, I think it's appropriate to mention one other group of people who might be overlooked unless I point out their profound impact on this project. Thank goodness I was reminded to include them in these acknowledgements by a stranger at a business dinner. He and I were discussing my *Wife for Life* research when he asked me, "Who did you find was the most helpful in writing your book, the successful wives or the experts?"

"The successful wives *are* the experts," I said.

So thank you one and all, experts or no, who have led and accompanied me down this path, and in the process, blessed my marriage, the marriages of my posterity, and God willing, the marriages of ten thousand others. I'll love you forever. –*Mona*

To write the author, please visit *ramonazabriskie.com*.

Books Cited & Index

Every effort has been made to locate all copyright-holders over a period of several months. In the event that we have unwillingly or inadvertently omitted the proper notification, the author and editor would be grateful to hear from the copyright-holder and to amend this book. The author is deeply indebted to all of the experts, authors, and resources listed below, as well as those cited in-text and heartily recommends their work. We also wish to acknowledge the Multnomah County Library in Portland, Oregon for their fine collection of books and people.

Beam, Joe. *Becoming One: Emotionally, Spiritually, Sexually.* New York, NY: Simon & Schuster, Inc.. Kindle Edition. 2010-06-10.

Belmonte, Kevin. *Hero for Humanity: A Biography of William Wilberforce.* Colorado Springs, CO: NavPress, 2002.

Bowman, Alisa. *Project: Happily Ever After: Saving Your Marriage When the Fairytale Falters.* Perseus Books Group. Kindle Edition. 2010-12-28.

Campbell, Joseph. *The Hero with a Thousand Faces: Commemorative Edition.* Princeton, NJ: Princeton University Press, 2004.

Chamberlain, Mark; Steurer, Geoff. *Love You, Hate the Porn: Healing a Relationship Damaged by Virtual Infidelity.* SLC, UT: Deseret Book. Kindle Edition. 2011-02-22.

Cowan, Connell, and Kinder, Melvyn. *Women Men Love, Women Men Leave.* New York, NY: Signet, 1987. Cunningham, Charlie and

Cunningham, Jackie. *Putty and Bess: Naval Aviation's Grand Couple.* Alexandria, VA: ANA., 1997.

Curie, Eve. *Madame Curie: A Biography* by Eve Curie, translated by Vincent Sheean. New York, NY: Doubleday, a division of Random House, Inc., 1937.

Doyle, Ursula. *Love Letters of Great Men.* New York, NY: St. Martin's Press, 2008.

Eggerichs, Emerson. *Love & Respect: The Love She Most Deserves, The Respect He Desperately Needs.* Nashville, TN: Thomas Nelson; Colorado Spring, CO: Focus on the Family, Kindle Edition. 2004.

Fisher, Helen E. *First Sex: The Natural Talents of Women and How They Are Changing the World.* Westminster, MD: Random House, Inc., 1999.

Fitch, Noel Riley. *Appetite for Life: the Biography of Julia Child.* New York, NY: Anchor Books, 1999.

Books Cited

Flaubert, Gustave. *Madame Bovary,* translated by Lydia Davis. Penguin Classics Deluxe Edition. Kindle Edition. 2010-09-23.Gill, Gillian. *We Two: Victoria and Albert: Rules, Partners, Rivals.* New York, NY: Ballantine Books, 2009.

Gottman, John, and Silver, Nan. *The Seven Principles for Making Marriage Work.* Crown Archetype. Kindle Edition. 2002.

Gottman, John. *The Science of Trust: Emotional Attunement for Couples.* Norton. Kindle Edition. 2011-04-11.

Gray, John. *Venus on Fire, Mars on Ice: Hormonal Balance – The Key to Life, Love and Energy.* Coquitlam, BC: Mind Publishing, 2011. Kindle Edition. 2011-03031.

Gurian, Michael. *What Could He Be Thinking? How a Man's Mind Really Works.* Macmillan. Kindle Edition. 2010-04-01.

Hannah, Kristen. *Distant Shores: A Novel.* New York, NY: Random House, Inc. Kindle Edition. 2002-07-16.

Harley, Willard F. *Fall in Love, Stay in Love.* Grand Rapids, Michigan: Revell, 2001.

Hibbert, Christopher. *Queen Victoria: a personal history.* New York, NY: Basic Books. 2000.

Johnson, Robert. *WE: Understanding the Psychology of Romantic Love.* New York, NY: HarperCollins, 1983.

Logue, Mark, and Conradi, Peter. *The King's Speech: Based on the Recently Discovered Diaries of Lionel Logue.* Quercus. Kindle Edition. 2010-11-25.

Lovric, Michelle, editor. *Love Letters, An Anthology of Passion.* New York, NY: Shooting Star Press Inc., 1994.

Lowenherz, David H., editor. *The 50 Greatest Love Letters of All Time.* New York, NY: Byron Press, 2002.

Lund, John. *For All Eternity: A Four-Talk Set to Strengthen Your Marriage.* [Audio recording]. American Fork, UT: Covenant Communications, Inc., 2003.

Mason, Mike. *The Mystery of Marriage: Meditations on the Miracle.* Colorado Springs, CO: Multnomah, a division of Random House, Inc. New York, NY: 1996. Kindle Edition. 2010-11-03.

McAdoo, Eleanor Wilson. *The Woodrow Wilsons.* New York, NY: The Macmillian Company, 1937.

McAdoo, Eleanor Wilson, editor. *The Priceless Gift: The Love Letters of Woodrow Wilson and Ellen Axson Wilson.* New York, NY: McGraw-Hill Book Co., Inc., 1962.

McCullough, David. *The Great Bridge: The Epic Story of the Building of the Brooklyn Bridge.* New York, NY: Simon & Schuster, 1972.

Moore, Thomas. *Soul Mates: Honoring the Mysteries of Love and Relationship.*

Books Cited

New York, NY: HarperCollins Publishers, 1994.

Myles, Monroe. *Understanding the Purpose and Power of Men.* New Kensington, PA: Whitaker House. Kindle Edition, 2001.

Orbuch, Terri. *Finding Love Again: 6 Simple Steps to a New and Happy Relationship.* Naperville, IL: Sourcebooks Casablanca. Kindle Edition. 2012.

Potter-Efron, Ron & Patty. *Reclaim Your Relationship: A Workbook of Exercises and Techniques to Help You Reconnect with Your Partner.* Hoboken, NJ: John Wiley & Sons, 2006.

Pounds, Norman. *The Medieval Castle in England and Wales.* Cambridge, UK: Cambridge University Press, 1993.

Reagan, Nancy. *My Turn: The Memoirs of Nancy Reagan.* New York, NY: Random House, 1989.

Thoele, Sue Patton. *Heart Centered Marriage: Fulfilling Our Natural Desire for Sacred Partnership.* Berkeley, CA: Conari Press, 1996.

Townsend, George Fyler. (Translator). *Aesop's Fables.* Kindle Edition, a public domain book.

Slattery, Julianna. *Finding the Hero in Your Husband: Surrendering the Way God Intended.* Deerfield, FL: Faith Communications, Inc.. Kindle Edition. 2010.

Waite, Linda J, and Gallagher. *The Case for Marriage: Why Married People Are Happier, Healthier, and Better Off Financially.* New York, NY: Broadway Books, 2000.

Weiner-Davis, Michelle. *Divorce Busting.* New York, NY: Fireside (Simon & Schuster), 1993.

Yost, Edna. *Frank and Lillian Gilbreth: Partners for Life.* The American Society of Mechanical Engineers, New York, NY: Van Rees Press. 1949.

Index

Index

Index

Index

Index

Index

Ramona Zabriskie's given name means "wise counselor" in Spanish, "mighty defender" in German, and "dreamer" in Arabic. All three come together in *Wife for Life: The Power to Succeed in Marriage.*

Known for her empathy, passion, and humor, Ramona's motivational speaking has taken her all over the country, from classrooms to stages, from chapels to college campuses, for over twenty years. She began focusing her live presentations on understanding men and marriage in 2008 in addition to writing three internationally popular blogs on the subject. Her subsequent personal involvement with readers and audiences from all over the world led to her work as a mentor and to the serious research and writing that became *Wife for Life.*

Prior to *Wife for Life*, Ramona spent thirty years writing and directing for the performing arts and chaired a number of service organizations and events focused on women, teens, and disability advocacy. She is the mother of four and wife-for-life to Dale Zabriskie, international keynoter and corporate evangelist. Her husband, children, in-law children, and grandchildren are her biggest fans and have all contributed their varied and professional talents to *Wife for Life.*

Though the Zabriskies raised their family in Orlando, Florida and have lived in London, England for a time; Ramona is actually a sixth generation Pacific-Northwestener. The couple now lives in their southwest Washington dream home called Blue House in the Woods, just over the river and through the woods from Portland, Oregon, where the author is always working on projects to help and inspire women.

Made in the USA
Columbia, SC
21 December 2020

29518538R00161